Annual Editions: Human Development, 47/e

Claire N. Rubman

http://create.mheducation.com

ISBN-10: 126019714X   ISBN-13: 9781260197143

Contents

i. Detailed Table of Contents 1

ii. Preface 5

Unit 1 7

1. Conception, Pregnancy and Prenatal Decisions 8

    1.1. The Pregnant Avatar: Seeing Oneself in C-Sections, Surrogates, and Sonograms by Theadora Walsh 9

    1.2. Two Dads and a Little Lady: Surrogacy Brings Tennessee Couple the Love of Their Lives by Beverly Prince-Sayward 13

    1.3. The Islamic Republic of Baby-Making by Azadeh Moaveni 16

    1.4. From Rubella to Zika: New Lessons from an Old Epidemic by Agnes R Howard 19

Unit 2 23

2. Development during Infancy and Early Childhood 24

    2.1. Vaccinations: Who Calls the Shots? by Liza Greve 25

    2.2. Obesity Prevention in Children by Alvin N Eden 30

    2.3. Good News, Bad News by Tom Curry 33

Unit 3 35

3. Development during Childhood: Cognition and Schooling 36

    3.1. New Faces of Blended Learning by Michael B. Horn and Julia Freeland Fisher 37

    3.2. Breaking the Silence by Troy Flint 41

    3.3. Immigrant Influxes Put U.S. Schools to the Test by Corey Mitchell 46

    3.4. Happy, Healthy Kids: Six Ways to Boost Mood, Calm ADHD, and Ease Anxiety by Lisa Turner 50

    3.5. Giving ADHD a Rest: With Diagnosis Rates Exploding Wildly, Is the Disorder a Mental Health Crisis — or a Cultural One? by Kate Lunau 52

Unit 4 57

4. Development during Childhood: Family and Culture 58

    4.1. Tough Fluidity: Complex Considerations for Trans Youth by Deborah June Goemans 59

    4.2. The Drugging of The American Boy by Ryan D'Agostino 63

    4.3. Responding to Defiance in the Moment 74

    4.4. Time to Lower the Drinking Age by Mary Kate Cary 77

    4.5. When to Worry about Your Child's Aggression by Jordana Mansbacher 79

    4.6. Displacement Crisis Grows as Boko Haram Increases Exploitation of Girls by Fredrick Nzwili 81

Unit 5 83

5. Development during Adolescence 84

5.1. Dangers of E-cigarettes and Liquid Nicotine among Children by Laura Friedenberg and Gary A. Smith 85
5.2. Secrets of Our Modern Youth by Brigitte Piniewski 88
5.3. Twenty Insider Tips for Working with Adolescents at Camp by Karen Goeller 90
5.4. Substance Abuse Concerns: Heroin and Prescription Drug Use on the Rise among Teens by PaperClip Communications 94
5.5. High Anxiety by Sandra Long Weaver 97
5.6. High-Tech Bullies by Ingrid Sturgis 100
5.7. Pathways to Adulthood by Jeremy Knoll 104
5.8. Pediatricians' Primer on Sexting by Pat F Bass 107

Unit 6 111

6. Development during Emerging & Early Adulthood 112
    6.1. Meeting the Needs of Student Parents by Rabiah Gul and Charles J Russo 113
    6.2. Stanford Sexual-Assault Case Reveals the Chasm that Privilege Creates by Naeemah Clark 116
    6.3. To Hell and Back by Julie Irwin Zimmerman 118
    6.4. Introducing the Topic of Self-harm in Schools: Developing an Educational and Preventative Support Intervention by Tina Rae 120
    6.5. The Real Science Behind Concussions by Michelle Taylor 126
    6.6. Our Miserable 21st Century by Nicholas Everstadt 130

Unit 7 139

7. Development during Middle to Late Adulthood 140
    7.1. PICK Your PATH to Retirement by Jane Bennett Clark 141
    7.2. Combat Age-Related Brain Atrophy by Barry Volk 145
    7.3. The Shock of Elder Abuse in Assisted Living by Lois Bowers 152
    7.4. Unique Magnesium Compound Reverses Brain Aging by Jamie Rivington 154
    7.5. Could Cooking a Different Dinner Save You from Alzheimer's? by Sarah Klein and Catherine Price 160
    7.6. No Country for Old People by David Bacon 163

Detailed Table of Contents

Unit 1: Conception, Pregnancy and Prenatal Decisions

The Pregnant Avatar: Seeing One-self in C-sections, Surrogates, and Sonograms, Theadora Walsh, *Afterimage*, 2017
Picture a pregnant Minion or a pregnant Cinderella – now you can see them on your computer! Read about an online pregnancy game. Read about how pregnant woman are now being represented through avatars. This online pregnancy and childbirth, however, is devoid of any human emotion, physical pain or hormonal impact. Learn about the similarities between this game and a clinic for surrogacy in Gujarat, India where "bodies" are chosen to grow children for infertile couples.

Two Dads and a Little Lady: Surrogacy Brings Tennessee Couple the Love of Their Lives, Beverly Prince-Sayward, *Gay Parent Magazine*, 2016
Read about a homosexual couple's search for a surrogate mother. Follow the story of Dell and Robert through disappointment and prejudice. Meet their daughter, Heiress, and read their parenting advice as they successfully navigate family life with their seven year old daughter.

The Islamic Republic of Baby-Making, Azadeh Moaveni, *Foreign Policy*, 2014
In Iran, the Ayatollah Ali Khamenei sanctioned sperm and egg donations in 1999. This fatwa, or legal pronouncement, led to the opening of 70 fertility clinics nationwide. Shiite and Suni clerics disagree about how the Quran applies to the bioethics of fertility clinics and the reproductive technologies that are practiced there.

From Rubella to Zika: New Lessons from an Old Epidemic, Agnes R. Howard, *Commonweal*, 2016
The Zika virus is discussed as a modern day epidemic. Parallels are drawn to the Rubella epidemic in the 1960s. The responsibilities of public health officials to contain the spread of this virus are outlined along with the responsibilities of women of child bearing age.

Unit 2: Development during Infancy and Early Childhood

Vaccinations: Who Calls The Shots? Liza Greve, *The New American*, 2016
The vaccination industry is a 24 million dollar business but does it really prevent disease and should vaccinations be mandated by our government? The possibility of infection after vaccination is discussed in light of the measles outbreak at Disneyland in 2015.

Obesity Prevention in Children, Alvin N. Eden, *Pediatrics for Parents*, 2017
Based on a longitudinal study in the New England Journal of Medicine, 25 percent of kindergarten children are overweight or obese. Read about these children in early childhood then follow them as they age. Do they lose their "puppy fat" or do they tend to remain overweight? Learn about the consequences of obesity from a medical and psychological perspective. Read as the blame shifts from sugar to parents to technology…

Good News, Bad News, Tom Curry, *Exceptional Parent (EP) Magazine*, 2014
Suggestions for parents and students to combat intimidation and bullying in the sports arena. Proactive advice includes positive reinforcement, seeking out good leadership and verbalizing concerns.

Unit 3: Development during Childhood: Cognition and Schooling

New Faces of Blended Learning, Michael B. Horn and Julia Freeland Fisher, *Educational Leadership*, 2017
Take a closer look inside today's classroom where technology is changing the face of education. Look at the difference that blended learning has created from the pace of the classroom to the successful completion of long and short-term goals. Read about how technology is enhancing the learning process and giving students ownership of their educational goals.

Breaking the Silence, Troy Flint, *Education Digest*, 2017
"POPS" and "Project WHAT" are support groups for children with incarcerated family members. Learn about the impetus to set up the POPS program – a letter written by a young incarcerated student to his former classmates. Read about the three million

children in the United States who carry the stigma, shame and burden of having an incarcerated parent or family member. Discover the social, emotional and psychological effect that this can have on a child.

Immigrant Influxes Put U.S. Schools to the Test, Corey Mitchell, *Education Week*, 2016
An inside look into some of the issues associated with the integration of immigrant children into the American school system from a cognitive, social and emotional perspective.

Happy, Healthy Kids: Six Ways to Boost Mood, Calm ADHD, and Ease Anxiety, Lisa Turner, *Better Nutrition*, 2014
Eating healthily can increase brain activity in children. Certain foods can enhance attention and concentration. Deficiencies in vitamins, copper, iodine and other nutrients can adversely affect a child's brain development. Conversely, appropriate levels of EPA, DHA and PharaGABA have been shown in research studies to enhance brain development.

Giving ADHD a Rest: with Diagnosis Rates Exploding Wildly, Is the Disorder a Mental Health Crisis—or a Cultural One? Kate Lunau, *Maclean's*, 2014
The rates of ADHD seem to have risen in America and other countries. This article looks to the possible causes such as increased educational pressures. The criteria for ADHD in the *Diagnostic and Statistical Manual of Mental Disorders (DSM)* and the effects of stimulants on the brain are discussed.

Unit 4: Development during Childhood: Family and Culture

Tough Fluidity: Complex Considerations for Trans Youth, Deborah June Goemans, *The Humanist*, 2017
What happens to children when there is a disconnect between their assigned gender and the gender that they identify with? Follow the story of Pat, a transgender child, who has identified as a girl since the age of three years old. Learn about Mike and his agonizing choices. Read about gender dysphoria, puberty blockers and the development of a gender-fluid identity. Think, as you read, about the cisgender and transgender population and the current laws in the United States.

The Drugging of the American Boy, Ryan D'Agostino, *Esquire*, 2014
The prevalence of ADHD diagnosis in young boys is discussed in relation to their behavior and schooling. The DSM-V criteria for diagnosis are discussed along with the funding for ADHD research.

Responding to Defiance in the Moment, *Education Digest*, 2017
Why do some children simply refuse to co-operate? Explore eight underlying reasons for non-compliance among children. Read about techniques to de-escalate defiant situations and promote co-operation. Learn about the importance of reflection and evaluation. Read about these while considering the bigger picture of discipline and family harmony.

Time to Lower the Drinking Age, Mary Kate Cary, *U.S. News & World Report*, 2014
The author makes the case for lowering the drinking age back to 18 as it was in the Reagan era. Lowering the age, she claims, would reduce binge drinking, illegal prescription drug use and sexual assault on college campuses.

When to Worry about Your Child's Aggression, Jordana Mansbacher, *Pediatrics for Parents*, 2015
Aggression is a natural part of our psyche but it is a parent's responsibility to interpret their child's overt behaviors and decide when intervention is necessary.

Displacement Crisis Grows as Boko Haram Increases Exploitation of Girls, Fredrick Nzwili, *Christian Century*, 2016
Read about the deplorable kidnappings and use of children by the terrorist group Boko Haram which operates in Nigeria and beyond. Young girls are forced to return home pregnant or carry out suicide missions for their captors.

Unit 5: Development during Adolescence

Dangers of E-cigarettes and Liquid Nicotine Among Children, Laura Friedenberg and Gary A. Smith, *Pediatrics for Parents*, 2017
What are the long term effects of e-cigarettes? Is second-hand vapor as dangerous as second-hand smoke? A 1,500 percent increase in calls to poison control concerning e-cigarette related issues suggests that they might pose a problem. Read about a recent study on e-cigarettes and their effect on children.

Secrets of Our Modern Youth, Brigitte Piniewski, *Pediatrics for Parents*, 2016
Hormonal chaos can be unleashed when overweight or obese children enter puberty. Learn about the social and emotional implications. Suggestions for prevention are also discussed.

Twenty Insider Tips for Working with Adolescents at Camp, Karen Goeller, *American Camp Association*, 2016
Increase your positive interactions with adolescents through these tips to promote positive leadership. As the adolescent brain grows and develops, follow these simple strategies to encourage better communication skills and decision making among our youth.

Substance Abuse Concerns: Heroin and Prescription Drug Use on the Rise among Teens, *Curriculum Review*, 2016
In light of the staggering increase in heroin and prescription drug use, the risk factors, signs and symptoms of addiction are highlighted. Health problems and behavioral changes are also discussed.

High Anxiety: Colleges Are Seeing an Increase in the Number of Students with Diagnosable Mental Illness, Anxiety, and Depression, Sandra Long Weaver, *Diverse: Issues in Higher Education*, 2016
A review of mental health records on college campuses suggests that 1:4 college students has a diagnosable illness, 1:6 students have been diagnosed or treated for anxiety in the past year and that 18% of college students have experienced suicidal ideation. Stressors and symptoms are discussed.

High-Tech Bullies, Ingrid Sturgis, *Diverse: Issues in Higher Education*, 2014
Bullying was once thought to be the domain of middle and high school students but it now appears to be a pervasive problem at the college level. Sites such as "College Wall of Shame" or "Juicy Campus" provide an ideal outlet for stalking, revealing secrets, or masquerading as somebody else.

Pathways to Adulthood, Jeremy Knoll, *Education Digest*, 2016
Are high school seniors lost? Are they clinging on to the traditional "senior year" activities to compensate for their fear of the future? Knoll suggests that the senior year of high school has become a "holding pattern" for many high schoolers replete with lost opportunities for personal growth creating an environment of "academic atrophy." Read about his ambitious challenges that he sets for his senior class as he implores them to introspect, reflect and discuss major issues about themselves and the world around them.

Pediatricians' Primer on Sexting, Pat F. Bass, *Contemporary Pediatrics*, 2016
Jessica Logan committed suicide while Amanda Todd resorted to drugs, alcohol and sex. Both were victims of sexting. Read about why 66 percent of teenagers report that they have sexted. Learn about their reasoning that ranges from flirting and attention seeking to fooling around and peer pressure. Learn about the legal implications of sexting and read advice from pediatricians.

Unit 6: Development during Emerging & Early Adulthood

Meeting the Needs of Student Parents, Rabiah Gul and Charles J. Russo, *School Business Affairs*, 2016
The rate of teen births has declined over the past 20 years. The question of educational goals for pregnant and parenting teens, however, still remains. Join the discussion on whether these teens should be educated separately or differently from their peers. Learn about the laws that protect pregnant and parenting teens. Read about the financial costs involved in implementing these educational requirements.

Stanford Sexual-Assault Case Reveals the Chasm that Privilege Creates, Naeemah Clark, *The Chronicle of Higher Education*, 2016
Read about the sentence that Brock Turner received from the court for raping a woman who was passed out at a college party. Decide for yourself what his Ivy League school and social status had to do with his sentence. Read about his social class, ethnicity and sportsmanship then decide what role they played in the outcome of his court case. Think about the father of this sexual predator and his reaction to his son's behavior. Finally, decide for yourself how this case has changed our perceptions.

To Hell and Back, Julie Irwin Zimmerman, *Cincinnati Magazine*, 2016
Learn what addiction feels like from Tracy. Follow her life from a shy, depressed high school student to a homeless heroin addict. Read about how she turned her life around and now advocates for others.

Introducing the Topic of Self-harm in Schools: Developing an Educational and Preventative Support Intervention, Tina Rae, *Education & Health*, 2016

Join our conversation on self-harm. Read about primary and secondary risk factors such as a sense of hopelessness or low self-esteem. We will define self-harm, discuss examples such as poisoning and mutilation. We will look at school based awareness programs and intervention techniques.

The Real Science behind Concussions, Michelle Taylor, *Laboratory Equipment*, 2016
Look at brain scans of football players to see CTE or Chronic Traumatic Encephalopathy – brain damage caused by repeated blows to the head. Read how memory, emotions and behavior are impacted by repeated blows to the head during sports such as football, ice hockey, wrestling, boxing and cheerleading. Recall the movie "Concussion" that was based on Dr. Omalu's work on the subject in 2015.

Our Miserable 21st Century, Nicholas Eberstadt, *Commentary*, 2017
It is important to discuss the social, emotional, cognitive and psychological development in relation to the world around us. Eberstadt paints a very gloomy picture of 21st Century America. It is nonetheless, the backdrop that development will occur within. Think about the effect that this will have on the development of the psyche as you read about fewer jobs, less social mobility and lower wages. Add to this the opioid epidemic of our times and the future certainly looks bleak.

Unit 7: Development during Middle to Late Adulthood

PICK Your PATH to Retirement, Jane Bennett Clark, *Kiplinger's Personal Finance*, 2015
Retirement has been redefined in the twenty-first Century as a result of increased life expectancy, more years in the work force, better health and higher levels of education.

Combat Age-Related Brain Atrophy, Barry Volk, *Life Extension Magazine*, 2015
The age-related causes of brain shrinkage are outlined along with suggestions to combat brain loss including the consumption of polyphenols (found in pomegranates) and resveratrol (found in red grapes). Increased intake of B vitamins and omega 3 fatty acids also helps to combat brain shrinkage.

The Shock of Elder Abuse in Assisted Living, Lois A. Bowers, *Long-Term Living*, 2014
Elder abuse including sexual abuse is discussed from the perspective of the nurse aides and the executive directors at assisted living facilities. Suggestions are made to combat this abuse that includes neglect, medication errors and sexually inappropriate behavior.

Unique Magnesium Compound Reverses Brain Aging, Jamie Rivington, *Life Extension Magazine*, 2016
Learn about how the brain can become more youthful with the addition of more magnesium to the diet in the form of a unique compound developed by MIT scientists. Read how magnesium can improve brain plasticity, impacting cognition, memory and leaning. The potential impact of this research on Alzheimer's disease and PTSD is discussed.

Could Cooking a Different Dinner Save You from Alzheimer's? Sarah Klein and Catherine Price, *Prevention*, 2016
Is it possible that the food that we each could contribute to Alzheimer's disease? Is it also possible to prevent the disease by eating differently? Consider how insulin levels contribute to this disease. Think about the effects of a high carbohydrate diet or the Mediterranean diet.

No Country for Old People, David Bacon, *Dollars &Sense*, 2016
Millions of our elderly citizens, according to David Bacon, are living undignified lives in their retirement. He describes their circumstances as "vulnerable and precarious," even suggesting that their human rights are being violated. He also reports on the blight of immigrants, legal and undocumented, as they try to survive in retirement.

Preface

The authors of this collection of articles collectively challenge the notion of the status quo: They question over-aggressive children, cyberbullies in homes and across college campuses, addiction, and the pervasiveness abuse of our senior citizens. They raise provocative questions such as:

- Are parents culpable if a child finds and uses their gun?
- What price do children pay when their parents are incarcerated?
- Can you simulate pregnancy with an avatar?
- Do undocumented students really have the same rights in the classroom as US citizens?
- What are the issues surrounding gender dysphoria?

This Annual Editions anthology generates new perspectives on a wide range of topics from life transgender children and their life choices to sexting, defiant children, and behavioral disorders. Read about current research on the pain and feelings of loneliness and isolation that the adolescent brain experiences. Learn about the lost girls in Nigeria at the hands of the Boko Haram terrorists. Find out what happens to the human brain as we age and discover techniques to keep our aging brains more dynamic.

These articles were compiled to promote thought and discussion using the Socratic Method (Socrates, 470–399 BC) to generate critical thinking as a powerful tool for learning. They are the ideal catalyst for student led discussions and student centered learning. They can be used as the stimulus for a debate, student presentations, or small group discussions.

The topics were selected to motivate and inspire you to think, read, discuss, and learn in an interactive environment. Take ownership of these issues and themes in human lifespan development. Using Bronfenbrenner's Ecological model (1994), think about how they impact you as an individual as well as society at large.

Claire N. Rubman
Suffolk County Community College

Editor of This Volume

DR. CLAIRE N. RUBMAN is a cognitive, developmental psychologist. She has numerous publications and radio interviews to her credit. She is frequently requested to present guest lectures, keynote addresses, and workshop presentation both within the United States and internationally.

Uniquely qualified to talk and write about cognitive development, Dr. Rubman has a refreshingly novel approach that appeals to students, teachers, parents, and experts in the field. Her conference presentations include titles such as:

- What's Next: Calculous in Kindergarten?
- Time Out Doesn't Work!
- A Line in the Sandbox
- Pixels in the Classroom
- The 21st Century Brain and Other Stories

Magazine articles include such titles as:

- Read-iculous: The Challenges of Reading through the Eyes of a Child
- The Big Fat Question of Obesity
- It's Never Too Soon to Plan for Kindergarten, is it?

Dr. Rubman is a professor at Suffolk County Community College in Selden, NY, where she has taught for the past 18 years. She has also spent time in the classroom as a kindergarten teacher in London, England, and California, USA.

Born and raised in Glasgow, Scotland, she earned her PhD and MA degrees in cognitive, developmental psychology from the State University of New York in Stony Brook. She holds a BA degree from Glasgow University and she also earned her Fellowship and Licentiateship (Teacher's Diploma) from the London College of Music in London, England, where she currently serves as an external examiner.

Dr. Rubman can be contacted through her website "Education and Parenting Matters" at www.clairerubman.com.

Academic Advisory Board Members

Members of the Academic Advisory Board are instrumental in the final selection of articles for each edition of Annual Editions. Their review of the articles for content, level, and appropriateness provides critical direction to the editors and staff. We think that you will find their careful consideration well reflected in this volume

Harriet Bachner
Pittsburg State University

Amanda Bozack
University of New Haven

Leilani M. Brown
University of Hawaii, Manoa

Shakira Cain-Bell
Jackson State University

Bruce Caine
Belmont University

Stephen S. Coccia
SUNY—Orange County Community College

John Connor
Daytona State College

Ric Ferraro
University of North Dakota

Kathleen E. Fite
Texas State University, San Marcos

Richelle Frabotta
Miami University, Middletown

Josephine Fritts
Ozarks Technical Community College

Michelle Fryer Hanson
University of Sioux Falls

Susan Hill
Arapahoe Community College

Melodie Hunnicutt
University of South Carolina Beaufort

Tesia Marshik
University of Wisconsin, La Crosse

Robert J. Martinez
University of The Incarnate Word

Bruce Munson
St. Louis Community College-Forest Park

Jessie Panko
Saint Xavier University

Mary Eva Repass
University of Virginia

Leo R. Sandy
Plymouth State University

Thomas R. Scheira
Buffalo State College

Susan Schlicht
St. Cloud Technical & Community College

John Shook
University of Dubuque

Daniel Stettner
Wayne State University

Fred Stickle
Western Kentucky University

Kim Taylor
Spokane Falls Community College

Lois J. Willoughby
Miami-Dade College

Unit 1

UNIT

Prepared by: Claire N. Rubman, *Suffolk County Community College, Selden, NY*

Conception, Pregnancy, and Prenatal Decisions

Consider what it takes to conceive, give birth, and make those first, vital parenting choices in this unit on prenatal influences on development.

Ever wondered what it might feel like to be pregnant or to give birth? Read about an online pregnancy game that claims to simulate pregnancy and childbirth! In "The Pregnant Avatar—Seeing Oneself in C-Section, Surrogates and Sonograms", Walsh (2017) discusses the physical, emotional, and hormonal aspects of pregnancy that technology may not be able to capture. Walsh explores the concept of surrogacy as just a body to grow a fetus within.

The surrogacy process is ideal for homosexual couples who are building their family. As the traditional two parent, heterosexual family paradigm has shifted, think about the increased demand for surrogates and for in vitro fertilization techniques. There were over 183,000 same-sex marriages in the United States in 2014 (New York Times, 2016). What qualitative differences, if any, do two fathers or two mothers make in child rearing? What are their parenting fears, concerns, and dreams? Meet Dell and Robert, a homosexual couple and read about their parenting decisions as they raise their daughter, Heiress. What issues do dads face and which problems are universal parenting concerns for all families? Read Prince-Sayward's article titled "Two Dads and a Little Lady: Surrogacy Brings Tennessee Couple the Love of Their Lives" (2016).

Read about the new technologies that are available to assist infertile and pregnant couples both in the United States and around the world. Read about couples in Iran who are finally able to take advantage of fertility treatments and technological advances in Moaveni's article titled "The Islamic Republic of Baby-Making" (2014). These technological advances have created new possibilities for some women whose religion used to preclude this type of intervention. In Iran, for example, the issuing of a fatwa on donor eggs or sperm by the Ayatollah Ali Khamenei cleared the way for the 20% of that nation's infertile couples to try new reproductive techniques. Moaveni's "The Islamic Republic of Baby-Making" explores the growth of 70 fertility clinics and takes a closer look at the root causes including male infertility which he describes as "the hidden story of the Middle East."

Regardless of how the embryo was conceived or the gender of the fetus' parents, all parents are charged with the enormous task of making life altering prenatal decisions from conception and birth throughout childhood and adolescence. One of the first issues is "pregnancy behavior." Research has clearly documented the deleterious effects of smoking, drinking, and drug use on the developing fetus, but today we face a new threat— the Zika Virus. Research has revealed that neonates born to women who contracted this virus may be born with Microcephaly. Their heads are extremely small and they may show signs of neural deficits (CDC, 2016). Armed with this knowledge, should men and women of childbearing age avoid countries that are affected by this possible teratogen. Would you give up a cruise or a two-week vacation because of this virus? By comparing old and newer epidemics, Howard (2016) looks at the responsibility of each individual parent and of the government in general.

Article   Prepared by: Claire N. Rubman, *Suffolk County Community College, Selden, NY*

The Pregnant Avatar: Seeing Oneself in C-Sections, Surrogates, and Sonograms

THEADORA WALSH

Learning Outcomes

After reading this article, you will be able to:

- Explain the concept of cognitive dissonance in relation to online pregnancy games.

- Discuss the importance of a sonogram during pregnancy especially for surrogate mothers.

- Describe how the Akanksha Infertility Clinic functions for surrogate mothers.

A quick Google search for "games for girls" yields a rather finite set of categories. There are cooking games, dress-up games, makeup games, shopping games, a few that feature household chores, childcare games, and pregnancy games. What exactly is a pregnancy game? How can the physical and emotional labor of forcing life into the world be conveyed as entertainment? Perhaps more pressingly, why does such a form of online engagement even exist?

Sifting through the hues of pink and purple that punctuate websites devoted to games for girls, I learned that pregnancy games are formulaic. Almost like recipes or the washing instructions on clothing tags, these games transform the travails of childbirth into a series of regimented and repetitive tasks. Through strictly enforced steps, the player may give the pregnant woman an ultrasound, send her a message, dress her in maternity clothes, or, quite ambitiously, perform a C-section.

I am interested in the way pregnancy games fit into understandings of gender and emotional labor in a world intimately linked through technological globalism. When young people identify with representations of pregnant women there are instructive assumptions about the Female body in labor implied by the constructed game. When technologies allow for the projection of the self into virtual worlds, identity is redefined by the structured and subjective realities of that representation. By enabling emotional identification with a rendered alternate experience, the avatar enables an extension of perspective. Avatars, icons that represent particular people, are both intimately linked to the person they represent and formally estranged. Considering the subjective association young girls might have with avatars in pregnancy games, I wonder how a relationship to one's own body might become representational during the lived experience of childbirth. In many ways, childbirth forces a sensitivity to futurity, as the pregnant woman must think about how her present choices will affect her child's future.

The pregnant female body becomes a representation, or symbol, of the child to be born. When people transfer the responsibilities and physicality of childbirth to a surrogate mother, the body of the woman carrying the unborn baby in the real world becomes even more like an avatar. When a mother proudly gazes upon a high-definition sonogram image, she has attained another virtual avatar for her unborn baby. New relationships formed through technology are paradoxical. They create possibilities for experiencing otherness but are limited by the inherent subjectivity that exists in building or entering any constructed world.

In the myriad of pregnancy games available, young players can select a number of culturally recognizable figures to act as their avatars. Elsa and her younger sister Anna from *Frozen* (2013, directed by Chris Buck and Jennifer Lee) give birth; they sometimes have twins. Barbie has a baby. Cinderella is pregnant, as are Belle, Rapunzel, and Ariel—the mermaid. My Little Pony gets knocked up, and so does a cartoon version of Beyoncé. Even a Minion from the Pixar film *Despicable Me* (2010, directed by Pierre Coffin and Chris Renaud) is gendered and then impregnated. The characters that young people impersonate are available to be anesthetized, X-rayed, and put under the knife.

In these pregnancy games, the Barbies and princesses and My Little Ponies are unaffected by the act of giving birth. Predisposed to a fabricated loveliness, they sit in operating chairs beaming and blinking enormous eyes. Their lips are painted red, their hair is prom-queen perfect, and their gowns are pushed up to expose a belly. Before the C-Section is performed, some of these online games let the player give the pregnant cartoon a face mask or makeover. Never are their recognizable faces distorted by pain or fear.

One of the major steps in most of the games is the conduction of an ultrasound. After a curled-up cartoon baby is shown on the screen, the player makes an incision. Soon the same image of the baby miraculously floats above the mother's belly. Something in the simplicity of the movement is particularly eerie. One can imagine the animator of the game selecting a preinstalled fade-in option, equating the process of birth to an aesthetic convention typically used in Microsoft PowerPoint presentations or car commercials.

I have two young cousins from Thailand. Before we were able to converse in English, I watched as they expertly searched for YouTube videos of Tinkerbell on their mother's iPad. Hyper-accessible images and scenarios can be preverbal for children living after the onset of the Internet. Before they were able to participate in American culture relationally or verbally, they could project themselves into the world through identification with the magical dispositions of impossibly formed cartoons.

Disney princesses and Barbies are cartoon caricatures of women, for the most part designed to represent the apex of androcentric desire. The use of these fantastical figures predisposes young players who already identify with these characters to project attachments and expectations into the game, endowing the play with an emotional poignancy. This can cause players to identify with the structurally limited iteration of femininity celebrated by patriarchal forces. We know all too well the way the world betrays young women. In *The Female Complaint* (2008) Lauren Berlant laments that "unlike other victims of generic social discrimination, women are expected to live with and desire the parties who have traditionally and institutionally denied them legitimacy and autonomy."[1] To attach a simplified version of childbirth to the already emotionally loaded image of Disney princesses necessarily connects pregnancy in the games with conditioned ideas about femininity. While a young player might emotionally identify with the woman giving birth, the games position the player as the doctor. From the perspective of a pair of sterilized and gloved hands, pregnancy looks simple. Seeing through the eyes of the doctor suggests a clean separation of mother and child. Hormonal changes, physical pain, postpartum depression—none of these bodily experiences are part of the perspective.

In *On Photography* (1977), Susan Sontag warns that "despite the illusion of giving understanding, what seeing through photographs really invites is an acquisitive relation to the world that nourishes aesthetic awareness and promotes emotional detachment."[2] The cognitive dissonance of the computer screen inundates the player with emotional neutrality toward childbirth. Pregnancy becomes understood as procedural, sterile, and distant. The game then replaces emotional distance with an abstract sense of fulfillment. With human complexity transformed by the game's design, the images function in a virtual plane in which the experiential spectrum of childbirth is aesthetically minimized.

The sonogram, which hovers in the games like a final goal or finish line, demands attention. The sonogram is received as a representation inside of a representation. In contrast to the two-dimensional sonograms of real life that offer a striking contrast with three-dimensional reality, the games' ultrasound machines render images of babies no different than the one that will later hover above the pregnant mothers' bodies.

The sonogram portrays the fetus as outline. Visible in a time before the complexity of relationality and development begins to shape personality, the sonogram shows the child as genetic image. Free from the realities of temporality, the sonogram is not yet imbued with character. Instead, the image allows for free association and projection. While sonograms have medical purposes, these pictures aesthetically remind one of the "Spirit photography" of late nineteenth-century America: they create an image that can be interpreted and given meaning without being constrained to actualities. The sonogram functions like an avatar. It is a representation that can be imaginatively customized by particular interpretation and preference.

Arlie Russell Hochschild's *The Outsourced Self: Intimate Life in Market Times* (2012) is an ethnographic collection of interviews with women involved in the rapidly expanding surrogacy market. In the field, Hochschild found an unquantifiable intimacy that often gets lost in market exchanges and global capitalism. Particularly interesting is the relationship between surrogate mother and sonogram that she encountered. Leela, a woman Hochschild met in Anand, Gujarat, India, said that she thought of the baby she carried as her own because "I saw his hands and legs on the sonogram . . . To this day I feel I have three children and one of them I gave as a gift."[3] The surrogate mother can become emotionally attached to the sonogram, using it as a tool of identification. The affective response allows for a sense of possession and a possibility to imagine the baby, which is inseparable from the mother's own body, empathetically. Sonograms allow both mothers—the surrogate mother and the genetic mother—to see the baby as their own avatar. However, while the surrogate looks at the sonogram with emotional attachment, the genetic parents also consider it as a source of evaluation.

Here there actually is a sort of "game" involved in the image of the fetus. The surrogate has "won" if the baby is healthy.

However, if the baby is miscarried or born with a disease, the surrogate will "lose," and suffer the economic consequences. To the adopting parents, the less quantifiable elements of the surrogate's "success" or "failure" at the "game" are estranged. The information comes remotely, often through a computer.

Games can create a space in the world that is not the world by rendering an alternate visual reality. Maurice Merleau-Ponty suggests that is it only through tools that the world as we see it becomes "apparent to us."[4] Yet the tool or lens of imaginative thought in pregnancy games feels more like an instruction manual than a place for exploration. The parameters in this interpretation of the world are formulaic and foreclosed. Arrows appear on the screen and instruct the player precisely how to interact with the pregnant woman. If the player deviates from the procession of the game, the action is simply ignored. An impossible way of being in the world is virtually composed. There is no way to lose the game, and, in this, there is no way to resist its presentation of the world. The capacity for communication and empathy is partially foreclosed as the phenomenological distance between perception and the body grows.

Dr. Nayna Patel runs the Akanksha Infertility Clinic in Gujarat, which was the subject of the film *Google Baby* (2009, directed by Zippi Brand Frank). The film follows the story of an Israeli couple who were unable to pursue surrogacy because of the high expense and homophobia in local clinics. They contact Patel, who helps them remotely select a surrogate mother for a fraction of the cost. The couple ships a mixture of their sperm, as well as a friend's egg donation, to India and face no personal questions from their removed partners in artificial insemination. Perhaps this global and remote way of obtaining a child mirrors what is demonstrated in the pregnancy game. A baby miraculously appears without the emotional or physical pains of pregnancy. The Akanksha Infertility Clinic functions in a Fordist model of production. The employees live, sleep, and eat at the clinic where their health is monitored. Once a woman agrees to become a surrogate, she must remain isolated in the clinic to ensure she refrains from sexual activity and follows the health stipulations the clinic requires. In the clinic, working as a surrogate means entering a virtual world, distinct from the rules, norms, and expectations that exist outside of it. For the duration of their pregnancy, the women are instructed to "think of your womb like a bag or a suitcase, carrying something that does not belong to you." The surrogate mother becomes an avatar in service of the adopting parents. She is selected as a temporary body that can be partially inhabited through paid access.

Patel gives each of her clients the opportunity to "customize" the woman who will work as their surrogate. Assured that all the women are completely healthy, those acquiring the services of a surrogate can make cosmetic and cultural selections. Just as the pregnancy games allow young girls to project personality onto the cartoon body of a Barbie or Disney princess, adopting parents can imagine a personality for their surrogate based on simple categorical information. One woman's file is shown in *Google Baby* quantified as: "complexion-wheatish, caste-Hindu, education-uneducated." None of this information seems obviously necessary to disclose. How would the woman's skin color, level of education, or caste affect the life of the baby? Why do people purchasing surrogacy services want this information? Perhaps it is because it allows the adopting parents to visualize the woman, within her foreign world, who will represent their bodies in the process of childbirth.

The ability to customize a surrogate is paralleled in the popular "sponsor a child" charity structure. People visit a website and personalize preferences for the child they would like to support. Like a video game avatar, a birthday can be chosen, as well as a sex, hair color, and age. These customized specifications remind me of my mother's *World of Warcraft* character. For $9.99 a month, she existed as an elf with milky-blue skin that could shape-shift into a bear. In the game, the politics of physical qualifiers can be suspended as arbitrary preferences. However, when similarly structured opportunities for customization are presented in real-world relationships, the problematic elements of selective representation become more pronounced.

The skin color of a surrogate mother defines how often she works, but it is up to the whim of families purchasing her services what skin color is desirable. This is the economic consequence of existing as avatar rather than "player." Will it be "wheatish" or "cardboard?"; will Jasmine or Cinderella receive a C-section?

The 2010 Tamil science-fiction blockbuster *Enthiran*, directed by Shankar Shanmugam, is about a Frankensteinian scientist who creates a super-intelligent robot in his image. The 65-year-old actor known by his mononymous stage name, Rajinikanth plays both the creator and his monster, which in itself is a technological feat of visual manipulation and careful editing. The film is primarily an extensive computer-generated imagery shot of a robot destroying cities and performing cloning acrobatics. Most of this absurd action film has no place in this discussion, but one scene set in a birthing room fits well with the dialogue of this essay.

Rajinikanth's fictional girlfriend is desperately trying to become a nurse specializing in female reproductive health despite her terrible grades and failing test scores. The robot becomes her personal study aid, memorizing her textbooks and silently dictating answers into a small headset during her exams. On a visit to the pregnancy clinic where she is training, the two encounter a medical emergency. A woman has gone into labor prematurely and both her life and that of her unborn child are threatened. Asserting himself, the robot brushes past the female head of the hospital, who insists that an emergency C-section must be performed. The robot silences her and informs the room that the baby will be born in an old-fashioned and traditional way.

The robot then proceeds to essentially pry the woman's hip bones open. The sequence is disturbing both because of the incredible pain it enacts on the female body and because of the suggestion that women's health should remain traditional even as medical technology becomes more advanced. From the very male robot's place of advanced knowledge, he can prescribe scientific regression for specifically female medical problems. Gendered knowledge is disguised as utopian futurism. Empowered constructions of technology, which already come from a privileged and predominately male position, are falsely erasing alternate perspectives from the project of development.

Before the violent arrival of her child, the woman at the clinic is delighted to see the artificial sonogram which the robot displays for her. It is the representation of the virtual child that helps the woman get through the extreme pain she experienced. The technologically rendered image distracts the pregnant mother from her emotional and physical present. The sonogram represents an end "goal" of pregnancy. Once again represented like a game, pregnancy becomes a process toward birth in the film. Almost as if the woman were a race car driver hurtling dangerously around corners, the movement toward a final goal emphasizes outcome over process.

The young player carving the cartoon body in the pregnancy games does so perfunctorily while a Barbie or Disney princess smiles and bats her eyelashes. Complacently, control rather than emotional fluctuations are experienced as a virtual knowledge of childbirth is constructed. It has been said many times that video games marketed to young boys encourage violence and desensitize the young brain to violence. It is equally likely that online pregnancy games teach girls to distance themselves from their bodies. Building on this impulse, these games suggest a future possibility—that if one is wealthy and white, like many of the cartoon princesses, the emotional and physical labors of pregnancy can be outsourced.

Though the complexities of pregnancy are edited out of the imagined world, the virtualization of pregnancy does not transcend the confines and realities of the gendered body. Instead, the virtual world performs a masking, building a space for erasure of actual inequality by presenting an image of technological utopia. In the future promised by these representations, people are disembodied. As life and technology increasingly intersect, the body can be more easily objectified and categorized into component parts. The capacity for customizing services online as global technology advances is bad for female bodies that have been historically repressed, is dangerous to the structurally impoverished, and is likely to intensify identification based on skin color.

To project oneself into another body expands personal scope and stretches the limitations of physical embodiment. However, the capacity to suspend reality and enter a virtual sphere is not without a material foundation. Though avatars allow for a temporary transcendence of condition, they also demand a physical surrogate host. Be it the silicon mined from the earth to construct computers, the workers assembling iPhones in Foxconn Technology Group's factories, or the body of a surrogate mother, the virtual does not exist outside of the power dynamics and social constructions that govern the actual. The desire to reproduce oneself in another body, a desire that motivates many to have children, has to be borne physically.

Notes

1. *Lauren Berlant, The Female Complaint* (Durham, NC: Duke University Press, 2008), 242.
2. Susan Sontag, *On Photography* (New York: Farrar, Strauss & Giroux, 1977), 111.
3. Arlie Russell Hochschild, *The Outsourced Self: Intimate Life in Market Times* (New York: Metropolitan Books/Henry Holt & Company, 2012), 98.
4. Maurice Merleau-Ponty, "Eye and Mind," in *The Primacy of Perception* (Evanston, IL: Northwestern University Press, 1964), 4.

Critical Thinking

1. List two advantages and two disadvantages of an online pregnancy game.
2. Give two reasons for and two reasons against contact between the biological parents and the surrogate mother during pregnancy.

Internet References

Differences between Surrogacy Pregnancy and Traditional Pregnancy
https://www.conceiveabilities.com/about/blog/differences-between-surrogacy-pregnancy-and-traditional-pregnancy

Gestational Surrogacy—Using IVF and Having a Surrogate Mother Carry the Child for You
https://www.advancedfertility.com/surrogacy.htm

What Are the Different Types of Surrogacy and What Are They Called?
http://www.modernfamilysurrogacy.com/page/different_types_of_surrogacy

Why I Was a Surrogate Mother
https://www.babble.com/pregnancy/be-a-surrogate-mother-surrogacy-story/

THEODORA WALSH makes animated text videos about space and sound that live at writingcircuits.com.

Article Prepared by: Claire N. Rubman, *Suffolk County Community College, Selden, NY*

Two Dads and a Little Lady: Surrogacy Brings Tennessee Couple the Love of Their Lives

BEVERLY PRINCE-SAYWARD

Learning Outcomes

After reading this article, you will be able to:

- Explain the parenting style that the dads called "honest rules."

- Describe Thomas and Bank's advice on surrogacy.

As gay men turn toward parenthood, many are choosing the route of using a surrogate. But where do you start? How do you choose a surrogate? Well, meet Dell Banks, Robert Thomas, and their beloved daughter Heiress Thomas-Banks, age 7. When Dell and Robert decided they wanted to be dads, they chose to use a surrogate and here is how it all happened.

Gay Parent Magazine (GPM): How did you start the surrogacy process? Did you use a service?

Dell Banks and Robert Thomas (Thomas–Banks): We pretty much handled the surrogacy on our own. We did all the research from how it works to where to locate a surrogate. We ultimately used an online site, which was set up much like an open forum or discussion board to find our surrogate. At the time, we were concerned about how an agency would perceive our relationship and how that would affect the process as a whole. We felt it would be best to do as much as we could without any obstacles.

GPM: How did you choose a surrogate?

Thomas–Banks: She was a part of the discussion board site we were on and we approached her. We had several lunches and dinners, cookouts and meet-ups, and we finally agreed on proceeding with the process of surrogacy.

Angela became our best friend, or even more like a sister, during and after the pregnancy and birth of Heiress. We had always agreed that we would be open about the process with Heiress when she was old enough to understand. We knew from the beginning that we would want Angela and Heiress to have the opportunity to get to know each other. We are firm believers that being open and honest about life's happenings with our child will make room for open communication and remove the element of fear and misunderstanding as much as possible.

Heiress and Angela have bonded. Angela has three other children and Heiress affectionately knows them as her brother and sisters. Recently, we took a trip up north to Michigan. Angela made brunch for us and Heiress got a chance to play with her siblings and take photos. To us all, it's like an extended family.

GPM: You mentioned that it was "taboo" in your community to pursue surrogacy in 2007. Can you explain more about that?

Thomas–Banks: At the very beginning of our surrogacy journey, we were contacted by an African-American woman who was having a tumultuous time with the father of her unborn child. The father of the child told her to have an abortion and she didn't want to go through with it. She reached out to us based on our ad on a website for surrogacy interests and we got truly excited, to say the least. We felt it was a blessing not only for us but also for the child whom may not have had a chance at life in any other case. Long story short, the mother told the father what she planned to do and he was totally against it and stated he would rather terminate the pregnancy than have his child raised by two gay, black dudes.

We were in talks with several other surrogates of other ethnic communities and we never experienced any kind of backlash or discrimination. It was only from our own African-American community that we experienced negativity. We finally realized, the hard way; this sort of thing just doesn't happen in our own community. To this day, we still get "looks" and "questions." However, the good always outweighs the bad.

*GPM: **Tell us about your family and what it is like having two dads and one little girl.***

Thomas–Banks: Our family is certainly not the usual "makeup" but we've managed to make what we have great!

Robert aka "Poppo" works from home for a large health insurance provider. He enjoys cooking, eating, traveling, bowling, and anything else that involves family quality time.

Dell aka "Daddy" is a self-published author and playwright who is the epitome of a DREAMER! [Dell Banks has published "Shady: A Novel" in 2011 which was then transformed into a stage play and just recently published "Shady 2: Pitch Black" with a release date of October 31, 2015. After seeing her daddy write a book, Heiress wrote her own book "The Adventures of Milo" which her daddies had illustrated by Aja Butler to be released December of 2015.]

Heiress is our 7-year-old cheerleader with tons of energy . . . tons. She's a second grader who reads on an advanced level and loves Elsa from Frozen.

In a nutshell, this is the makeup of our multiracial, sexually diverse, unusually normal family. Like most families, we have homework time, dinnertime, and bedtime. On weekends and during times when there is no work and/or school, we play board games and have bowling competitions on XBOX. Heiress often tries to out dance her Poppo on the dance video games . . . and she's usually successful. We have moments of fun and laughter and also moments of teaching and discipline.

The fact that there are two dads and one little girl never becomes a factor. When we have questions specific to raising a little girl such as proper hygiene techniques, what to expect and when, we look to our supportive families. Heiress affectionately calls Robert's mother Nana. Dell's mother is her Grammy. Robert's grandmother is her GiGi. Dell's grandmother is her Granny. With their support, we're quite all right.

*GPM: **What was it like when you first realized that you were going to be dads?***

Thomas–Banks: We were ecstatic and over the moon. For Robert, it took a while for it to really sink in. It was unreal! Holding her for the first time was beyond what words could explain, there was a joyous outpouring from our souls. That feeling of first holding her is something that can never be forgotten. It was the start of the greatest gifts of our lives.

*GPM: **You mentioned that your parenting style could be considered "Honest Rules." What does that mean to you?***

Thomas–Banks: Being honest and upfront is the key to a successful parenting journey. There are so many children being born into situations based and built upon lies and deceit, which makes room for a lot of pain and grief. We could have created some grandiose story for Heiress about how she got here and how she has two dads. We chose not to because when she gets older and wants answers, our credibility would already have been shot because we parented her based on lies; it's selfish, heartless, and flat-out wrong. So when our daughter asks questions about anything, we tell the truth.

*GPM: **Is there any advice you would give to other gay couples or single men wishing to pursue surrogacy as a route to becoming parents?***

Thomas–Banks: The advice we would give is to make sure that you're ready financially, physically, emotionally, and socially. Surrogacy can be a great and rewarding experience if it's well planned. There are so many kids being brought into this world without people considering the aforementioned elements. It takes a lot to raise a child; no child deserves to be brought into an unstable environment. Be honest and upfront with all parties involved; make sure your wants and desires are thoroughly discussed before going into any situation . . . this is a lifelong commitment.

Critical Thinking

1. Discuss two ways that perspective parents can plan for a more successful surrogacy experience.
2. Give two advantages and two disadvantages of acting as a surrogate mother.
3. How does gender influence parenting style?

Internet References

A Gay Dad's Tips for Successful Parenting
https://www.huffingtonpost.com/2013/07/21/gay-father-parenting-advice_n_3631741.html

Homosexual Parenting: Is It Time for Change?
https://www.acpeds.org/the-college-speaks/position-statements/parenting-issues/homosexual-parenting-is-it-time-for-change

How Families with Two Dads Raise Their Kids
http://theconversation.com/how-families-with-2-dads-raise-their-kids-77386

Overview of Lesbian and Gay Parenting, Adoption, and Foster Care
https://www.aclu.org/fact-sheet/overview-lesbian-and-gay-parenting-adoption-and-foster-care

What Does the Scholarly Research Say About the Well-being of Children with Gay or Lesbian Parents?
http://whatweknow.law.columbia.edu/topics/lgbt-equality/what-does-the-scholarly-research-say-about-the-wellbeing-of-children-with-gay-or-lesbian-parents/

Article   Prepared by: Claire N. Rubman, *Suffolk County Community College, Selden, NY*

The Islamic Republic of Baby-Making

How the supreme leader's revolutionary acceptance of cutting-edge fertility treatments is changing lives in Iran—and unsettling the deeply conservative Sunni Middle East

Learning Outcomes

After reading this article, you will be able to:

- Detail the consequences of infertility before the Ayatollah's fatwa in 1999.
- Explain the outcome of "consanguineous" marriages in Iran.
- Describe how the "hidden story" of the Middle East has impacted the Shiite and Sunni communities.

On a sultry evening last fall, a private fertility clinic in the southern Iranian city of Shiraz was so busy that the harried receptionist struggled to accommodate all the women seeking its services. On a mantelpiece rested a framed fatwa from Ayatollah Ali Khamenei providing religious sanction for sperm and egg donations—placed there, perhaps, to reassure these women that they had the supreme leader's approval for what they were about to do. Many had traveled long distances from smaller towns to reach the clinic, and the packed waiting area was abuzz with conversation, as women swapped stories about treatment, drugs, and their shared struggles to conceive a child.

"I couldn't afford this five years ago, but I've saved up now and am ready to try," said one 30-year-old woman seated in the waiting room.

While the world's attention has been focused on Iran's nuclear program, the country has been quietly working on a different sort of breakout capacity. The Islamic Republic—governed by its strict mullahs, who've managed to botch progress in fields ranging from domestic manufacturing to airport construction—has unexpectedly transformed itself into the fertility treatment capital of the Muslim Middle East. Iran now boasts more than 70 clinics nationwide, which attract childless couples, Sunni and Shiite alike, from throughout the region. This initiative has raised challenges to traditional views on parenthood and marriage and has helped chip away at taboos about sexual health—even as it has left some of Iran's conservative Sunni neighbors aghast.

"Doctors in the Gulf are horrified by the way the Iranians have allowed this," says Soraya Tremayne, an Oxford University professor and an expert on fertility in Iran. "They say, 'We would never allow this among us.'" For generations of Iranians, infertility was once a marriage-unraveling, soul-decaying trauma. It was memorialized in films like Dariush Mehrjui's *Leila,* in which a conniving mother bullies her son into taking a second wife when his first fails to conceive. The first wife, ashamed of her infertility and still in love with her husband, goes along with the plan, but the emotional strain destroys their marriage and the husband is ultimately left with a child, but bitterly alone. The film screened just a few years before Khamenei's 1999 fatwa and was a major hit, resonating with the multitude of Iranian women and men facing the prospect of a childless marriage and the intolerable alternative of polygamy.

Iran, like other Middle Eastern countries, has an extremely high infertility rate. More than 20 percent of Iranian couples cannot conceive, according to a study conducted by one of the country's leading fertility clinics, compared with the global rate of between 8 and 12 percent. Experts believe this is due to the prevalence of consanguineous marriages, or those between cousins. Male infertility is "the hidden story of the Middle East," says Marcia Inhorn, a Yale University medical anthropologist and a specialist on assisted reproduction in the region. Couple that with a shocking, multidecade decline in the average number of children born per woman, and it means that fertility treatment is needed in Iran more than ever.

Still, the pressure on a married couple—and particularly the woman—to produce children remains intense.

"We live in an Eastern society, and having children remains a very significant thing in our culture," says Sara Fallahi, a physician who practices in one of Shiraz's three fertility clinics. "Even for this generation that's getting married later and wanting smaller families, most still definitely want one child."

Iran's first in vitro fertilization (IVF) clinic opened up in Yazd, a desert city in central Iran, more than 20 years ago. It immediately found itself inundated with clients. By the mid-2000s, it was so popular that lines stretched out the door. Couples who had traveled from rural areas would camp outside in hopes of getting an appointment. More clinics soon opened in Tehran and across the country.

IVF quickly gained acceptance in other parts of the Middle East, but physicians ran into religious restrictions prohibiting more advanced forms of fertility treatment. Standard IVF involves fertilizing an egg with sperm in a laboratory and then returning the embryo into the womb, a process requiring that both the egg and sperm of the respective partners be viable, which is not always the case. The next step in treating infertility requires a third party—that is, an egg or sperm donor from outside the couple. In Islam, the ethics of such treatment are murky: Patients initially worried they might be committing adultery or that children born of such unions would be illegitimate.

But childless couples continued to demand a way to conceive. In Iran, medical specialists set about finding a religious solution, seeking the support of sympathetic mujtahids (clerics qualified to read and interpret the Quran).

The Shiite tradition of reinterpreting Islamic law was central to the clerics' willingness to go along—in stark contrast to Sunni jurisprudence's focus on scholarly consensus and literal readings of the Quran, which has meant few fresh legal rulings on modern matters.

Although, to Westerners, Iran's Shiite clerics might appear reactionary, they are downright revolutionary when it comes to bioethics. In recent years, they have handed down fatwas allowing everything from stem-cell research to cloning.

Their edicts did necessitate some Quranic contortions, however. The religiously acceptable solutions offered at first, like temporary marriage between an egg donor and the fertile male partner, proved too complicated, requiring a married donor to endure a flurry of divorces and remarriages. And some clerics who disagree with Khamenei's fatwa still advocate temporary marriage as a way of avoiding the adulterous implications of third-party donations. But this approach is easier for husbands, who can contract a temporary marriage with a female egg donor without needing to divorce the infertile wife; for a fertile wife to be able to receive sperm from a donor, she must divorce her husband, wait a religiously mandated 3 months before marrying the sperm donor, then divorce him, and finally remarry her original husband.

Iranian clerics' willingness to issue innovative religious rulings coincided with a changing political and demographic climate that also spurred fertility treatments. In the wake of the 1979 revolution, the country embarked on a quest to boost population, but by the late 1980s and early 1990s, as Iran struggled to rebuild in the aftermath of its devastating war with Iraq and with the baby boom in full effect, many questioned whether the country's economy, schools, and cities could handle the population growth. So the authorities reversed course, implementing a set of policies that gently persuaded traditional Iranians to have fewer children.

According to Oxford's Tremayne, authorities carefully avoided words like "reduction" and "control" and instead proposed "regulation of the family," emphasizing that the policy was intended not only to reduce family size but also to enable infertile couples to have families. The bargain worked, as traditionalists embraced the government's antinatal policies and Iran's fertility treatment centers multiplied. By promoting contraception and vasectomies, among other strategies, and withdrawing state subsidies after the second child, Iran managed to reduce its population growth rate from 3.8 percent in 1986 to 1.5 percent in 1996. But it may have worked too well: today, Iran finds itself below the replacement rate of 2.1 children per woman.

In 1999, Khamenei issued his landmark fatwa making third-party sperm and egg donation permissible. "Both the egg donor and the infertile mother must abide by the religious codes regarding parenting," the ayatollah decreed, setting out the various conditions that made the act permissible before God. Through Khamenei's edict, the Islamic Republic had made clear at the highest level that the state was ready to sanction Iranians' efforts to make babies—whatever it took.

Today, the era when infertility was discussed in hushed tones is giving way to a lively culture of intervention and openness. Women chat openly about IVF on state television, couples recommend specialists and trade stories on Internet message boards, and practitioners have begun pushing insurance companies to cover treatment. And the state runs subsidized clinics, so the cost for treatment is lower than almost anywhere else in the world: a full course of IVF, including drugs, runs the equivalent of just $1,500, according to Fallahi.

Khamenei's fatwa was revolutionary for Shiite Muslims everywhere, and it cleared the way for many clinics in Lebanon, which has a significant Shiite population, to follow suit. But according to Yale's Inhorn, Sunnis are also responding to the ruling, with some infertile couples from the Arab world heading to Tehran clinics that employ Arabic interpreters. Sunni countries like Egypt, Turkey, and the United Arab Emirates practice classic IVF widely, but offer no treatment options for men and women who require third-party reproductive assistance to conceive.

"Some Sunni couples have been able to wrap their minds around egg donation," says Inhorn. "They can tell themselves, 'Well, at least there's one fatwa that says it's OK. Some branch of Islam says so.' This makes them more at ease."

Still, Fallahi, the physician, says that anxious clients at her clinic in Shiraz often raise the question of religious approval. "They want to be sure what they're doing is not haram," or forbidden by Islamic law, she says. Parliament legalized embryo donation in 2003, providing some legal backing to the supreme leader's religious ruling. Fallahi stresses, however, that Khamenei's edict is the opinion of one marja, or source of emulation, and that not all ayatollahs agree. "We tell people that parliament has approved this, but that they need to check with the marja they follow to see if he gives permission." In some ways, fertility treatment may be the rare area where the Iranian regime has moved forward before society is ready. Although legislators approved embryo donation, they overruled Khamenei on sperm donation, banning the procedure in 2003. As a result, the practice was pushed underground, and those clinics that quietly offer the treatment are vulnerable to prosecution. Sara Bamdad, a researcher in Shiraz who conducted a survey on public attitudes about assisted reproduction, found that only 34 percent of respondents approved of egg donation. "Lawmakers should be thinking about the future and what is going to happen to these children when they're older," says Bamdad. "If a society can't accept a child that's born of assisted reproduction, then there'll be so many problems in the future."

Iran's legal system has yet to catch up with the implications of third-party fertility treatments. Under Iran's Islamic family law, babies born of sperm or egg donation fall into the legal category of adopted children and stepchildren, who are not permitted to inherit property from non biological parents. Couples thus must find alternative ways to put aside assets to provide for these kids, and the rights and responsibilities of biological parents (the egg or sperm donors, who are meant to remain confidential but whose identities are sometimes disclosed in practice) remain unclear. But if religious rulings are still murky, the baby-making revolution may be gently removing cultural taboos around other areas of sexual health. The Avicenna Infertility Clinic in Tehran, the country's most prominent fertility treatment center, has recently opened a health clinic that treats sexual dysfunction and sexually transmitted diseases.

Tremayne recounts visiting a fertility clinic where a large room full of men and women sat watching a video transmission of a surgery to fertilize a woman's egg on a giant television screen. "Our intention is to create a new culture so that people understand how babies are conceived and how infertility can be treated," a doctor told Tremayne. Scenes like this are part of a broader effort to educate the public, and while it may take years for infertility to lose its stigma in Iranian culture, the discussion of bodies and their biological functions and failings may be gradually helping Iranian men and women share responsibility for what has for centuries been the profound nang, or dishonor, laid at the feet of women.

The pursuit of cutting-edge baby-making has launched a process that could ultimately change what it means to be married and infertile, what it means to be a parent, even what it means to be kin in the Islamic Republic. As Iran struggles with the collision between its people's evolving values and the tenets of Islamic law, its success with fertility treatment suggests that it just may be possible to reconcile these competing pressures. But whether it will catch on in the Sunni Middle East is an open question.

"Iran is surging ahead using [these technologies] in all their forms," Tremayne says, "going places where the Sunni countries in the region cannot follow."

Critical Thinking

1. How do infertility rates in Iran compare with other countries such as the United States?

2. How do marriage laws in Iran conflict with fertility treatments that are currently available and future treatments such as artificial sperm or uterus transplants?

Internet References

Central Intelligence Agency The World Fact Book Total Fertility Rates
https://www.cia.gov/library/publications/the-world-factbook/field

faculty.washington.edu Modernization and Consanguineous Marriage in Iran
http://faculty.washington.edu/charles/pubs/1994-ModernizationConsanguineousMarriageIran.pdf

Islamweb.net Infertility: the Struggle to Conceive
http://www.islamweb.net/womane/nindex.php?page=readart&id=149490s/2127.html

IVF.net IVF Clinics Middle East
http://www.ivf.net/ivf/royan-institute-o3899.html

The National Center for Biotechnology Information Making Muslim babies: IVF and gamete donation in Sunni versus Shi'a Islam
http://www.ncbi.nlm.nih.gov/pmc/articles/PMC1705533

UN.org Recent Changes and the Future of Fertility in Iran
http://www.un.org/esa/population/publications/completingfertility/2RevisedABBASIpaper.PDF

Moaveni, Azadeh. "The Islamic Republic of Baby-Making." *Foreign Policy*. 2014 (January, 2014): 1–8. Used with permission.

Article   Prepared by: Claire N. Rubman, *Suffolk County Community College, Selden, NY*

From Rubella to Zika
New Lessons from an Old Epidemic

AGNES R. HOWARD

Learning Outcomes

After reading this article, you will be able to:

- Discuss where the Zika virus came from.

- Explain the effects of the Zika virus on pregnant and non-pregnant women.

- Compare the similarities between the Zika virus today and the rubella outbreak in the 1960s and explain the lessons that we have learned.

A woman feels under the weather, achy and feverish, and then recovers. All is well until she learns soon after that she is pregnant. Her mild bout of sickness could leave her baby with developmental delays, mental impairment, and lifelong suffering. In 2016, that is the fearful scenario associated with the Zika virus, which arrived in the Western Hemisphere last year and is now spreading rapidly. But in the 1960s, the same scenario was associated with rubella here in the United States. Remembering responses to the rubella crisis might inform our reactions to the current one. Advocacy for mothers, care for children with disabilities, and appreciation for the fragile, essential work of pregnancy should be our priorities, not recourse to abortion.

In 1964, an epidemic of rubella, or German measles, hit the United States. The disease had come before under different names in the late nineteenth century. But its arrival in 1964 was much more alarming. Researchers in Australia discovered a correlation between rubella and serious birth defects in 1941. Dr. Norman Gregg, a Sydney ophthalmologist, had noticed cataracts and unusual behavior among infants whose mothers had rubella during pregnancy. Other doctors observed more birth defects from gestational rubella, a group of problems eventually labeled

congenital rubella syndrome (CRS), including complications with the heart, vision, and hearing, and delays in mental development. Maternal rubella could also cause miscarriage or infant death. In 1960s America, the fear rubella generated was sharpened by the thalidomide scandal that preceded it. While the drug thalidomide was not approved for use in the United States, it had been widely prescribed in Germany and the United Kingdom in the 1950s and declared safe for pregnant women. But children exposed to it in utero were born with missing or malformed limbs. Pictures of "thalidomide babies," which circulated widely in the United States, heightened public concern about the dangers of maternal behavior. They showed that a mother's actions could, wittingly or unwittingly, wreak harm on her unborn child.

As historian Leslie J. Reagan argues in her study of America's rubella epidemic, *Dangerous Pregnancies: Mothers, Disabilities, and Abortion in Modern America*, the outbreak helped reshape abortion debates in the United States, building support for termination when the fetus was likely to be disabled. Consistent with mid-twentieth-century emphases on family planning and responsible parenthood, women who sought abortion because of rubella were portrayed in news reports as acting conscientiously, sparing children from suffering, protecting a family's other children from the difficulties and costs of a disabled sibling. While women could not be sure their children would be affected, the risk was especially high if the disease came early in pregnancy. Fears of having a "damaged" child helped make abortion a socially acceptable choice for white middle-class families and not only for the marginal. When the disease struck in the 1960s, therapeutic abortion was legal in some parts of the United States but access was limited, granted by hospital committees on a case-by-case basis. Testimony of "damaged" babies and agonized accounts of parents denied abortions and struggling to care for severely disabled children helped tip the balance of public opinion in favor of liberalized abortion laws.

Efforts to expand access to therapeutic abortion strengthened the push for abortion rights more broadly. Rubella-inspired reform efforts dovetailed with movements for women's rights and reproductive health changes. In California, a group of doctors, lawmakers, and citizens collaborated to advocate a Humane Abortion Act, though by the time it was passed in 1967 (and signed by Governor Ronald Reagan), it was more moderate than the law changes many abortion-rights advocates sought.

Catholics were prominent in opposing abortion as a response to rubella. Amid California's 1965–1966 debates, Catholic clergy, doctors, and laypeople testified against abortion in front of legislative committees. Priests preached against abortion at Easter Sunday Masses in California. In New York, amid that state's 1967 debates, bishops signed a letter against abortion and ordered it to be read at Mass in churches across the state. Of course, Catholics were not united against abortion, and some organized groups to endorse legal access to it. But before and after *Roe v. Wade*, Catholics were conspicuous in opposition to legalized abortion.

The Zika virus now plaguing Latin America replays some features of the 1960s rubella epidemic. First identified in 1947, the virus was named for its source, the Zika Forest in Uganda. It spread through Africa and Asia, then to the South Pacific in 2007, and arrived in Brazil in May 2015. While the virus sometimes travels by sexual contact, it is mostly borne by two species of mosquitoes: the *Aedes aegypti* and *Aedes albopictus*. Like rubella, the Zika virus was tolerated without great alarm until a connection to birth defects was discovered. Though the link is still unclear, a spike in the number of cases of microcephaly—a condition in which babies are born with an unusually small head and brain—suggests causal connection between maternal exposure to Zika virus and fetal damage. Brazil has found over four thousand cases of microcephaly since October 2015. In February, public health officials predicted the Zika virus would move through all of the Americas, except Canada.

Though the worry about Zika has spread widely, those most at risk are a very particular group. A few who get sick from Zika are at risk for Guillain-Barre syndrome, which causes temporary paralysis. Others experience symptoms like the flu, symptoms generally milder in strength than those caused by related viruses, dengue fever, and chikungunya. But about 80 percent of those who get the Zika virus experience no symptoms at all. Public health officials are mainly concerned about childbearing women, who can pass the virus on to their unborn children, on whom it seems to have much more serious effects.

In contrast to the 1960s rubella outbreak, the Zika virus arrives with only a strong correlation rather than a confirmed understanding of how maternal sickness causes harm to babies. While consensus for therapeutic abortion was just beginning to form in the 1960s, childbearing women now face heavier pressure not to bring to term a pregnancy with serious

fetal problems. In the United States, where abortion is legal and accessible, abortion for therapeutic reasons has become a fairly standard feature of medically supervised reproduction. Diagnostic procedures and genetic counseling are integrated into prenatal care regimes, with abortion made available when abnormalities are detected. While parents in the 1960s had to make decisions about continuing pregnancy based on probabilities, fetal imaging now allows parents to detect abnormalities early and with considerable certainty. In contrast to the United States, abortion laws tend to be more restrictive in Latin America. It is illegal in Chile, Nicaragua, El Salvador, and the Dominican Republic, and subject to limitations in other Latin American countries. Some Brazilian legislators are aiming to tighten their country's abortion laws in response to the virus.

Latin American clergy have offered a range of responses to the Zika crisis. Though 70 percent of Latin American adults still identify as Roman Catholic, the use of birth control is common. Bishop Leonardo Ulrich Steiner, secretary general of the National Council of Bishops of Brazil, upholds the traditional Catholic position against contraception, denouncing its use to control the Zika virus. But some church officials have taken a different line. Cardinal Odilo Scherer of São Paulo, for instance, acknowledges the use of contraception among Brazilian Catholics, which is likely to increase because of the virus. Strengthening the plausibility of birth control as a partial response to this crisis, in a February interview Pope Francis implied that contraception might be permissible under these circumstances since "avoiding pregnancy is not an absolute evil." He cited the purported approval of Pope Paul VI for the use of contraceptives by nuns in the Congo who were at risk of being raped.

But while there has been a range of responses to the question of whether contraception can be used to combat the Zika virus, Catholic officials consistently reject aborting microcephalic babies. Cardinal Óscar Rodríguez Maradiaga of Honduras, an advisor to Pope Francis, observes that therapeutic abortions do not cure—they kill. Urging "due vigilance" in response to the Zika virus, Archbishop Bernardito Auza, the Vatican's Permanent Observer to the United Nations, insists that "regardless of the connection to the Zika virus, it is a fact of human existence that some children develop conditions like microcephaly, and that these children deserve to be protected and cared for throughout their lives."

Protecting these children must begin with protecting their mothers. Archbishop Auza has addressed the problem with compassion, but Catholic opposition to abortion is sometimes expressed without much sensitivity to the realities of pregnancy. Stern warnings not to use Zika as a justification for abortion can suggest that pregnant women are looking for any excuse to abort. What should come first is recognition of the struggle and sorrow of women who are unable to protect their children from the Zika virus and other such threats. The bearing of children entails special labor, relationships, and disciplines. There is a great deal to be done and said about this new threat to childbearing before abortion ever enters the discussion.

Alarmed at the dangers posed by the Zika virus, some have placed the responsibility for preventing harm squarely on women themselves. U.S. travel warnings advise women who are pregnant not to visit areas where Zika infection is possible. That might be doable. But Brazil, Ecuador, El Salvador, Colombia, and Jamaica have advised women to delay getting pregnant for a year or two. That recommendation is obviously much harder to follow. Not all pregnancies are planned, after all; nor are all women in a position to make and enforce unilateral decisions about contraception or abstinence. The counsel that women avoid danger by not conceiving seems as unrealistic as recommendations in the 1960s that women avoid exposing themselves to rubella, even though many of them already had children who brought the sickness home from school and needed to be cared for. The whole logic of prenatal precautions can magnify expectant mothers' fear and sense of guilt, since everything from canned tuna to a glass of wine might harm an unborn baby. (The Center for Disease Control recently announced its recommendation that women who drink any alcohol at all should be using birth control.)

Pregnant women have long been blamed when anything goes wrong between conception and birth. For centuries people in the West accepted the Aristotelian theory that men provided the seed of a new person, while women merely provided a place and matter for its growth. If that place turned out to be inhospitable, it was the mother's fault. Hence, men got all or most of the credit when reproduction went well, and women got most of the blame when it did not. Belief in "maternal impressions"—the idea that frightening sights or events encountered by the mother could be stamped on the child—continued even into twentieth-century America. Cravings were considered strong enough to mark an unborn baby: if a pregnant woman who wanted strawberries did not get them, the baby might be born with a tell-tale red blotch. In the middle of the twentieth century, doctors denounced belief in "maternal impressions" but warned women that their prenatal psychological problems could sicken, maim, or expel their babies. And in the past several decades, women have faced criminal prosecution for substances they deliver to a fetus. Cocaine use in the 1980s raised worries of an epidemic of crack babies, and more recently, methamphetamine and opioid addiction have drawn critiques of women who harm their children through those drugs.

The fact that the Zika virus wreaks its most serious damage through the bodies of pregnant women naturally focuses our attention on pregnancy itself. A woman expecting a child spends the months of her pregnancy doing a range of works intended for the child's benefit, the chief of these being provision of nutriment and protection from harm. Some of this work is unconscious, as the pregnant body reconfigures organs to accommodate the fetus. But much of the work women do to protect their unborn children is intentional and difficult: avoiding certain foods or medicine, abstaining from alcohol, changing jobs, moving from one place to another, even taking to bed if there are complications.

Environmental hazards reach the next generation through the bodies of mothers. Many threats to a fetus are outside the control of the expectant mother, who may be unable to avoid drinking contaminated water or consuming toxins from food, soil, or air. As with many environmental harms, the poor are particularly vulnerable. The Zika virus, like rubella and certain environmental threats, perniciously inverts the protective nurture of pregnancy, leaving a woman powerless to ward off danger—or, worse, delivering harm to a child through her mother's body.

What, then, is to be done about the Zika virus? Public health officials can work to limit contagion, eliminate breeding grounds for mosquitoes, educate populations at risk, improve understanding of the link between the disease and birth defects. Above all, they can work to develop a vaccine. Researchers now say that a vaccine for the Zika virus is at least eighteen months away. Past experience with rubella vaccination is instructive here. Nearly five years after the height of the American epidemic, large-scale public and private investment did finally lead to a rubella vaccine, but persuading people to get themselves and their children vaccinated was not always easy. It required making arguments about the common good and taking collective responsibility for the health of the children yet to be born. Most vaccines are intended to benefit the people to whom they are administered, but the rubella vaccination in the late 1960s and early 1970s was different. It prioritized children not in order to spare them the rash and fever, but for the protection of their mothers, their future siblings, and their own future offspring. Similarly, a vaccine for the Zika virus should be targeted to protect the work of childbearing, keeping children safe by protecting their mothers.

But maybe the most important lesson we can learn from the rubella scare is that the fear of birth defects should not lead to the further embrace of therapeutic abortion. We are already all too willing to accept the elimination of fetuses with defects or disabilities. Instead, the fact that the Zika virus has its worst effects on the unborn should refocus our attention on the welfare and safety of those who bear the burdens and risks of pregnancy and suffer most of the sorrow this virus can cause.

Critical Thinking

1. What are we doing to educate sexually active teens about the effects of the Zika virus?

2. What should couples who are hoping to conceive in the foreseeable future do to modify their behavior and/or travel plans in light of the Zika virus?

Internet References

10 Zika Facts You Need To Know Now
time.com/4318624/zika-virus-and-birth-defects-what-you-need-to-know/

About Zika: CDC
https://www.cdc.gov/zika/about/

AGNES R. HOWARD is an assistant professor of history at Gordon College in Wenham, Massachusetts.

Unit 2

UNIT

Prepared by: Claire N. Rubman, *Suffolk County Community College, Selden, NY*

Development during Infancy and Early Childhood

When you look at a newborn baby, what is he or she capable of? How long will it be until this little bundle of joy steals, plays video games, or feels sorry for a friend? Whether this is our child or a child we are taking care of, what can we do to enhance development? What are the best decisions in terms of vaccinations at the doctor's office or toys in the toy box?

One of the first decisions that a mother must make for her neonate is whether vaccinate her infant. To provide our infants with the best possible start in life, the potential exists to vaccinate infants against such childhood diseases as polio, measles, mumps, and rubella. Is it possible, however, that the very vaccines that were developed to protect our infants from disease could, instead, be harming our children? Many parents fear that vaccinations cause Autism. This is fueled, in part, by a 1998 study by a researcher in England, Dr. Andrew Wakefield. Wakefield claimed that the vaccine itself caused intestinal damage and a release of toxins which affected the brain. Similarly, it was widely believed that the neurotoxin, Thimerosal, caused Autism in children but since its removal from children's vaccinations, the rates of autism have not decreased accordingly lending credence to the notion that it was not the root cause of Autism. Greve (2016) looks at the $24,000,000 vaccination industry and highlights the dangers of not vaccinating your infant. She focuses on the measles outbreak at Disneyland in 2015.

There are other times when parents have less control over the decision-making process. Curry's article on bullying and harassment in the sports arena highlights the role that parents can play, quite literally, from the sidelines. As a coach, Curry (2014) discusses the importance of a parent's positive attitude.

The environment that we raise our children in has a direct impact on their development. The final two articles in this unit discuss the effects of a well-balanced diet and a safe home environment.

According to the CDC (2017), 17 percent of our children are characterized as obese. That's a staggering 12.7 million children and adolescents! In our Kindergarten population, 25 percent are classified as either overweight or obese. Is this just "puppy fat" or does it have more serious ramifications? Read about the life-long consequences of obesity from a medical and psychological perspective in "Obesity Prevention in Children" by Eden (2017).

Our final article in this unit concerns the home environment and child safety. As the issue of gun control dominates our headline news, do parents take time to consider the implications of keeping a gun in their home? What happens when a child finds that weapon? Is a parent culpable if his or her child shoots that gun? Is a parent legally or morally responsible if a child shoots himself or herself with a gun found in the home? Is this a tragic accident or is this a crime? Read about 4-year-old Eli and 11-year-old Sienna who died in two separate and unrelated incidences related to guns in their homes. Karras (2016) explores this emotionally charged issue in "The #1 Gun Safety Question Every Mother Should Ask."

Article   Prepared by: Claire N. Rubman, *Suffolk County Community College, Selden, NY*

Vaccinations: Who Calls the Shots?

Liza Greve

Learning Outcomes

After reading this article, you will be able to:

- Explain the concept of the "vaccine herd immunity."

- Explain the concept of the "safe herd immunity."

- Elaborate on the "greater good" rhetoric in relation to vaccines.

Vaccine choice—whether to give one's own children vaccines for various viral maladies—has become a household topic, even working its way into the presidential debates. The debate has been characterized by most media and many politicians as a fight between those who are concerned about public health and those who ignorantly disregard public safety, and endanger others via their decisions not to inoculate, because of overblown fears of vaccine dangers. But the controversy has not been accurately presented. As someone who has been on the front lines fighting for parental choice, it's apparent to me that it would be more precise to say that the battle is between those who trust themselves to weigh the potential benefits and dangers of vaccines and those who wish to give the power to make parental decisions to the state (as if government is all-wise).

The year 2015 began with a media frenzy over a measles outbreak at Disneyland. It captured attention like never before and started a firestorm of debate. Thankfully, there were no deaths or serious complications. But that is not unusual. The Centers for Disease Control reports that approximately 0.2 percent of the measles cases in the United States from 1985 to 1992 resulted in death. In fact, it would have been unusual if someone had died, because no one has died from measles in this country since 2004. Compare that to CDC findings about the flu:

> It is estimated that in the United States, each year on average 5% to 20% of the population gets the flu and more than 200,000 people are hospitalized from seasonal flu-related complications. Flu seasons are unpredictable and can be severe. Over a period of 30 years, between 1976 and 2006, estimates of flu-associated deaths in the United States range from a low of about 3,000 to a high of about 49,000 people.

So at the very least, the media frenzy over measles at Disney was overblown. It was also very one-sided—against parents' rights. Interestingly, what one didn't hear in the media coverage was a separate fact from the CDC: According to the CDC, since 2004, more than 100 people have died from the measles (MMR) vaccine. Based on the CDC's own data, there is actually a greater risk of dying from taking the vaccine than there is from catching the measles.

Also pertinent is the observation that if the vaccinations work, how is it possible that the unvaccinated kids are endangering *everyone*? Shouldn't the vaccinated children be safe?

As a parent who has investigated the facts after seeing one of my children injured, I believe that the vaccine, in the case of measles, is more deadly than the disease, and I choose not to take that risk with my other children. While the knee-jerk reaction by the all-powerful government crowd would be to accuse me and those like me of recklessness, irresponsibility, or worse, the simple fact is that I believe not only that my children are my responsibility and should be guided by me, but that it is the number one job of parents to decide what risks their children will be allowed to take, as they already do in most other areas.

Consider that Stanford Children's Health reports that in the United States about 30 million children between the ages of five and 14 participate in some form of organized sport, and 3.5 million of them (more than 10 percent) are injured, with many getting traumatic brain injury and some even dying. Stanford clarifies:

- Sports and recreational activities contribute to approximately 21 percent of all traumatic brain injuries among American children.
- Almost 50 percent of head injuries sustained in sports or recreational activities occur during bicycling, skateboarding, or skating incidents.

Some parents respond to sports-injury statistics by not letting their children participate in certain sports, such as football or skiing, or by not letting their children skate without helmets or forbidding trampoline use; others encourage all athletic activities, with the mind-set not only that athletics chisel properly functioning bodies, but that sports build character, and the only thing worse than a child who is physically injured is a child with a damaged psyche. But the important thing is that parents choose—as is their right.

An Outbreak of Legislation

Notwithstanding the facts that vaccine mandates are really mandates to restrict parental rights, and fueled by the media attention, legislation popped up around the nation with the purpose of abolishing nonmedical vaccine exemptions or "opt-outs" for schoolchildren. Americans were led to believe that the Disneyland outbreak was the result of unvaccinated children and that all Americans were in danger as a result of the unvaccinated. Again, assertions diverged from reality.

According to the CDC, the outbreak likely started from a traveler who became infected overseas, then visited Disneyland while infectious. Analysis by CDC scientists showed that the measles virus type (B3) was identical to the virus type that caused the large measles outbreak in the Philippines in 2014. Whether the foreign carrier had been vaccinated is unknown.

Moreover, claims made about the efficacy of the vaccines and the dangers spawned by unvaccinated children were grossly inaccurate. Legislators who authored bills to require vaccinations claimed herd immunity—defined as a "general immunity to a pathogen in a population based on the acquired immunity to it by a high proportion of members over time"—was at an all-time low because parents were abusing their personal and religious exemption rights by not inoculating their children. But vaccine-based herd immunity is largely a myth.

The original concept of herd immunity was coined by Dr. A.W. Hedrich in the 1930s, based upon his epidemiological studies of measles. His theory applied to the protection that occurs when a population contracts and recovers *naturally* from infections. Later on, immunologists adopted the phrase, and they established a desired 68 percent vaccination rate to acquire "safe herd immunity" in a population. Later they increased the desired vaccination rate to 95 percent of the population to garner herd immunity, though nothing new was learned about disease pathology to account for the increase. But even that vaccination rate doesn't guarantee safety from infection.

Outbreaks still occur even in populations where 99 percent of the group has been vaccinated. In 1986, for example, a school in Corpus Christi, Texas, had a measles outbreak even though 99 percent of the students were vaccinated. Not only does this fact make a mockery out of herd immunity, it draws attention to the fact that *people who have been vaccinated can still become infected*—thus condemning the arguments of the big-government people.

Outbreaks among the vaccinated are common. In 2011, a 22-year-old woman, also known as "Measles Mary," developed measles shortly after being vaccinated. Despite having received both of her two "recommended" doses, she turned out to be unwittingly contagious. Ultimately, she transmitted the measles to four people, of whom, not surprisingly, two had been fully vaccinated.

Also, some parents report their children developing "measles-like" rashes after being vaccinated with this live virus. One Oklahoma family, the Tylers, witnessed their one-year-old little boy become instantly lethargic after his MMR. Three days later, he spiked a high fever and then proceeded to scream all night for the first three days of the fever. Once the fever broke, he broke out in a "measles-like" rash. Needless to say, the Tyler family did not vaccinate him for the second MMR; therefore, this child needs an exemption to attend school.

Another weakness in the argument for herd immunity is based on adult coverage. Adults outnumber children three to one, yet currently this demographic of the "herd" cannot be said to be vaccinated. Natural immunity to a disease *can* last a lifetime; vaccine-induced immunity often does not. Vaccine efficacy rates depend on the vaccine. The Centers for Disease Control admits, "In the first year after getting vaccinated, whooping cough vaccines for adolescents and adults (called Tdap) protect about 7 out of 10 people who receive them. There is a decrease in effectiveness in each following year. About 3 or 4 out of 10 people are fully protected 4 years after getting Tdap." Therefore, over half of our community of adults is unvaccinated, as most *do not* get boosters. Hence, our communities have never achieved a 95 percent vaccine-induced herd immunity, yet we still have managed to eliminate many serious diseases. So there must be other factors, such as better sanitation and nutrition, that explain our successes.

A Problem-causing Solution

The theory of vaccine-induced herd immunity is being sold in an attempt to achieve an agenda: forced vaccinations for all, beginning with our children, and increased government power over the people. What better way to achieve these goals than by legislation camouflaged in "greater good" rhetoric?

My home state of Oklahoma was one of the states threatened with legislation. State Senator and Doctor Ervin Yen attempted (unsuccessfully) to eliminate both the religious and personal exemptions to vaccinations that Oklahoma has long upheld. In response, thousands of concerned citizens quickly organized to oppose this violation of rights. Oklahomans for Vaccine and Health Choice was founded, and concerned parents (many with vaccine-injured children) began contacting their state legislators in record numbers. These parents began to coordinate e-mail campaigns, educational movie screenings, and town hall meetings to educate both legislators and fellow citizens on the issue of vaccine choice.

One town hall meeting was structured in a debate-like forum and featured Senator Yen and Dr. Stephanie Christner, a licensed psychiatrist, whose own infant daughter died of vaccine-induced SIDS. First, Dr. Christner gave her presentation, which detailed peer-reviewed studies demonstrating vaccines are not always safe or effective. Countering, Senator Yen defended his bill with two arguments: the theory of herd immunity and the claim that vaccine injury is extremely rare, at "one in a million."

The claim about herd immunity is, as we noted, speculative, at best, and the second assertion is misleading. The CDC reports that one *patient is compensated* by the vaccine court for every one million vaccine *doses* given, not that only one person out of a million people is injured. Far more have likely been injured and not received compensation, because it is very difficult to get compensation for injury.

Pharmaceutical companies, to ensure their profitability, lobbied Congress for years to pass legislation to become virtually immune to prosecution. In 1986, the National Childhood Vaccine Injury Act was passed. The act removed liability for drug-caused injuries and effectively closed the courthouse doors to the injured.

In the place of standard trials for injury via vaccines, the National Vaccine Injury Court was formed. It is not a true court because it has no judge, no jury, no legal precedent, and no public hearing. It pays injured claimants from a fund created by confiscating part of the purchase price of each vaccine—if you can get into the "court" and win your case.

To make it before the court, an individual files a petition with the U.S. Court of Federal Claims. Next, the U.S. Department of Health and Human Services medical staff reviews the petition and determines if it meets the medical criteria for compensation. The U.S. Department of Justice develops a report that includes the medical recommendation and legal analysis and submits it to the court. The report is presented to a court-appointed special master, who decides whether the petitioner should be compensated, often after holding a hearing in which both parties can present evidence. If compensation is awarded, the special master determines the amount and type of compensation. Finally, if a family is able to navigate through each of the governmental steps, the court orders the U.S. Department of Health and Human Services to award compensation. Application must begin before the expiration of a two-year statute of limitation from time of injury or death.

To date, of the approximately 14,000 cases selected, only 4,000 were determined to be compensable, thus leaving almost *10,000 cases dismissed.* Sadly, most families living through the after-effects of injuries or death *never file a petition*, so the above numbers are just a fraction of what could and what should have been paid. The majority of vaccine-injured never see a penny. Despite the drawbacks of the new system for plaintiffs, to date, over $3.2 billion has been paid out to victims.

Soon after legal immunity was granted, protecting pharmaceutical companies from lawsuits, the CDC increased the vaccine schedule for America's children, and to date the schedule has tripled, with children receiving upwards of 70 vaccines. Vaccine revenues have soared from $510 million in 1985 to $24.3 billion in 2014. There has also been an increase in autism rates during this time, though the government disputes the fact that vaccines can even cause autism, despite its own court judgments and other findings.

For example, a study done by the *Pace Environmental Law Review* in 2011 revealed 83 compensated cases of autism, showing that the government has known about a link between vaccines and autism for many years now.

In June 2007, in a remarkably clear decision, Special Master Richard Abell ruled in a case accusing the MMR shot of causing Bailey Banks to acquire autism when he was 15 months old that the Bankses had successfully demonstrated that "the MMR vaccine at issue actually caused the conditions from which Bailey suffered and continues to suffer." In his conclusion, Abell ruled that the MMR had directly caused a brain inflammation which, in turn, had caused the autism.

Moreover, a 2013 report published by the Institute of Medicine concluded that the federally recommended birth-to-six-year-old child vaccine schedule has *not* been fully scientifically evaluated; therefore, we may have traded the fear of contracting short-term illnesses for living a life with long-term chronic illness:

> Most vaccine-related research focuses on the outcomes of single immunizations or combinations of vaccines administered at a single visit. Although each new vaccine is evaluated in the context of the overall immunization schedule that existed at the time of review of that vaccine, elements of the schedule are not evaluated once it is adjusted to accommodate a new vaccine. Thus, key elements of the entire schedule—the number, frequency, timing, order and age at administration of vaccines—have not been systematically examined in research studies.

Many activists in the pro-parental-choice movement are parents who have had a child experience traumatic injury as the result of vaccines. They witnessed children change for the worse after vaccinations, with many reporting autism occurring.

Since the 1990s, there has been an explosion in the number of cases of autism. A disorder that was once very rare, according to the Centers for Disease Control, is now estimated to affect one in 50 Americans.

The disease was once so rare that very few doctors had ever seen anything like it. In April 1943, a psychiatry journal called *The Nervous Child* published an article entitled "Autistic Disturbances of Affective Contact." Written by Leo Kanner, a Johns Hopkins child psychiatrist who is widely considered the founder of the field, the article discusses his observations of a few cases where he states that a new and unknown disorder—autism—was beginning to appear:

> Since 1938, there have come to our attention a number of children whose condition differs so markedly and uniquely from anything reported so far, that each case merits—and, I hope, will eventually receive—a detailed consideration of its fascinating peculiarities.

Elsewhere, he called autism "a behavior pattern not known to me or anyone else theretofore." And the increase in autism is so great that it cannot be explained on the basis of better diagnosing. If one in 50 now have autism, then where are all the elderly people with autism? There would have to be approximately two percent of our elderly population who have had a life of autism. That cohort doesn't exist.

Despite, or because of, the explosion of autism in children, government is so intent on attacking claims of vaccine-induced autism that it literally trashed data finding that inoculations did cause autism. In the summer of 2014, Dr. William Thompson, a senior scientist at the CDC, stated that in 2004, he and his study co-authors intentionally threw away information relative to the autism-MMR link. He revealed that the CDC possessed evidence showing that the MMR increases the risk of autism in African American boys by 340 percent if given before the age of 36 months. Instead of warning the public, the CDC's top scientists actively conspired to bury, and even destroy, that evidence.

Congressman Bill Posey (R-Fla.) quoted Dr. Thompson in testimony before Congress, saying, "The coauthors scheduled a meeting to destroy documents related to the study. The remaining four coauthors all met and brought a big garbage can into the meeting room and went through all the hard copy documents that we had thought we should discard and put them in a huge garbage can."

Dr. William Thompson has not testified before Congress about the allegations. Congressman Posey has requested a congressional hearing take place, but one has not been scheduled, as the incident is still under investigation, according to Congressman Jason Chaffetz' office. Chaffetz (R-Utah) serves as the chair of the Oversight and Government Reform Committee, yet for over a year has made no public attempt to subpoena Dr. William Thompson.

Going on the Offense

Aware of all the foregoing information, the pro-parental-choice movement in Oklahoma strove to find legislators who were both willing to listen to the facts and would be open to going on the offense to protect vaccine choice. State Representative Randy Grau and State Senator Nathan Dahm took the lead by authoring a bill that would require doctors to present a more balanced approach to informed consent that includes potential risks/benefits, ingredients, and knowledge about the lack of liability should injury or death occur.

The bill was in line with recommendations from the American Medical Association. That group says about medical procedures and the requirements for informed consent and the ability to refuse treatment:

> The patient's right of self-decision can be effectively exercised only if the patient possesses enough information to enable an informed choice. The physician's obligation is to present the medical facts *accurately* to the patient or to the individual responsible for the patient's care and to make recommendations for management in accordance with good medical practice. The physician has an ethical obligation to help the patient make choices from among the therapeutic *alternatives* consistent with good medical practice.

On February 8, 2016, Representative Grau introduced his bill, HB 3016, the Parental Rights Immunization Act, at Health Freedom Rally 2016. He announced to the crowd, "I know you did not pick this fight. This fight came to you when there was a proposal to take away your choice, to take away your rights." Speaking about Yen's bill, he continued, "Just like in education, where parents are the primary teacher, I believe parents are the first and primary health care provider." The crowd cheered.

State Representative Mike Ritze, DO, a physician and surgeon, coauthor of the bill, also spoke at the rally: "Parental oversight of their children, in regard to vaccine choice, is the basic government that God has given to or in the family structure. With over 70 vaccines suggested by government today the parents should decide which is needed with advice and consent of their family physician."

And just as Americans want to know the ingredients in their food, many parents want to know what ingredients are being injected into their children. HB 3016 would ensure that parents could receive that information prior to vaccinations. Vaccine ingredients include heavy metals, such as aluminum; known carcinogens, such as formaldehyde; and human and animal cells, such as aborted fetal cells that are used as cultures to grow live viruses.

On February 17, 2016, Oklahoma's HB 3016 unanimously passed out of committee. When it hit the House floor on March 9, it received little opposition and passed 89-6. HB 3016 passed its first Senate committee, the Health and Human Services Committee, by a vote of seven to one. The only senator to vote against informing parents was Senator Ervin Yen.

HB 3016 was eventually cleared by the Oklahoma legislature and sent to Governor Mary Fallin for her signature. Fallin vetoed the measure on April 29. As of this writing, proponents of HB 3016 are hoping to override the veto.

Strategizing for Forced Vaccinations

In response to opposition to his own bill, Senator Yen changed his original bill, which had removed both personal and religious exemptions, so that it only removed personal exemptions. Despite the change, State Senator Rob Standridge, chair of the Senate Health and Human Services Committee, refused to hear Yen's bill on the basis that the legislature should not get involved in decisions best left to doctors and parents. This was a victory, but it was a temporary victory. In the afternoon of Friday, February 19, 2016, grassroots activists were notified that another committee, the Education Committee, was going to hear the bill, SB 1478, the following Monday. Oklahomans for Vaccine and Health Choice-PAC immediately sent out action alerts. By the end of the weekend, hundreds of Oklahomans had e-mailed, as well as filling legislator's voicemails to capacity. By Monday concerned citizens were waiting in the halls at the Capitol. After one hour of debate, the bill was killed, but only by one nail-biting vote. Senator Yen has vowed to not give up, and in his closing statements, he stated to the dismay of the crowd, "I don't know why parents want exemptions. I think parents opt out of vaccines because it is easier than taking their kids to the doctor"—an obvious ad hominem attack, especially since it is easier to go to the doctor than the capitol.

The Elephant in the Room

For any parent who has ever opted out of vaccines, it is a reality that refusing to vaccinate is in no way easy. From the moment your child is born, vaccines are pushed, beginning with the hepatitis B shot at birth. This disease is mainly passed via sexual intercourse and IV drug use; yet the vaccine is given to newborns, and then parents are pressured to follow a hefty schedule of over 70 vaccines by the time the child is 18. If parents refuse, they are often made to feel guilty.

We are at a crossroads on who "calls the shots" over our health and freedom. With over 200 vaccines in development, this is not just about children anymore. All of us will be targets to meet the quota for "herd immunity." We either give over complete control of health decisions to government and the trillion-dollar pharmaceutical industry or fight this type of legislation now! Our nation has become the most vaccinated nation on Earth, and Americans are under the threat of being denied education or employment if they don't comply with vaccinations. When we consider that vaccines come with risk (thousands of reported injuries), are often not effective (outbreaks have occurred in populations where 99 percent were vaccinated), have no consumer product liability, and are given in numbers today that have never been tested in totality, it seems that the pursuit by legislators to remove personal and religious exemptions is tyranny in its highest form, so we opt to fight.

Critical Thinking

1. Make the case for and against your child interacting with other children who were not vaccinated against measles, mumps, rubella, chickenpox, and other childhood diseases.

2. How do parents decide if vaccines are safe for their children?

3. Should religious and personal exemptions exist for vaccines for government-funded programs and state schools?

Internet References

Defending the Religious Exemption to Vaccinations
   http://www.nvic.org/nvic-vaccine-news/june-2016/defending-religious-exemption-to-vaccination.aspx
Measles Cases and Outbreaks
   http://www.cdc.gov/measles/cases-outbreaks.html
Vaccine Law Information
   http://www.nvic.org/vaccine-laws.aspx

LIZA GREVE is a codirector of Oklahomans for Vaccine and Health Choice.

Article Prepared by: Claire N. Rubman, *Suffolk County Community College, Selden, NY*

Obesity Prevention in Children

ALVIN N. EDEN

Learning Outcomes

After reading this article, you will be able to:

- Describe the cultural climate that has contributed to significant weight gain in children over the last 40 years.
- Explain the "10 commandments" to beat obesity.

In 1975, I published my first book, *Growing Up Thin,* which addressed the problem of obesity in children. It was a huge success and received a great deal of publicity. Yet despite these efforts, 40 years later, children are fatter than ever.

So what happened during these past 40 years?

1. More and more meals are being eaten in "fast-food" establishments.
2. Portions sizes are now larger.
3. Besides TV, we now have computers, cell phones, and tablets for children, all which increase sedentary time—what I call "S.O.B. Syndrome" (Sitting On Butt).
4. Physical education time in schools has become more limited.
5. More safety issues have become associated with outdoor play, such as increased automobile traffic and fear of abduction.

In truth, the obesity problem actually dates back to the 1950s, during which period food production in the United States dramatically increased. Starting at that time, billions of dollars began being spent to produce and market high-density, high-calorie foods at a relatively low expense to the consumer.

According to a New York Times report in August 2008, sugar consumption rose by nearly 33 percent due to the use of high fructose corn syrup alone. The average American was now eating 1.8 more pounds of food each week.

The statistics are frightening. About 6 percent the 1950s, rising to 25 percent by the 1970s. Today, the figure is about 35 percent. The prevalence of childhood obesity has also increased significantly—two- to three-fold—just in the past few decades.

An early childhood longitudinal study of over 7,000 children published in the *New England Journal of Medicine* (July 2014) showed that over 25 percent of children entering kindergarten were either overweight or obese. These overweight and obese kindergarteners were four times as likely to have remained obese into the eighth grade, as compared to children of normal weight entering kindergarten.

In fact, nearly two out of every three children who enter kindergarten obese will remain obese as teenagers; in turn, most of those will end up obese as adults. In other words, if your child starts kindergarten overweight or obese, he will be at an extremely high risk of remaining that way throughout childhood and beyond.

The current childhood obesity epidemic is in large measure due to the modern high-density, high-calorie sugar-laden diet. This, together with a more sedentary lifestyle, explains why today we have so many overweight and obese children (and adults).

Yet the consequences of developing obesity as a child are well known: in addition to reducing an individual's overall lifespan, other negative results include the development of type 2 diabetes, elevated cholesterol, orthopedic problems, sleep apnea, and a variety of psychological/social problems brought on due to a lack of self-esteem and self-worth. Obese children are also more likely to be bullied and socially isolated.

What's worse, this epidemic of childhood obesity has remained with us despite massive efforts to halt it in place—or at least slow it down. Up to this point, the majority of our efforts have been unsuccessful, if well intentioned. The answer is obvious.

Having been a practicing pediatrician for over 40 years now, with a particular interest in this subject, my experience (as well as that of many other pediatricians caring for obese children) strongly suggests that the treatment of both school-age and adolescent obesity is almost always unsuccessful. Sad though it is to say, the treatment of obese school-age children and older teenagers is usually doomed to fail.

The basic problem is that neither the pediatric community nor the parents of young children are taking early-onset obesity seriously enough. It is often difficult to convince parents that during the first five years of a child's life there even is a problem. In truth, most pediatricians do very little to encourage parents toward lowering the risk of obesity in their very young children. It is of interest to note that, within the recommendations of the American Academy of Pediatrics "Bright Futures" program, none of the well-child visits for children aged 2–4 years list either diet or nutrition as a priority.

What has become increasingly obvious to me is that the only way to make any inroads into the problem of childhood obesity is not to let it happen in the first place. In other words, prevention—rather than treatment—is the key to success. The earlier you start, the better chance you have of preventing obesity from ever becoming a problem for your child.

And that is what this book is all about.

Quoting from an editorial in *JAMA Pediatrics*, August 2013, in an issue devoted to childhood obesity: "Targeted interventions aiming to prevent obesity before it is established . . . may offer the potential to break the vicious cycle of obesity."

The article goes on to say, "Infancy and the early childhood years are 'sensitive' periods of growth and development, presenting the opportunity to either reduce or increase the risk of later obesity."

Based on the results of many studies on the treatment of childhood obesity, the authors conclude that parental motivation plays a strong role in predicting the effects of childhood obesity intervention. Further, family-based interventions have been found to be most effective, and the earlier they are started, the better.

When the entire family works together, intervention becomes much more successful. There is nothing magical about this program. It is simple, straightforward, and safe. It is based on extensive experience as a practicing pediatrician, as well as the most recent scientifically proven studies about childhood obesity. Learn to take an active role in your children's health. Protect your child from ever having to worry about being overweight or obese.

The 10 commandments for "Winning the Obesity Battle"

1. Monitor your child's weight percentile regularly
2. Encourage outdoor physical activity each day
3. Less TV
4. More sleep
5. Cut down on juice
6. No soda or sweetened fruit drinks
7. Healthy snacks
8. Never use food as reward
9. Feed your child a nutritious, well-balanced diet
10. Eat family meals together

Gardasil Compliance

Determining the most effective immunization schedule requires consideration of many factors: immune response ability of the child, the age of the child, the duration of the immunity, and convenience are just a few. Gardasil 9 is a vaccine designed to protect against nine strains of the Human Papillomavirus, a pathogen known to be a factor in the development of cervical, vaginal, vulvar and anal cancers and genital warts in girls and women and anal cancer and genital warts in boys and men.

A recent study compared two immunization schedules for teens for Gardasil 9: giving at the same visit as the Neisseria meningitidis or the Tdap (diphtheria/tetanus/acellular pertussis) versus at a visit when no other vaccine was given. The question was whether there was better compliance receiving the Gardasil vaccination if it was given at the same time as another vaccine.

The first consideration of the researchers was whether giving the vaccinations at the same time affected the teens' immune response. In other words, did giving two vaccines at the same time decrease the teens' protection from these vaccine-preventable diseases. The answer was no—the responses were the same.

Another factor to consider is the rate of adverse reactions. None of the 1,241 teens in the study had any significant adverse reactions. The group that received two vaccinations at the same visit had a little more injection-site swelling than the other group.

The authors conclude that giving the Gardasil vaccine at the same time as another vaccine is safe, doesn't affect the immune response, and may improve compliance by lessening the number of office visits required.

Critical Thinking

1. Why is a longitudinal study the best research method for this type of study on obesity?
2. How could technology be used to fight the weight battle?
3. Does technology contribute to the weight gain that has been reported in children?

Internet References

Childhood Obesity and Technology—What's the connection?

https://www.floridahospital.com/blog/childhood-obesity-technology-whats-connection

Childhood Overweight—The Obesity Society

http://www.obesity.org/obesity/resources/facts-about-obesity/childhood-overweight

Obesity in Action Coalition

http://www.obesityaction.org/understanding-obesity-in-children/what-is-childhood-obesity

Obesity in Children and Technology

https://www.livestrong.com/article/46320-obesity-children-technology/

The State of Childhood Obesity

https://stateofobesity.org/childhood-obesity-trends/

ALVIN N. EDEN is the chairman emeritus of the Department of Pediatrics, Wyckoff Heights Medical Center, Brooklyn, New York and a clinical professor of pediatrics, Weill Cornell Medical Center, New York, NY. He practices in Forest Hills, NY. His latest book is Fit from the Start, How to Prevent Childhood Obesity.

Article   Prepared by: Claire N. Rubman, *Suffolk County Community College, Selden, NY*

Good News, Bad News

Despite efforts to curb harassment, intimidation and bullying, these issues still make their way to our headlines each season. What can you do to protect your child from such incidents?

TOM CURRY

Learning Outcomes

After reading this article, you will be able to:

- Describe eight possible measures for parents to identify and combat poor conduct in sports.

- Explain the power of positive thinking in relation to bullying, harassment and intimidation in sports.

I have been in the coaching profession since I was 18 years old. Starting as a volunteer at our local church coaching the 8th grade basketball team, I also coached the Babe Ruth league baseball in our town, along with numerous other sports at various times. That covers 44 years of coaching various sports at many levels. I have been the athletic director at three schools since 1990. I have seen so many positive things happen in and around athletics and have been privileged to work with some of the finest people I have known in and out of the business. Good people, good coaches and administrators, along with concerned parents and adults, all trying their best to help kids make good decisions and be productive citizens.

It has become alarming that, despite efforts to curb harassment, intimidation and bullying (HIB), these issues still make their way to our headlines each season. Schools and organizations go the extra mile to discuss with teachers, coaches and students the problems and laws concerning HIB and the potential for serious harm to all concerned. Yet, recent stories indicate that there is still a lot more to do. What can you, as a parent do to protect your child from such incidents as they grow up in these times?

Pay attention to what is going on in the sports programs your child is involved in. Are there traditions or rituals that are making your child uncomfortable or not want to attend practices or

games? Do the coaches reinforce positive behaviors, good team ideals and embrace good leadership ideas and skills? Are you uncomfortable with a particular tradition or policy that seems to be "a business as usual" policy?

Create a dialogue with your child, other kids and parents about things other than wins and losses! What do you want your child to take with him or her from this sports program? Continue this dialogue with coaches, supervisors, principals and community leaders. Let good character development be the focal point of your programs and developing responsible citizens be the goal of sports programs everywhere.

Promote leadership and sportsmanship in youth and school sports and activities. Be the role model for positive parent behavior at games, events and practices. Many times as parents, we must fight the urge to be a negative part of the experience our children face in athletics. If we fail to set a good, positive example for our children, we may actually do more harm than good to their future. Ask yourself some questions . . . Am I trying to re-live my life through my child? Am I affecting his or her experience in a positive way or is the outcome negative? Many parents think they are helping their child by "sticking up" for him or her. I heard of a story recently where a mother went to a lower level baseball game to watch her son pitch. The young man struggled through the first two innings and the coach decided after 10 runs that maybe he should switch positions with another player. The mother took exception and it took the local police department to get her off the field from the pitcher's mound where she had sat on the beach chair she brought, refusing to move. The young man quit the team the next day, suffering from a good case of embarrassment.

Know your child. Watch for signs of disinterest or not wanting to attend practices or games. Are any of their habits changing? Sleep? Diet? School? Friends? Talk about things other than playing time and winning games. Point out positive behaviors you see athletes exhibiting at the professional and college levels. Cite examples of some of our leaders in all walks of life and what they did in athletics to help them along the way. Frequently discuss situations in sports that are not what sports are really about. Tell your child why you think something is wrong and how they should be behaving while on the field or in the gym

Speak up if you think something is amiss, but do it in the right way. Going after a coach or anyone in public is not a good way to make a point. Ask to speak to the coach privately about your concern. If you think there is a case of HIB, give the coach a chance to correct the situation. It could just be inappropriate behavior by a kid or kids which can be addressed by the coach or leadership. Zero tolerance is the only answer for harassment, intimidation and bullying, but it is also important to recognize that not every incident is an HIB incident. A discussion with the coach or leadership may resolve the problem and would go a long way to make everyone more accountable and make everyone more on the lookout for potential problems. Sometimes it is best to think "evolution, not revolution." Today our kids are bombarded with examples of poor behavior on some of the reality television shows on the networks and on cable. Behaviors which may seem funny on television may actually be quite wrong and hurtful in real life.

Reward good behavior. Society looks to punish poor behavior and people who may be the aggressor and in some cases the victims. I suggest that we really recognize those teams, schools and organizations that do things the right way. See a good example of sportsmanship and write that school or organization a note telling them you noticed. It amazes me that, each day our students do some extraordinary things and some things that are really above and beyond the norm. Let's all start to recognize those efforts instead of always dwelling on the negative things that can and do come up.

Bad news is everywhere. The media descends on stories with "the latest on the 'whatever' scandal" is on that day. The details about the situation, the people involved bring correspondents, news teams and reporters in droves to the scene for immediate updates on the crisis.

Good news travels slower. The media sometimes runs "feel good stories" but the day-to-day things our kids, coaches and teachers may do often go unnoticed. Maybe we, as parents, coaches, educators and community members should and could pay more attention to those things that really make us who we are. By doing so, we just might change the tide of the poor behavior and actions that can make us hang our heads and say, "How could this happen?" There are three types of people in the world . . . those that make things happen . . . those that watch things happen . . . and those who wonder, what happened? I think we know what group is best to be in! Let's make that good news travel faster and be the force of change. The time has come to act against harassment. intimidation and bullying and the action against HIB starts inside each of us.

Critical Thinking

1. How can children be empowered to speak up if they see injustice?
2. How does television contribute to the climate of intimidation, harassment and bullying in sports?

Internet References

Coach Bullying: More Frequent than You Might Think
    http://www.cnn.com/2014/01/13/health/coaches-bullying/index.html

Help us Fight Bullying in Sports
    http://www.youthsportspsychology.com/youth_sports_psychology_blog/?p=621

Stomp Out Bullying: Bullying and Sports
    http://www.stompoutbullying.org/index.php/information-and-resources/about-bullying-and-cyberbullying/bullying-and-sports

The Real Damage Bullying Coaches Can Inflict on Kids
    http://time.com/5382/the-real-damage-bullying-coaches-can-inflict-on-kids

---

Tom Curry has been an Athletic Director in Bergen County, New Jersey, as well as an adjunct professor in the Wellness and Exercise Science Department at Bergen Community College for 24 years. He has coached high school basketball and golf and was voted Bergen County Basketball Coach of the Year in 2002. He has spoken at the New Jersey Medical Society Sports Symposium and to parent groups on various issues pertaining to youth sports. He was inducted into the NJ Coaches Hall of Fame in 2012.

Unit 3

UNIT

Prepared by: Claire N. Rubman, *Suffolk County Community College, Selden, NY*

Development during Childhood: Cognition and Schooling

This unit considers the educational needs of a child from their school situation to the food that they eat and the emotional baggage that they carry with them.

Are all children in the United States educated equally regardless of their documentation status? What are some of the problems associated with education children from other countries? Consider how many languages a school must allow for and the cultural nuances associated with each ethnicity. How do schools embrace all children?

Over 23 percent of children in public schools today come from immigrant homes. This is a ubiquitous problem that has grown from 11 percent in the 1990s. Although they have had a legal right to be educated since 1982, Konings (2017) highlights the barriers that exist for these immigrant children. These problems include language barriers, cultural sensitivity, documentation issues, and interrupted education. Read about the cognitive, social, and emotional impact on children in "Protecting Immigrant Children's Right to Education" and Corey's (2016) "Immigrant Influxes put U.S. Schools to the Test".

Regardless of ethnicity, what does it mean to "educate" a child? Is there a list of facts that all children should know at any given age or is quality education comprised of a less tangible type of knowledge or skill set? Are we demanding too much from our children and, when we perceive that they are underperforming, are we inadvertently overmedicating them to compensate? Depression, attentional issues, and a lack of concentration seem to plague our educational paradigm. According to the Center for Disease Control, 6.4 million American children were diagnosed with ADHD in 2013. Two thirds of these children were prescribed medication such as Ritalin or Adderall. Read about diagnostic rates, environmental irritants, and educational pressures that are affecting our children and the rates of ADHD in our society in "Giving ADHD a Rest: With Diagnosis Rates Exploding Wildly, Is the Disorder a mental Health Crisis—Or a Cultural One" by Linau (2014). We continue this discussion by looking at alternatives to medication, for example, could the food that we eat impact our concentration and attention levels? Could eating healthily increase our cognitive abilities? Read about the essential vitamins and minerals that a child requires for healthy brain development in "Happy, Healthy Kids: Six Ways to Boost Mood, Calm ADHD and Ease Anxiety" by Lisa Turner (2014).

Some children attend school carrying a hefty load of baggage that is primarily their parent's responsibility. These children bear the guilt of their parents' poor choices. Over 3,000,000 children in the United States have parents who are currently serving prison sentences. These children are trying to educate themselves while shouldering the burden of their parents' crimes. They carry the stigma and shame with them throughout their school day. Learn about the "POPS" program and "Project WHAT" that have been established as support groups for children with incarcerated family members. Read about the impetus for the POPS program in "Breaking the Silence" by Troy Flint (2017).

Article   Prepared by: Claire N. Rubman, *Suffolk County Community College, Selden, NY*

New Faces of Blended Learning

Innovative schools are combining online and face-to-face learning to personalize education in a variety of ways.

MICHAEL B. HORN AND JULIA FREELAND FISHER

Learning Outcomes

After reading this article, you will be able to:

- Describe the instructional and infrastructure role that technology plays in the classroom today.

- Explain three trends that have emerged in blended learning situations, situation rotation, pacing, and flipped instruction.

The blended learning model—the combination of online learning and brick-and-mortar schooling—is not new. But as this model continues to evolve and mature, it's producing new kinds of learning experiences. Blended learning began decades ago as a practical solution to fill gaps in access to curriculum content. Schools that couldn't offer certain advanced or elective coursework found an answer in online courses that could affordably deliver content to students anytime and anywhere, often reaching across district and state lines. Although students continued to take traditional face-to-face classes, they could supplement these courses with online courses.

Online coursework was a breakthrough in its own right. But these course offerings eventually expanded to include a wider array of instructional models, taking advantage of the power of technology to rethink the choreography of the traditional classroom. Early blended models took the flexibility and accessibility of online learning and integrated it into brick-and-mortar classrooms, creating more differentiation while still maintaining age-based cohorts and course structures. By shifting some instruction online, teachers could devote more of their limited time to face-to-face coaching and small-group instruction, mainstays of any differentiated model. And online software

tools could also collect more and better data on how students were performing, thus enabling teachers to differentiate even more effectively.

In more recent years, the twin drumbeats of personalization and deeper learning have grown louder. The urge to use technology to meet the individual learning needs of every student undergirds a shift in blended learning that is well underway.

Teachers in this latest style of blended learning use technology not only to differentiate with greater precision but also to do away with the strict silos of bell schedules, courses, and age-based cohorts and to create richer experiences that produce deeper learning, such as projects spanning several weeks. In these blended learning models, technology does not just play an instructional role, delivering content and assessment on a flexible basis as students are ready. It also plays an infrastructure role, coordinating scheduling, testing, and student progress. These models often offer various learning pathways and modalities, rather than a single pathway or progression. Consequently, students have greater choice over what and how they learn.

Three Trends in Blended Learning

Over the last five years, the Clayton Christensen Institute has tracked the growth of these models in our Blended Learning Universe directory (www.blendedlearning.org), which profiles more than 400 blended learning schools. The data we've collected over the past six months points to three trends we're watching as schools continue to expand and evolve their blended approaches.

Schools Continue to Adopt Station Rotation

Station Rotation is one of the most popular blended learning models and the fastest-growing model, according to our data. Station Rotation is particularly popular among elementary schools because its basic structure fits naturally into many traditional elementary classrooms. Historically, elementary school teachers have used *centers*—dividing young students into small groups and rotating them among different learning stations—to organize and manage classroom learning. Adding a station with online learning to an existing center model comes naturally.

For example, at Bella Romero Academy, a K-8 public school in Greeley-Evans School District in Colorado, Station Rotation powers the school's goal of increasing the degree of personalization in each student's education. Principal Jonathan Cooney didn't mandate any particular model of blended learning; instead, his team identified principles that any instructional model should incorporate. "We articulated that the model used by each professional should include four key elements: tight feedback loops, targeted instruction, student ownership of learning, and high-quality peer-to-peer interactions." Cooney found that most teachers adopted Station Rotation as the best entry point to guarantee these key elements while increasing personalization.

Deagan Andrews, director of instructional technology for Greeley-Evans, has seen the same pattern in other schools across the district. "Our design teams, composed of teachers and principals, seem to gravitate toward a rotational model. I think Station Rotation provides a concrete place to start, and they can see how to implement and incorporate digital content, collaboration, and small-group instruction," he said.

Of course, Station Rotation merely describes the choreography of a classroom; any number of activities or designs can occur within and between given stations. Teachers at Bella Romero are finding ways to better differentiate instruction to align more precisely to students' needs. For example, students complete different work at the "same" station, based on their individual needs. "Students needing fluency use Achieve3000 as a digital tool, while those working on comprehension use i-Ready," Cooney said. "On their paper-and-pencil learning guide, different standards are highlighted to guide what work students will complete based on teacher analysis of student work already completed."

These efforts to differentiate instruction with greater precision are paying off. At Bella Romero, 93 percent of students qualify for free or reduced-price meals, 89 percent are ethnic minorities, and 60 percent are English language learners. Since adopting blended learning, the school has seen marked growth. In just three years, it has transformed from a struggling school to one that earned Colorado's highest designation for schools.

According to internal testing data, the school is showing significant growth for English language learners and students who qualify for free or reduced-price meals.

Schools Explore Ways to Unlock Flexible Pacing

It's unlikely that the growth of Station Rotation will slow down anytime soon. However, educators are also starting to look for elbow room around pacing and flexibility within their rotation models by freeing students and teachers from stringent time-based practices.

At Bella Romero, for example, teachers have often found that rotating students strictly on a timer—for instance, 20 min per station—may conflict with efforts to make the most effective use of digital content. A student may be required to change stations just minutes before finishing, or may start a lesson with only minutes remaining at the station. "Timer-based rotation seems less sensible to students and often causes them to budget their effort. If a student is finished with a lesson and five minutes remain, he simply kills the time," Cooney said.

To avoid time being wasted, Bella Romero teachers have loosened strict time allotments and instead designed a "tap-out" system that keeps students on task. Students are paired or put in groups of three, and when one student finishes his assigned lesson on the digital tool, he notifies the partner, who then takes her turn on the device.

In the coming years, we anticipate that middle schools may lead the way in pushing Station Rotation models even further toward the flexible use of time and pace, both within rotation models and by shepherding new models into the mix. At Piedmont Middle School in Piedmont, Alabama, for example, school leaders had observed that advanced students were not being challenged enough and struggling students were not receiving sufficient help from teachers to make meaningful progress. Although Piedmont had a 1:1 laptop program at the time, and several teachers were using Station Rotation, school leaders were not seeing the growth in student achievement they desired.

To address this challenge and give students more ownership of their learning, Piedmont shifted to a new model in 2014. Students now spend their time in three blocks each day: Class Time, Team Time, and My Time. This structure enables students to progress at their own pace and gives teachers ample time to work with students individually and in small groups.

Class Time is a rotation learning period during which students work independently and at their own pace on online content in math and reading and then apply the concepts and skills they gained from the online content in interdisciplinary projects. Each project is linked to standards and is assigned to students when they reach those specific standards.

During Team Time, students meet in a small team with a teacher who serves as a mentor to help them set short-term and long-term goals, build relationships, and explore personal interests. A given team stays with the same teacher throughout middle school. "We wanted to create a family atmosphere inside the school so every student has an adult here who monitors them and knows them from year to year," Snow said. Teachers use formative assessments to monitor and focus their team's efforts. During this time, students also have the opportunity to split off individually and take "à la carte" online high school courses to work on content above their grade level.

During My Time, students drive their own learning and apply the self-directed learning strategies they developed during Team Time. They use an adaptive online curriculum to progress independently on specific goals they set with their teachers, focusing on the core subjects in which they are furthest behind as determined by their scores on the Northwest Evaluation Association's MAP assessments. Students who are fully caught up can choose which core subjects to work on during My Time. Students also have opportunities to collaborate with a teacher, an intern, or their peers to improve their learning. Teachers spend half of the My Time period reflecting on students' data with their grade-level teams; they spend the other half providing targeted instruction to students.

High Schools Disrupt Traditional Structures with the Flex Model

At the high school level, given that older students have different development and instructional needs and teachers are more focused on teaching specific subjects and courses, we see different blended learning models thrive. These disruptive innovations tend to start outside mainstream classrooms, and then make their way to the core after they've proved effective.

For example, in 2014, Western Wayne Schools in Pershing, Indiana, created an alternative blended learning program to support high school students who were failing courses and in danger of dropping out. Although the district's students had a 90 percent passing rate on state exams in elementary and middle school, high school teachers complained that some students were entering high school academically unprepared. The alternative program began as a school-within-a-school model, in which students could enroll in online courses to recover credits while also enrolling in traditional courses. Students could complete their credit-recovery courses at any time instead of re-enrolling in courses and completing them on a semester schedule.

Recognizing that this flexibility in pacing could benefit all students, the district recently expanded the program to offer online courses as an option for all high school students. Students can choose to enroll in an online course, which they complete at their own pace in a flexible classroom environment with a teacher during the school day. These flexible learning environments often look more like tutoring or group-study sessions than traditional classrooms.

In describing the changes the district has made to support these blended efforts, assistant superintendent George Philhower said, "We have made adjustments to how we look at traditional school timelines (grading periods, semesters, class periods, grade levels) and have begun to shift to a system that guarantees learning instead of seat time. Instead of receiving credits at the end of the semester, students at our high school are earning credits based on when they complete their coursework."

Wayne's new model has been especially powerful for students who had often fallen through the cracks. "In the traditional system, students who failed a class had to repeat it the following semester, sometimes the following school year. They would often fall into a 'failure trap,' where it soon becomes impossible to pass while juggling other course loads," Philhower said. "Now, students have the flexibility to complete coursework in whatever way works best for them."

Districts like Wayne are seeing promising results with a disruptive blended learning model that upends, rather than reinforces, seat time. Such a model also tends to disrupt the traditional role of teachers as deliverers of content. As Chris Walter, a blended learning math and science teacher at Innovations Early College High School in Salt Lake City, Utah, said, "One of the biggest struggles for me is giving away a lot of control." Walters's school operates a Flex model of blended learning, in which students access all the assignments and learning resources for most of their courses online. "I am no longer responsible for making each student do my assigned task at the time appointed by me. Instead, I've needed to shift to identifying and helping the students that need additional support."

That shift, although a promising on-ramp to more flexible learning environments, may not come quickly in high schools where teachers are used to overseeing specific content areas and delivering content through traditional lectures and course structures. Therefore, we expect that models that preserve course structures—particularly flipped classroom models, in which teachers record their own lectures or leverage open education resources and then use class time for projects or differentiated instruction—will continue to increase in popularity.

Moving Forward

These three trends are consistent with the manner in which innovations tend to unfold. On the one hand, classrooms are quickly turning to models like Station Rotation and flipped instruction, which sustain but improve on traditional time and cohort-based classrooms. On the other hand, disruptive instructional models are taking root beyond the traditional classroom as schools strive to move beyond stringent pacing and course structures.

With an eye on innovative models and better outcomes, blended learning is still in flux, in the best sense of the word. Schools are innovating rapidly; indeed, in the past six months, we've seen at least a dozen schools that have shifted from using a single model of blended learning to using multiple models. More than 81 of the now 400-plus active schools in our database use a combination of two or more blended learning models. As we talk to educators, our intuition is that this is a sign of things to come.

Blended Learning Models

The majority of blended-learning programs resemble one of four models:

1. **Rotation Model:** Students rotate on a fixed schedule or at the teacher's discretion between learning modalities, at least one of which is online learning. Other activities might include small-group or full-class instruction, group projects, individual tutoring, and pencil-and-paper assignments. The students learn mostly on the brick-and-mortar campus, except for any homework assignments. Variations include Station Rotation, in which all students rotate through the same stations within a contained classroom, and Flipped Classroom, in which students participate individually in online learning off-site and then attend the brick-and-mortar school for teacher-guided practice and projects.

2. **Flex Model:** Online learning is the backbone of student learning, even if it directs students to offline activities at times. Students move on an individually customized, fluid schedule among learning modalities. The teacher of record is on-site, and students learn mostly on the brick-and-mortar campus, except for any homework assignments. The teacher or other adults provide face-to-face support on a flexible and adaptive as-needed basis through activities such as small-group instruction, group projects, and individual tutoring.

3. **À La Carte Model:** Students take one or more courses entirely online to accompany other

experiences they are having at a brick-and-mortar school or learning center. The teacher of record for the online course is the online teacher. Students may take the online course either on the brick-and-mortar campus or at the learning center.

4. **Enriched Virtual Model:** Students attend required face-to-face learning sessions with their teacher of record and then are free to complete their remaining coursework remotely, apart from the face-to-face teacher. The same person generally serves as both the online and face-to-face teacher.

Source: From *Blended: Using Disruptive Innovation to Improve Schools,* by M. B. Horn and H. Staker, 2014. San Francisco: Jossey-Bass. Copyright © 2014 Michael B. Horn and Heather Staker. Used with permission.

Critical Thinking

1. How has technology changed the way you learn and think?
2. Which subjects in the school curriculum are enhanced by technology?

Internet References

3 Ways to Maximize Kids' Learning with Technology
https://www.commonsensemedia.org/blog/3-ways-to-maximize-kids-learning-with-technology

10 Reasons Today's Students NEED Technology in the Classroom
https://www.securedgenetworks.com/blog/10-reasons-today-s-students-need-technology-in-the-classroom

Technology and Children
http://www.naeyc.org/content/technology-and-young-children

Technology in Early Childhood Education
http://www.child-encyclopedia.com/technology-early-childhood-education/according-experts/learning-digital-age-putting-education-back

Technology Is transforming What Happens When a Child Goes to School
https://www.economist.com/news/briefing/21725285-reformers-are-using-new-software-personalise-learning-technology-transforming-what-happens

MICHAEL B. HORN is a cofounder and distinguished fellow of education research at the Clayton Christensen Institute (www.christensen institute.org).

JULIA FREELAND FISHER is a director of education research at the Clayton Christensen Institute (www.christenseninstitute.org).

Horn, Michael B.; Fisher, Julia Freeland. "New Faces of Blended Learning," *Educational Leadership*, March 2017. Copyright ©2017 by Association for Supervision & Curriculum Development. Used with permission.

Article   Prepared by: Claire N. Rubman, *Suffolk County Community College, Selden, NY*

Breaking the Silence

A growing coalition is working to support and give greater voice to students with incarcerated parents.

Troy Flint

Learning Outcomes

After reading this article, you will be able to:

- Explain the "spill-over effect."

- Describe the purpose of groups such as POPS.

- Discuss how parental incarceration impacts children's lives such as social exclusion, low self-esteem, poverty, depression, and obesity.

It had been a year since Dennis Danziger had last seen John, the most talented writer in his English class at Venice High School. Now, the teacher and former sitcom writer was making the long trip up Interstate 5 to reunite with a favorite student. Danziger had taken a special interest in John, pushing him toward college and asking his coworkers to monitor his progress, make sure he stayed on track. So, it was bittersweet—more bitter than sweet—when Danziger sat down across from his prized pupil.

"The guy waiting for me, John, who had been one of my favorite students ever, had been inside for a year. I was just six feet away and I didn't recognize him," Danziger recalled. "He had lost a tremendous amount of weight. I was actually asking him certain questions to make sure who he was."

Twelve months into a 22-year sentence for drunkenly shooting a man in the shoulder, John had shed his boyish fat and exchanged any semblance of a normal adolescent life for a thoroughly adult existence. New Folsom Prison has that effect on people; it's a transformative experience of the most unpleasant kind. Though John's appearance had changed dramatically, he retained his connection to Venice High.

When Danziger returned home, he received a letter from John, who asked him to read the letter to his class. Next week in class, he read the letter: "Dear Student, I sat in his classroom a year ago and now I'm doing 22 inside. The only thing I ever promised my mother was that she would see me walk across the stage and now she'll never have that and who knows if she'll ever see me alive again. So do what your teachers say."

The words sat heavily in the air and then an unlikely voice rang out.

"This one lady with a 0.0 average who just slept the whole time sat up and talked," Danziger recalled. "No one had ever heard her speak. She said, 'My brother is in New Folsom' and she talked and talked and there was this link between the letter I read from John and what she had to say."

That night, Danziger relayed the story to his wife, Amy Friedman, who responded, "Let's start a club!" That gave birth to Pain of the Prison System (POPS), a nonprofit organization that supports high school students who have a connection to an incarcerated loved one or have themselves been incarcerated. POPS began with just six students in a Venice High classroom and now has seven affiliates (six in California and one in Minnesota). It's the only school-based program of its kind in the country. Friedman is committed to establishing POPS clubs in schools nationwide, a quest that has roots in her own biography.

"In the 1990s, I was a newspaper columnist who went into prison [on a writing assignment] and fell in love with a prisoner and raised his children. My girls were very young when their father went to prison and preadolescent and young teenagers when they came into my life," Friedman recalled.

"They never spoke of their father and where he was. They became world class liars as a result and really struggled in school and socially because of their secret. This secret came from them having been stigmatized when they were younger and believing people would judge them. I saw that by carrying around this secret, they were hurting themselves. They're in their 30s and still carry this around."

Parental Incarceration

Friedman's daughters are far from alone. The current rate of imprisonment is roughly four times higher than in 1970 and more than 2 million people are currently incarcerated in the United States. About 3 million children in the United States have an incarcerated parent—a figure which doesn't include those in local jails. Christopher Wildeman, associate professor of Policy Analysis and Management at Cornell University and senior researcher at the Rockwell Foundation Research Unit in Copenhagen, Denmark, began to explore the effects of parental incarceration in 2006.

"I became interested in parental incarceration through my interest in family inequality. I read a lot of the research and it highlighted neighborhood conditions, family structure, and social class, but really little of it talked about contact with the criminal justice system," Wildeman explained. "That seemed like a big oversight given what I knew about the consequences of incarceration. I poked around thinking there should be some big research literature that looks at the family impacts of incarceration, but there wasn't much there. I decided to fill that in to get a better sense of how this life experience affects some of the most vulnerable kids we have in educational institutions."

Wildeman found that the negative impact of parental incarceration was even more severe than he expected initially, with an incarcerated father roughly doubling the risk of homelessness for a child. He also identified a strong connection between parental incarceration and gaps in student health and academic outcomes, which he documented in a book with Rutgers University-Newark Professor Sara Wakefield. *Children of the Prison Boom: Mass Incarceration and the Future of American Inequality* shows that the rate of parental imprisonment generally has skyrocketed and that racial disparities in parental incarceration rates are growing and a significant source of social inequality.

One in 40 White children born in 1978 went on to have a parent imprisoned. For White children born in 1990, just 12 years later, the figure was one in 25. For Black children born in 1978, the rate of parental imprisonment was one in seven; by 1990 the rate had jumped to one in four. And among Black children born in 1990 to high school dropouts, more than half (50.5 percent) had a father imprisoned. As *Children of the Prison Boom* describes it, "These estimates, robustness checks, and extensions to longitudinal data indicate that parental imprisonment has emerged as a novel—and distinctively American—childhood risk that is concentrated among black children and children of low-education parents."

"What was surprising to me was just how much higher rates of parental incarceration, combined with these negative individual level effects, exacerbated racial inequality in child well-being," Wildeman said. "So, depending on the outcome or set of outcomes, mass incarceration increased racial disparities in school well-being between 10 percent and 60 percent. When we think about one factor that affects racial inequality, that's a pretty big one."

Overall, 45 percent of incarcerated parents are Black, 28 percent are White, and 21 percent are Latino, but the impact of incarceration is not limited to the imprisoned and their families. Holly Foster, associate professor of sociology at Texas A&M and John Hagan, the John D. MacArthur Professor of Sociology and Law at Northwestern University have been studying the effects of parental incarceration since 2007. When asked for their most significant findings, they cited the link between parental incarceration and social exclusion and the negative impact of parental incarceration on educational outcomes—even for students whose parents aren't imprisoned.

"Parental incarceration leads to children's social exclusion in late adolescence and early adulthood through the mechanism of education. If these students were given the support to attain higher levels of education, their social exclusion may be prevented," Foster and Hagan wrote in an e-mail. "Also, schools with higher concentrations of incarcerated fathers lead to lower education among children who themselves have an incarcerated father, as well as among students who don't have a father incarcerated.

"This work speaks to the phenomenon of 'spillover effects' and suggests parental incarceration is a social problem that has broad-reaching implications for students."

While the effects of parental incarceration are profound, they are not equally distributed. Parental incarceration has severe consequences for educational behavior and health that are often concentrated in low-income and heavily minority neighborhoods. Youth who have experienced parental incarceration are at higher risk for depression, anxiety, obesity, and asthma. Similarly, a 2015 study published in the *Journal of Health and Social Behavior* showed that youth with incarcerated parents are more likely to exhibit developmental delays and attention deficits.

"Children suffer when they have a parent incarcerated, but not all children suffer in the same way and the deleterious consequences of parental incarceration are stronger for some groups of children than other children," said Kristin Turney, associate professor of sociology at the University of California, Irvine and author of "The Unequal Consequences of Mass Incarceration for Children." Turney adds, "Children who are racial and ethnic minorities and poor children are more likely to experience parental incarceration. Therefore, just because more of these children are exposed to parental incarcerations, parental incarceration may increase racial/ethnic and social class inequalities in educational outcomes."

While there is no easy answer to this societal problem, support programs can be the start of a broader solution.

Support Programs

"A good example is Pains of the Prison System, Turney says. "They are creating a supportive space for children affected by parental incarceration."

POPS has earned a wealth of media coverage, hosted visitors from the *Los Angeles Times* and National Public Radio, and even seen its students visit the White House as youth ambassadors.

"It is amazing. They bring in incredible people; they write and do a lot of poetry. Then end up taking what could be a negative and channel it toward the positive," said Venice High Principal Oryla Wiedoeft. "I look at the kids and think, 'I would never know your dad is in jail because you have it so together.' It's all about being super constructive and giving the kids a safe place to talk and challenge their feelings."

At the outset, POPS had three basic principles: meet at lunch to make the club available to everyone and to bond over the breaking of bread; adhere to the rule that no one has to say why they're attending; and incorporate an art-based component to promote creative and cathartic expression.

"It was magical from the getgo," Friedman remembered. "The very first day, the very first meeting, this little 10th-grader walks into the room and takes a peanut butter and jelly sandwich and sits down. Then the second girl walks into the room and they're both 10th-graders and they go—'you?!' These two girls had been friends since kindergarten and hang out together and never knew that they both had parents who were incarcerated. It created this incredible bond."

Encouraged by the early returns, Friedman quickly looked to expand the program to other schools, but met with resistance. "People say that we don't have that population; I say that's just not true. My girls always thought they were the only ones and I knew damn well that wasn't true. The other response is 'we don't want to target that population.' Well, you're not targeting them, you're not forcing people to join. It's not like 'go get counseling.'"

Far from being forced, some of POPS's biggest advocates have reached out to Friedman and Danziger for help in starting programs at their own schools.

Another major change agent in the crusade to support youth with incarcerated parents is Project! WHAT, a Bay Area-based group. WHAT! stands for "We're Here and Talking" and the people doing the talking are students. The program uses youth who have experienced parental incarceration to develop curriculum and facilitate trainings aimed at improving policies and services for peers experiencing the same hardship and adults who want to learn more about the needs of this population.

Project WHAT! takes its inspiration from the Incarcerated Parents Bill of Rights that was created at San Francisco State University. The group has two cohorts, one in Oakland that's focused more on presentations and lobbying and another in San Francisco that emphasizes campaign work. Project WHAT! candidates fill out applications with essay questions designed to measure their commitment and suitability for a job which can involve door-to-door canvassing, counseling, meeting facilitation, political advocacy, and policy analysis. The youth team members on the review committee evaluate the responses with a matrix that emphasizes important qualities like respect and capacity for teamwork. Those who make the grade participate in a summer orientation before being deployed to the field when school starts in the fall.

"They get people to think about children," said Alisha Murdock, a peer mentor for Project WHAT! and a program alumna. "Our main goal is to raise awareness about something that's never talked about. We're starting a conversation about how to start a conversation with students of incarcerated parents."

That conversation is about to get a lot bigger thanks to an expanded partnership between Project WHAT! and the San Francisco Unified School District. In March, the San Francisco USD Board of Education resolved to assess its curriculum in order to determine how the district can better serve the needs of students with incarcerated parents. Project WHAT! helped write the resolution which, among other items, could result in standardized training for district staff and the introduction of videos and literature that sensitize adults to the plight of students experiencing parental incarceration.

"As far as I know, we're the first school district to develop a specific policy or plan to support school districts with incarcerated parents. The students themselves felt heard and valued and that's a huge part of why we did this," said San Francisco Unified School Board President Matt Haney. "We wanted to communicate that their schools are on their side, and to the extent that they haven't been, we want to work with them to address that."

Haney introduced the resolution along with Vice President Shamann Walton after participating in a Project WHAT! training session for SFUSD counselors, social workers, and support staff in 2015. Impressed by what he saw, Haney requested a report from district staff on what they knew about youth with incarcerated parents and the services that SFUSD offered the population.

"What came out of that was a clear need to do more and to build on and expand the efforts that had already started. We met with students from Project WHAT! and heard about their experiences, their needs and some of the ways in which their schools could better understand them. We then consulted organizations that work with students with incarcerated parents and put together a set of policies and approaches to address this population and their unique set of needs."

One recurring theme was that misunderstandings about students with incarcerated parents created barriers to learning and participation and feelings of stigma and exclusion. The students agreed that if school staff follow best practices on how to discuss the issue, identify resources, and facilitate communication, better academic and social experiences would result.

"When a child comes to school and says I saw my dad hit my mom last night, the teacher knows what to do and can offer them resources," Murdock said. "With incarcerated parents, they hear 'Oh, my mom just went to jail' and they don't know how to deal with that when it should be 'Maybe you should email this person, contact Project WHAT!, or go to camp at Project Avary.' One of the biggest things is making sure teachers know how to deal with it."

The first step toward dealing with parental incarceration is identifying the affected students. Castaic Union School District Trustee Victor Torres explained that this is an underrecognized challenge that districts need to address more aggressively. Torres compared it to the way in which foster youth and homeless students were often overlooked and underserved before their designation as groups requiring additional support in California's new school funding system.

"The jail is right there in Lancaster. Our parents from L.A. get convicted, end up going to that jail, and the families move up to my area," Torres said.

California Inspector General Robert Barton notes that's a common occurrence in a state the size of California where prisoners are often located far from home. His office, which is responsible for providing oversight of 10 different aspects of state prison operations, encourages visits from loved ones in part because he sees them as a key to rehabilitation.

"It's important because everyone has a different trigger that causes them to change and often it's their children. They don't want them to follow in their footsteps; they want to be a better example and get out and provide for them. You can't measure the impact of incarceration without taking into account the children outside. And to a large extent, those children are a forgotten demographic."

Torres is pushing for solutions to support students in his district who are experiencing parental incarceration, an effort that is challenging at the most fundamental level.

Identifying Students

"One of the most significant problems we have with this population is not being able to identify them because it's not one of those social norms where people say 'my husband's in jail and that's why we're here.' These students have a traumatic experience in their lives that goes unknown, so it's not until after the kid is acting out or gets into trouble that some of these things come to the surface."

Torres advocates opening the lines of communication and working with families to remove the stigma of parental incarceration in the hopes that greater transparency will aid school districts in supporting students with incarcerated parents. He is also exploring the idea of an after-school program that focuses more on socialization than academics, to relieve some of the burden on parents and reduce the feelings of exclusion that are often a product of parental incarceration. That approach aligns with the one recommended by Cornell's Wildeman who, noting the financial impact of an incarcerated parent, suggests extended childcare and programs that defray expenses for the remaining parent as valuable supports.

"Mentoring programs can do a lot of good, but if schools wanted to design an intervention, I'd push them beyond that toward interventions that support the primary caregiver who's left behind," Wildeman said. "When you talk to folks who have family members in prison, you tend to hear about things that could diminish their costs a little bit and they tend to talk about time constraints and the stigma of incarceration and not wanting people to know."

Similarly, Foster and Hagan recommend that school districts supplement mentoring programs with an investment in academic programs for students experiencing parental incarceration to help ensure high school completion and preparation for college success and consider funding scholarships that would help offset economic disadvantages.

All researchers agree that further investigation is needed to determine how to facilitate better outcomes for youth with incarcerated parents.

"As a first step, school boards and elected officials could be particularly helpful by facilitating and allowing access to schools to study this pressing social problem," Foster and Hagan wrote. "More detailed data on how parental incarceration effects work would allow researchers to better understand the types of programs that need to be introduced to ensure all students succeed."

In the meantime, the tried-and-true method of letting students know that adults and educators care for them comes highly recommended from those who have been through the struggle and come out the other side.

"When I was in 6th grade, no one asked me what was going on when I started missing school; none of my teachers paid attention," said Murdock. "Something as simple as asking if someone is OK makes a difference. Just asking the question opens the child up to all different kinds of possibilities. Let children know it's OK to talk about and give them their voices back."

Critical Thinking

1. Discuss three ways that the school system could support children whose parents are incarcerated.

2. What can incarcerated parents do to support their children?

Internet References

Children of Incarcerated Parents
https://www.ncsl.org/documents/cyf/childrenofincarceratedparents.pdf

Office of Children and Family Services—Children of Incarcerated Parents
http://ocfs.ny.gov/main/incarcerated_parents/default.asp

Supporting Children and Families of Prisoners
https://www.childwelfare.gov/topics/supporting/support-services/prisoners/

When Parents Are in Prison the Children Suffer
https://well.blogs.nytimes.com/2016/04/26/when-parents-are-in-prison-children-suffer/

Why Children with Parents in Prison Are Especially Burdened
https://www.theatlantic.com/politics/archive/2015/12/why-children-with-parents-in-prison-are-especially-burdened/433638/

TROY FLINT is the California School Boards Association's senior director of communications.

Article   Prepared by: Claire N. Rubman, *Suffolk County Community College, Selden, NY*

Immigrant Influxes Put U.S. Schools to the Test

COREY MITCHELL

Learning Outcomes

After reading this article, you will be able to:

- Articulate three issues associated with educating immigrants in the United States.

- Explain the "cultural disconnect."

Bishar Hassan spends his days navigating the halls and classrooms of Talahi Elementary School, working to embrace and empower the dozens of Somali students who have arrived since the start of the year.

Across town, his brother, Ahmed Hassan, fills a similar role at Discovery Community School, another campus that has experienced a recent surge in enrollment of Somali students.

The Hassan brothers are part of a growing community of Somali residents in this central Minnesota city of 65,000. The recent influx of immigrant students is nothing new in the St. Cloud school district, where English-language-learner enrollment has spiked by 350 percent in the past 15 years.

Today, roughly 20 percent of the district's 10,000 students are English-language learners, many of them with ties to the East African nation of Somalia.

Similar situations are developing in districts around the country.

The United States is now home to the largest number of foreign-born black people in its history—and many are K-12 students enrolled in public schools. The English-learners among them are overwhelmingly native Spanish, French, or Haitian Creole speakers, but districts have had to adjust on the fly to meet the needs of students who arrive communicating in less frequently spoken languages, such as Amharic, Haitian Creole, and Somali.

Nationwide, nearly 35,000 K-12 students report that they speak Somali at home, making it the eighth most common native language for English-learners in public schools, according to federal data from the 2013–2014 school year.

Somali families began resettling here in large numbers at the turn of the century, and their children have become fixtures in St. Cloud's schools. About 1,625 of the district's English-learners are Somali. And as educators in the St. Cloud district have found, language is often just the first hurdle they encounter when new immigrant communities arrive.

Social service agencies often look to place refugee families in communities where they have access to jobs and other support services, even in places that are not traditional magnets for newcomers.

"They could pop up in places that maybe even haven't had English-learners before," said Delia Pompa, a senior fellow for education policy at the Washington-based Migration Policy Institute. "It's always a challenge to work with English-learners . . . but you can't overlook the effect of culture and language."

The Minnesota chapter of the Council on American–Islamic Relations filed a federal civil rights complaint against the St. Cloud school district in 2011, alleging a hostile environment for the district's Somali students that included widespread and frequent harassment based in large measure, on religion. The majority of the Somali community is Muslim.

Five years later, remnants of that tension remain.

"The St. Cloud school district is a long way away from really being a place where all students feel completely welcome," said Jaylani Hussein, the executive director of the council's Minnesota chapter.

Cultural and Linguistic Liasions

The Hassan brothers are on the front lines of St. Cloud's efforts to better serve its ever-expanding English-learner population and integrate the Somali community.

They officially work as bilingual communication support specialists. Their duties range from providing verbal and written translations into Somali and English, advising students, cultural navigation, and working to bridge the language and cultural gaps that emerge between district staff members and Somali families.

"We're in between two stones when it comes to bridging that gap between the communities we serve and the institutions we work for," Ahmed Hassan said.

One day, the brothers are explaining to parents that all of their children, including those who have disabilities, have the right to a public education. The next, they're helping colleagues understand that Somali students who don't make eye contact aren't being disrespectful; in their culture, children are expected to look down when adults speak to them.

The district has ramped up its efforts to recruit Somali residents, like the brothers, who can relate to the students, many of whom are refugees of the civil war between ethnic groups that erupted in their country decades ago and continues today.

Sundis Ibrahim, 15, arrived in Minnesota two years ago from a Kenyan refugee camp, knowing little English. She's a sophomore here at Apollo High School, where nearly a quarter of the 1,400 students are Somali.

For Sundis and her classmates, the promise of the bright future their families envision in America is housed within the school walls.

The soft-spoken teenager has made connections since coming to Minnesota, but language remains a barrier. She struggles with science and English/language arts classes, but said that teachers often praise her effort.

"I understand the questions, but I don't always know the answers," Sundis said.

The same could be said of school district staff.

"Sense of Belonging"

Natalie Prasch, St. Cloud's director of English-learner programs, recruited the Hassan brothers, at separate times, when they came to the district's Welcome Center to enroll their younger siblings in school.

All told, eight of their siblings have attended or are attending school in St. Cloud; the youngest is a seven-year-old second grader.

For their brothers and sisters, "everything looked different, the system, the people they interacted with, the culture," said Bashir Hassan, who is 29. "That sense of belonging was the first struggle."

The same holds true for Ahmed Hassan, 30. He still remembers the day he came to the United States from a Kenyan refugee camp. His arrival in September 2008 ushered in a new life and new hopes, but so much uncertainty. His brother Bashir was his guide.

"He was my counselor, my adviser of what to do and where to go when it comes to being successful in this country," Ahmed Hassan said.

Schools across the country are educating more than 800,000 immigrant students who have been in American schools for less than three years. And as that population has grown, the U.S. Department of Education has announced plans to work more intently to address the needs of both refugee and black English-learner students in public schools.

Those populations intersect in St. Cloud, where Somali students who spent their entire lives in the desert and tropical climates of Africa must adjust to Minnesota's brutal winters.

"We're taking kids who grew up in the desert and sticking them in iceboxes," Prasch said.

During the winter months, the district is often tracking down coats, hats, and gloves for students at the same time they're administering home-language surveys—a set of questions used to identify the language or languages an ELL student speaks and understands.

Some students suffer from malnutrition and its mental and physical aftereffects. Those children often hoard food in their lockers because they're so used to going without.

Then, there are the students with no formal education; for them, pencils and books are foreign objects.

Teachers and Somali staff members alike say the students who've had little to no experience with schooling are easy to spot. To address their needs initially, more time is spent focusing on structure and order than curriculum and learning English.

In its high schools, St. Cloud has "English Academy" courses designed to aid newcomer English-learners and struggling long-term ELLs get up to speed while teaching core subjects such as biology and math.

In social studies classes, teachers tailor lesson plans to incorporate a global view of events, both past and present. In several classrooms at Apollo High, maps of Africa and Minnesota are posted side-by-side on classroom walls.

Counselors also work to integrate students in English-only courses to help their language development. Almost all the courses have Somali-speaking paraprofessionals at the ready to translate and address student questions.

Despite recognition from the U.S. Department of Education for its efforts to educate ELLs, the district hasn't been able to close a yawning achievement gap between English-learners and native English speakers—a problem that vexes most school systems.

Talahi Elementary, where roughly 45 percent of students are Somali, is a state "priority school," a label attached to Minnesota's most persistently low-performing Title I schools. With test scores among the bottom 5 percent in the state, the state department of education is closely monitoring Talahi's performance and turnaround plans.

"We view language as an opportunity [not] a deficit," said Principal Kate Flynn, "but we're always nervous about test scores."

Cultural Disconnect?

While St. Cloud works to support the English-language development of its students, district officials say it has been just as important to make Somali students and their families feel welcome in schools and part of the community, which remains a work in progress.

In the district's middle and high schools, Muslim students have access to private rooms with prayer rugs for the five daily prayers. Districtwide, school lunch menus provide pork-free options for students, and staff members try to spur the newcomer students' interest in sports, culture clubs, and other extracurricular activities to develop connections beyond the classroom.

Somali student–athletes played key roles on Apollo High's 2014 state championship soccer team, and track and field teams have drawn plenty of Somali participants. The district has partnered with the University of Minnesota to develop uniforms for female athletes who wear hijab, the headscarves worn by some Muslim girls and women.

St. Cloud's Technical High School, the site of Somali student protests last spring over anti-Muslim harassment, began an international club that allows English-learner students to showcase their cultural heritage.

"When you're separated, it's really hard to feel like you're a part of the community," assistant superintendent Marsha Baisch said. "You feel different, you feel other."

Some students still feel that way.

A 2011 settlement ending a federal civil rights investigation of the treatment of Somali students in St. Cloud requires the school district to report all allegations of harassment.

Under the agreement, the district must make its schools more welcoming to Somalis.

But the agreement didn't signal an end to the resentment and clashes in the district.

Last spring, racial and religious tensions at Technical High School erupted when students and parents, most of them Somali, alleged that school officials did not adequately respond to bullying incidents and anti-Islamic discrimination.

A social media post that implied a Technical High student had ties to the Islamic State terrorist group whose adherents have been responsible for deadly attacks, sparked the protest.

The postroiled St. Cloud's tight-knit Somali community. The ensuing unrest drew the attention of Minnesota Gov. Mark Dayton, who attended community forums in the city.

Several of the Hassan brothers' younger siblings graduated from Tech High, the site of the mass walkout last spring. As employees, they wonder if enough efforts have been made to hire Somali teachers and administrators.

Struggle to Find Black Teachers

Finding and attracting Somali-speaking teaching candidates have proved challenging. Only one of the district's 700-plus teachers is Somali. Not many of the district's teachers are black.

As an adjunct instructor at local St. Cloud State University and the nearby College of St. Benedict, Prasch is always on the lookout for teaching candidates. The district is teaming with St. Cloud State to groom more Somali teaching candidates, including an effort to provide a pathway to help district staff already working as paraprofessionals to earn degrees.

Hiring trusted community members is key to building a rapport, said Pompa, of the Migration Policy Institute. But the strategy could take time to produce results in St. Cloud.

Many students rely on loans to help pay for college, but under Islamic law, devout Muslims are prohibited from taking on interest-based loans. So many of the Somali St. Cloud schools employees have to work their way through school, often at a slower pace than their peers.

Bishar Hassan, who is a semester away from earning his bachelor's degree at St. Cloud State, couldn't peel away from his job in the district to be a full-time student.

He and his brother felt duty-bound to support his family and the city's Somali community.

"We found Minnesota to be our home," he said. "This is my favorite thing to do in my life, [making] a difference in the lives of others."

Critical Thinking

1. Discuss the challenges that arise as non-English speaking immigrants are welcomed into schools and communities.

2. Discuss the cultural difficulties that Somalis and other immigrants face as they assimilate into the American culture in their new communities.

3. How can American communities make the influx of new immigrants feel more welcome?

Internet References

Big Influx of Non-English Speakers Challenges Educational System

http://projects.ctmirror.org/fairfielded/index.php/big-influx-non-english-speakers-challenges-educational-system

Immigration and Cultural Diversity—Public Eye

http://www.publiceye.org/ark/immigrants/CulturalDiv.html

New Somali Refugee Arrivals in Minnesota Are Increasing

- http://www.startribune.com/new-somali-refugee-arrivals-in-minnesota-are-increasing/281197521/#1

Why Immigration Is Not about Making "Them" More Like "Us"

http://www.theatlantic.com/politics/archive/2015/10/should-immigration-require-assimilation/406759/

Article   Prepared by: Claire N. Rubman, *Suffolk County Community College, Selden, NY*

Happy, Healthy Kids

Six Ways to Boost Mood, Calm ADHD, and Ease Anxiety

LISA TURNER

Learning Outcomes

After reading this article, you will be able to:

- Articulate how many children and adolescents in the United States experience mental health issues.

- Describe the role of fats and additives in good mental health.

- Explain how vitamins, protein, and herbal alternatives can alleviate some mental health issues such as depression, anxiety, or sleep disorders.

Only 30 years ago, it was thought that children did not experience depression or other mental health issues. We now know that an estimated 4 million children and adolescents in the U.S. suffer from serious mental disorders, and that as many as 21 percent of kids ages 9–17 have a diagnosable addictive or mental disorder that causes impairment.

Mental disorders in children range from depression, anxiety, and attention deficit disorder (ADD), to psychosis and schizophrenia. These conditions may be mild enough to cause only occasional, temporary distress—or severe enough to disrupt and damage lives.

But treating kids for mental disorders is tricky, especially since the effects of medications can vary, and side effects can be severe. If you suspect that your child has a mental disorder, it's critical to get a good diagnosis from a doctor or health care provider who specializes in pediatric mental health. In severe cases, medication and/or psychotherapy may be required.

However, many mental health conditions in kids, including ADHD, anxiety, and mild depression, can be soothed with natural alternatives. Even if medication is required, supplements and herbs can often enhance the treatment. Be sure to check with your health care provider first, and then consider some of these natural alternatives:

1. **Subtract the additives.** Studies suggest that food additives—including colorings, preservatives, artificial flavors, sugars, and MSG—exacerbate hyperactivity and can worsen symptoms of attention deficit hyperactivity disorder (ADHD). Gluten, added to many sauces, soups, and other products, may also be a problem. In one study, undiagnosed celiac disease was found to cause a number of issues, including ADHD and behavior disorders. And the artificial sweetener aspartame is broken down in the brain into aspartic acid, which can lead to anxiety and depression and inhibit serotonin production.

2. **Focus on fat.** It's crucial to brain health, maintaining flexibility of cell membranes to ensure they can better send and receive information. But the type of fat is important. Saturated fat may impact brain plasticity, and has been linked with symptoms of anxiety in some people. Omega-3 fats, however, keep nerve cell membranes flexible, and several studies suggest they help alleviate ADHD-related symptoms and depression. Some studies have also suggested that a deficiency in DHA, a type of omega-3, hampers transmission of serotonin, norepinephrine, and dopamine, neurotransmitters involved in mood. Wild Alaskan salmon, sardines, walnuts, and flax seeds are good food sources of omega-3s. Or choose a high-quality omega-3 supplement.

3. **Try herbal cures.** Some herbs have been shown in clinical trials to be both safe and effective. In one study of more than 100 kids under the age of 12, St. John's wort alleviated symptoms of mild to moderate depression. (But because it can interact with other

medications, it's especially important to talk with a doctor before using St. John's wort.) Valerian has been shown to alleviate anxiety and improve sleep, and studies show that lemon balm combined with valerian can safely treat restlessness and sleep disorders in children. And in another study, passionflower combined with St. John's wort and valerian significantly lessened depression, anxiety, and sleeplessness.

4. **Push B vitamins.** They're critical for normal neurological functioning. One study of 6,517 boys and girls ages 12–15 found that higher intake of B vitamins, especially folate and vitamin B_6, was associated with a lower prevalence of depression in early adolescence. Vitamin B_6 (pyridoxine) is a major cofactor in the synthesis of serotonin; vitamin B_{12} may also form SAM-e (S-adenosylmethionine), a compound linked with mood. Folate is also a factor in forming serotonin, norepinephrine, and SAM-e, and deficiencies of folate have been found in people with depression and anxiety.

5. **Eat to beat the blues.** Protein is key—a shortage can exacerbate anxiety and/or depression. Best sources: turkey, cheese, chicken, fish, beans, and almonds. Magnesium, found in leafy greens, pumpkin seeds, and beans, can ease depression. Zinc helps the brain produce GABA, a compound that combats anxiety and irritability. It's abundant in oysters and can also be found in crab, turkey, lentils, and yogurt. Vitamin E keeps nerve cell membranes flexible, allowing information to be smoothly transmitted. You'll find it in sunflower seeds, almonds, and other nuts.

6. **Teach relaxation.** Show kids how to unwind: Lie down with your child on the floor and do a simple body scan, imagining each part of the body—from toes to head—melting like an ice cube on a warm sidewalk. Help your child learn to follow her inhales and exhales; this helps her focus on her breath and calms the central nervous system. Start small, with a 5-minute session, and make it a daily ritual—right after school is a perfect time for keyed-up kids who need to unwind.

Critical Thinking

1. Why are so many of our children lacking the essential vitamins, fats, and nutrients for optimal brain development?

2. How can we promote healthy fats such as saturated fats while encouraging families to avoid less healthy foods?

Internet References

5 Foods that Negatively Affect Your Child's Mood
http://childdevelopmentinfo.com/adhd-add/five-foods-negatively-affect-childs-mood

Anxiety and Mood Disorders Center
http://www.childmind.org/en/clinics/centers/anxiety-and-mood-disorders-center

Mood Disorders & ADHD
https://www.healthychildren.org/English/health-issues/conditions/adhd/Pages/Mood-Disorders-ADHD.aspx

Scientists learn how what you eat affects your brain—and those of your kids
http://newsroom.ucla.edu/releases/scientists-learn-how-food-affects-52668

LISA TURNER is a certified food psychology coach, nutritional healer, intuitive eating consultant, and author. She has written five books on food and nutrition and developed the Inspired Eats iPhone app.

Article   Prepared by: Claire N. Rubman, *Suffolk County Community College, Selden, NY*

Giving ADHD a Rest: With Diagnosis Rates Exploding Wildly, Is the Disorder a Mental Health Crisis—or a Cultural One?

KATE LUNAU

Learning Outcomes

After reading this article, you will be able to:

- Define and give examples of symptoms of ADHD as defined by the DSM.

- Explain the "accountability rates" in North Carolina schools and the authors' assumed relationship with rates of ADHD diagnosis.

- Explain the term "brain doping."

Any visitor to North Carolina and California will know that the two states have their differences. The former is a typically "red state"; California is staunchly "blue." Each has certain geographic, ethnic and cultural peculiarities, different demographic makeup, family income levels, and more. Yet perhaps the most surprising divide, one many wouldn't expect, is that North Carolina appears to be a hotbed for attention deficit hyperactivity disorder, or ADHD—especially when compared to California. A child who lived in North Carolina instead of California in 2007, according to U.S. academics Stephen Hinshaw and Richard Scheffler, was 2½ times more likely to be diagnosed.

In their forthcoming book *The ADHD Explosion*, Hinshaw and Scheffler—a psychologist and health economist, respectively, at the University of California at Berkeley—examine the causes behind the startling and rapid rise in diagnosis rates of ADHD, a neurobehavioural disorder that has somehow become epidemic. In the U.S., more than one in ten kids has been diagnosed; more than 3.5 million are taking drugs to curb symptoms, from lack of focus to hyperactivity. While ADHD typically hits middle-class boys the hardest, rates among other groups are steadily rising, including girls, adults, and minorities. Kids are being tested and diagnosed as young as preschool. In North Carolina, as many as 30 percent of teenage boys are diagnosed. Scheffler says, "It's getting scary."

According to psychologist Enrico Gnaulati, who is based in Pasadena, California, ADHD is now "as prevalent as the common cold." Various factors seem to be driving up the numbers, factors that extend from home to school to the doctor's office and beyond. "So many kids have trouble these days," says longtime ADHD researcher L. Alan Sroufe, professor emeritus at the University of Wisconsin at Madison. "I doubt it's a change in our genetic pool. Something else is going on."

A closer look at the case of North Carolina and California may be instructive. According to Hinshaw and Scheffler, North Carolinian kids between the ages of four and seventeen had an ADHD diagnosis rate of 16 percent in 2007. In California, it was just over 6 percent. Kids with a diagnosis in North Carolina also faced a 50 percent higher probability they'd get medication. After exhaustively exploring demographics, health care policies, cultural values, and other possible factors, they landed on school policy as what Scheffler calls "the closest thing to a silver bullet."

Giving ADHD a Rest: With Diagnosis Rates Exploding Wildly, Is the Disorder a Mental Health Crisis — or a Cultural One? by Kate Lunau

53

Over the past few decades, incentives have been introduced for U.S. schools to turn out better graduation rates and test scores—and they've been pushed to compete for funding. North Carolina was one of the first states with school accountability laws, disciplining schools for missing targets, and rewarding them for exceeding them. "Such laws provide a real incentive to have children diagnosed and treated," Hinshaw and Scheffler write: Kids in special education classes ideally get the help they need to improve their test scores and (in some areas) aren't counted in the district's test score average.

The rate of ADHD diagnosis varies between countries; as Hinshaw and Scheffler have shown, it even varies significantly within countries. This raises an important question: Is the ADHD epidemic really a mental health crisis, or a cultural and societal one?

ADHD is a "chronic and debilitating mental disorder," Gnaulati says, one that can last a lifetime. It's believed to affect between 5 and 10 percent of the population, and boys still seem especially prone. (Nearly one in five high school boys have ADHD, compared to 1 in 11 girls, according to the U.S. Centers for Disease Control and Prevention.) Kids with ADHD can have a hard time making and keeping friends. In one study of boys at summer camp, Hinshaw found that after just a few hours, those with an ADHD diagnosis were far more likely to be rejected than those without one. The disorder can persist into adulthood, raising the risk of low self-esteem, divorce, unemployment, and driving accidents; even getting arrested and going to jail, according to a report from the Centre for ADHD Awareness, Canada.

In fact, the brains of people with ADHD are different. They're short on receptors for the neurotransmitter dopamine, and their brain volume looks to be slightly smaller. But no medical test or brain scan can yet give a definitive diagnosis. The gold standard comes from the *Diagnostic and Statistical Manual of Mental Disorders*, or *DSM*, from the American Psychiatric Association. The latest version of this "bible of psychiatry," released in May, lists nine symptoms of inattention (making careless mistakes on homework; distractibility; trouble staying organized), and nine of hyperactivity or impulsivity (interrupting others; climbing when it's inappropriate; and excessive talking, to give some examples). They'll sound familiar to anyone who's spent time with kids. "Every child is to some extent impulsive, distractible, disorganized, and has trouble following directions," says Gnaulati, author of *Back to Normal*, an investigation of why what he calls "ordinary childhood behaviour" is often mistaken for ADHD.

The *DSM* specifies that a child should be showing many symptoms consistently, in two or more settings (at home and at school, for example), a better indication that he isn't just acting out because of a bad teacher, or an annoying sibling. "Studies show that if you stick to the two-informant requirement, the number of cases falls by 40 percent," says Gnaulati. Surprisingly often, the diagnoses seem to be hastily given, and drugs dispensed.

It was once thought that stimulants affected people with ADHD differently—calming them down, revving up everyone else—but we now know that's not the case. Virtually everybody seems to react the same in the short term, Sroufe says. "They're attention-enhancers. We've known that since the Second World War," when they were given to radar operators to stay awake and focused. Those with true ADHD show bigger gains, partly because their brains may be "underaroused" to begin with, write Hinshaw and Scheffler. (About two-thirds of U.S. kids with a diagnosis get medication; in Canada, it's about 50 percent.) Stimulants have side effects, including suppressing appetite, speeding up the heart rate, and raising blood pressure. Kids who take them for a long time might end up an inch or so shorter, according to Hinshaw and Scheffler's book, because dopamine activity interferes with growth hormone. And those who don't need them will eventually develop a tolerance, needing a greater and greater quantity to get the effect they're after.

"Brain doping" is by now a well-known phenomenon among college and university students across North America. Many students don't see stimulant use as cheating: One 2012 study found that male college students believe it's far more unethical for an athlete to use steroids than for a student to abuse prescription stimulants to ace a test. "Some red-hot parents want to get their kid into Harvard, Berkeley or Princeton," Scheffler says. "They're going to need a perfect score, so they're going to push." With an ADHD diagnosis, students can seek special accommodations at school, like more time on tests including the SAT, a standardized college entrance exam. With parents, students, and even school boards recognizing the potential benefits that come with diagnosis, ADHD is occurring with increasing frequency among groups other than the white middle class, where rates have typically been highest: According to Hinshaw and Scheffler, African American youth are now just as likely, if not more, to be diagnosed and medicated.

Drug advertisements could also be driving rates of diagnosis upward. Hinshaw and Scheffler describe one ad from Johnson & Johnson, maker of the stimulant Concerta, which shows a happy mother and a son who's getting "better test scores at school" and doing "more chores at home," the text reads. "The message is clear: the right pill breeds family harmony," they write. Sometimes, another underlying health problem will be mistakenly diagnosed as ADHD. In his new book, *ADHD Does Not Exist*, Richard Saul documents 25 conditions that can look like ADHD; most common are vision and hearing issues. "Until you get glasses, it's very hard to understand what [the teacher] is speaking about if you can't see the board," he says.

"Same with hearing." Conditions ranging from bipolar disorder to Tourette's syndrome can also be mistaken for ADHD, Saul writes. Despite the strongly worded title of his book, he believes that 20 percent of those diagnosed are "neurochemical distractible impulsive" and have what we'd term ADHD. The rest are being misdiagnosed, and as a result, he says, "the right treatment is being delayed."

Sleep deprivation is another big cause of misdiagnosis. "It's paradoxical, but especially for kids, it does create hyperactivity and impulsivity," says Vatsal Thakkar of New York University's Langone Medical Center. Given mounting academic pressures, and the screens that populate virtually every room, many kids simply aren't getting enough downtime. A child's relative immaturity can factor in, too. In 2012, a study in the *Canadian Medical Association Journal* found that the youngest kids in a classroom were more likely to have an ADHD diagnosis, and to be prescribed medication. Those born in December are nearly a full year younger than some of their peers, a big difference, especially in kindergarten. (In the U.S., half of all kids with ADHD are diagnosed before age six.)

Gnaulati, who has a son, worries the deck's been stacked against boys, who are more prone to blurt out an answer, run around the classroom, or otherwise act out. "During the kindergarten years, boys are at least a year behind girls in basic self-regulation," he says. Gnaulati notes that school teachers, pediatricians, and school psychologists are all more likely be female—which he argues could be a contributing factor. "In a sense," he writes, "girl behaviour has become the standard by which we judge all kids."

In Canada, we don't track ADHD diagnosis rates as closely as in the U.S. But the rate of diagnosis does look to be picking up here, and elsewhere, too. A study by Hinshaw and Scheffler compared the use of ADHD drugs to countries' per capita gross domestic product. "Richer countries spend more [on ADHD medications]," Scheffler says. "But some countries still spend more than their income would predict." They found that Canada, the U.S., and Australia all had a greater use of these drugs than GDP suggests. A 2013 paper in the *British Journal of Medicine* notes that Australia saw a 73 percent increase in prescribing rates for ADHD medications between 2000 and 2011. The Netherlands had a similar spike—the prevalence of ADHD, and the rate at which ADHD drugs were prescribed to kids, doubled between 2003 and 2007.

Peter Conrad of Brandeis University, outside Boston, is studying how the *DSM* definition of ADHD (which we use in Canada) has been exported around the globe, leading to more kids diagnosed and treated. "Until the late '90s, most diagnosis in Europe was done under the World Health Organization's *International Classification of Diseases*," which is much more strict, he notes. (The *ICD*, for example, required symptoms of inattention, impulsivity, and hyperactivity, while an older version of the *DSM* required only two.)

European countries began to adopt the *DSM* definition, a response to the fact that so much research on ADHD comes out of the U.S.—and the *DSM* began to be seen as the standard. "France and Italy still have low rates," says Conrad, "partly because they don't use the *DSM*." A 2013 study from the University of Exeter found that U.K. kids were much less likely than those in the U.S. to be diagnosed with ADHD, which may be due to tougher criteria, or to parents' resistance to medicating their kids. Even so, other countries are catching up. According to Hinshaw and Scheffler, the use of ADHD medication is rising over five times faster around the world than in the U.S.

Many of the same pressures that motivate diagnosis in the U.S. are at play in Canada, although in different ways. Given the tight job market and increasing academic demands, students are under more pressure to succeed than ever. And while our school test results aren't tied to funding like in the U.S., "high-stakes testing" is increasingly important, says Elizabeth Dhuey, a University of Toronto economist who studies education.

For one thing, it's a point of pride for schools. Results from Ontario's EQAO standardized test are reported in the media and used to rank and compare institutions. ("EQAO: How did your school fare in Ontario's standardized tests?" reads one 2012 *Toronto Star* headline.) What constitutes an "exceptionality" and triggers special services also varies between provinces. In Newfoundland, ADHD has been an "exceptionality" for the past two decades; in Ontario, it isn't considered a special category, but ADHD students can access special education and other extra help on a case-by-case basis. And in B.C., school districts can get supplemental funding for students with ADHD, according to the ministry of education.

These pressures aren't abating—if anything, many are getting stronger—and so, it seems likely we haven't yet reached peak ADHD. Scheffler and Hinshaw raise the possibility that, within the decade, ADHD rates in the U.S. might reach 15 percent or higher; and that as many as four-fifths of those diagnosed could have a prescription.

The hope lies in finding better scientific markers—a definitive test that could confirm true cases of ADHD, and those who will benefit most from treatment, including medication. Otherwise, we're facing the prospect of a generation of kids living with a serious mental health diagnosis, and quite possibly taking powerful drugs long term into adulthood, with all

Giving ADHD a Rest: With Diagnosis Rates Exploding Wildly, Is the Disorder a Mental Health Crisis — or a Cultural One? by Kate Lunau

55

the potential side effects they entail. Whatever is contributing to ADHD's startling rise, it's clear that this isn't a contagious disease kids are swapping on the playground. In many cases, we're giving it to them.

Critical Thinking

1. Explain the relationship between academic pressure and rates of ADHD diagnosis.

2. Why have countries such as Australia and the Netherlands seen a spike in their rates of ADHD diagnosis while other countries such as the UK or are much less likely to see such diagnoses?

Internet References

7 Facts You Need To Know About ADHD
http://www.adhdawarenessmonth.org/adhd-facts

ADHD Not a Real Disease, Says Leading Neuroscientist
http://themindunleashed.org/2014/10/adhd-real-disease-says-leading-neuroscientist.html

Attention-Deficit/Hyperactivity Disorder (ADHD) Symptoms and Diagnosis
http://www.cdc.gov/ncbddd/adhd/diagnosis.html

DSM-5TM - ADHD Institute
http://www.adhd-institute.com/assessment-diagnosis/diagnosis/dsm-5tm

Unit 4

Prepared by: Claire N. Rubman, *Suffolk County Community College, Selden, NY*

UNIT

Development during Childhood: Family and Culture

In our fast paced, high pressure, technologically oriented society, parents shoulder an enormous burden. They are, after all, legally and morally responsible for their children's behavior. Parents have the unenviable task of protecting their children from the perils of bullying, underage drinking, inappropriate posts on Twitter, Facebook Instagram or other social media, and the general dangers of children roaming on an unsupervised "information highway." As their children develop into adolescents, parents also have to contend with the changes associated with puberty and the neurological changes that define adolescent thought and behavior.

In an attempt to keep up, D'Agostino claims that we are coping by "drugging" our children. In his article, "The Drugging of the American Boy," he claims that we, as a society, are "pathologizing boyhood." D'Agostino (2014) suggests that the increased pressure on schools from government programs such as the "Race to the Top" have contributed to the increased rates of diagnosis with extra time or excluded exam scores as an incentive.

Parenting is fraught with challenging situations but not all of them rise to the level of medical intervention. How do you know, for example, if your child's behaviors fall within the normal range? When should you take your child to be tested, when should you medicate your child and when should you worry about your child's aggressive behaviors? What are the red flags that parents should watch for—hurting small animals, teasing siblings, and so on? How much hostility is too much? What do those childhood behaviors represent and how should we interpret them—are they a cry for help or normal childhood responses? Read Mansbacher's article (2015) titled "When to Worry about Your Child's Aggression."

Sometimes it is a child's daily behaviors that can be the most disconcerting for parents. What happens, for example, when your child simply refuses to co-operate? What's in our arsenal of parenting tools that may equip us to respond to our child's noncompliance? Learn how parents can de-escalate defiant situations and work to promote cooperation in the home. Think about discipline and family harmony as you read "Responding to Defiance in the Moment" (2017). Read about mental health issues that plague our children and may contribute to their inappropriate behaviors. Gascoigne (2014) outlines the psychological well-being of three children in her discussion of conduct disorders, self-harm, and anorexia nervosa. Read about the Porter family, Amy, and Valerie and learn about their triggers.

Focusing on the developing teenage brain, Cary (2014) discusses the failure of current government policies to address the problems associated with underage drinking in her article "Time to Lower the Drinking Age." She hypothesizes that lowering the drinking age would make teens less likely to binge drink or turn to alternatives to alcohol such as illegal prescription use, especially on college campuses.

Our discussion on family and culture ends with an article on the freedom that we may, inadvertently, take for granted. The exploitation of young girls in Nigeria includes the kidnapping of children by Boko Haram terrorist group. As we celebrate the release of these young girls to their families, it is vital to appreciate the relative freedom that most children in the United States of America enjoy on a daily basis while remembering the torture, incarceration, and rape of these young girls in Nigeria. Read about their harrowing journey in Nzwili's article (2016) as we focus on our global commitment to children of all nations.

Article   Prepared by: Claire N. Rubman, *Suffolk County Community College, Selden, NY*

Tough Fluidity: Complex Considerations for Trans Youth

Deborah June Goemans

Learning Outcomes

After reading this article, you will be able to:

- Articulate the difference between gender identity and sexual preference.

- Explain the terms cisgender, transgender, dysmorphia, and gender dysphoria.

- Explain "social transitioning" and the role of "puberty blockers."

Snips and snails

And puppy-dogs' tails

That's what little boys are made of. Sugar and spice

And all that's nice

That's what little girls are made of.

Last year was a big year for "Jan." She was in first grade and her parents had agreed to let her transition from her assigned gender, which was male, to the gender she identifies as, which is female. This is an enlightened age and Jan lives in an enlightened country (South Africa), and so her elementary school principal gathered the students and their parents around and informed everyone that Jan was now going to live as "a girl with boy bits."

Jan's mother explained how we're all different and that she, Jan's mother, is different because she has one foot bigger than the other. After the adults finished speaking, they asked if any of the children had questions. Two boys raised their hands. The first said he felt sorry for Jan.

"Oh?" said the principal. "But you know Jan wants to live as a girl and not a boy."

"Yes," he replied, "but that's not why I'm sorry. I'm sorry for Jan because her mom has one foot bigger than the other." And the other little boy? He said he knew exactly how Jan felt because he was half-fish.

The teachers didn't know how to respond to an identity they hadn't heard of, but okay—transgender, gender-fluid, half-fish—they weren't going to judge. The gobsmacked response of the adults to the innocence of a child identifying as half-fish (because his mother said he swims like a fish) reveals why gender identity is such a hot topic; it's part evolutionary debate, part human rights issue, part kindness and respect, and part sociological Wild West as we grapple with changing norms, changing language, and changing expectations.

A quick lesson to start. Many people confuse gender identity with sexual preference, but they're two different things: gender identity is one's own body image—the element that makes a boy identify as a boy, a girl identify as a girl, a girl identify as a boy, or vice versa—while sexual preference is the sexual identity of the person with whom one wants to have sex. So, your sexual identity may be cisgender male (with penis and testes intact) but your sexual preference can be gay.

Sexual identity is clearly complex, but everyone has a sex that is determined by three things:

1. The sex chromosomes—XY for boys and XX for females, and sometimes other variants, such as when girls have one X chromosome or an extra X chromosome and boys have an extra X chromosome. The chromosomes govern the synthesis of various hormones responsible for forming the gonads (the ovaries or testes), the genitals (the vagina and the penis), and the sexual parts of the brain. Our sex chromosomes are set at conception and do not change throughout our lives. Their action, however, can be

influenced by hormones, including hormones administered by physicians.

2. The sexual organs are undetermined during the first seven weeks of gestation. During this period, the basic architecture of the fetus is laid out fish-like: head to tail, right and left, and ventral to dorsal, and the tissues for the gonads are essentially there and starting their journey, but it's not visually obvious if they will produce female or male sexual organs, or both, or neither. Over the next five weeks in utero, we can see the sexual organs beginning to develop. This process, known as differentiation, is controlled, for the most part, by hormones under the control of the sex chromosomes but is also influenced by the mother, the embryo itself, or other inhabitants of the womb, like a twin. So the development of the assigned sex, like every other trait, has both a genetic and environmental component. During puberty, which can take place anywhere from 9 to 16 years old, the secondary sexual characteristics develop, such as facial and pubic hair and increased muscle mass in men and curves, menstruation, and the development of breasts for women.

3. The third aspect of sex development is gender perception, which is a body image issue. This is tied into the structure of the brain and differences in the brain between men and women. Gender perception starts during the second half of pregnancy, when sexual differentiation of the brain begins. According to Dick F. Swaab and Alicia Garcia-Falgueras of the Netherlands Institute for Neuroscience in Amsterdam, "[S]ince sexual differentiation of the genitals takes place in the first two months of pregnancy and sexual differentiation of the brain starts in the second half of pregnancy, these two processes can be influenced independently, which may result in transsexuality." As far as happiness and self-fulfillment are concerned, for everyone—transgender or cisgender—sexual perception is one of the most important elements of self and body image.

Which brings us to "Pat," the daughter of a friend in my humanist group. Pat is ten years old and has healthy XY chromosomes and male sexual organs, but she has identified as a girl since she was three years old. My friend has two younger children who are cisgender (male) and says the gender difference between Pat and her brothers is stark. Pat is terrified of going through puberty. She doesn't want to be fluid; she wants to grow up to be a woman and she wants her sexual organs and her outward appearance to match her identity. For my friend, trying to force her daughter to be a boy is as cruel and bizarre as trying to turn her cisgender children transgender.

While most people can understand the need for medical intervention for those whose genitals and chromosomes don't match and have been assigned incorrectly at birth, even some of the most open-minded will balk at the concept of using a lab to allow a child with matching chromosomes and genitals but a different sexual identity to transition medically and hormonally. Here's what *Sexual Personae* author, Camille Paglia (who self-identifies as a "transgender being") told Sam Dorman of the *Washington Free Beacon* recently:

> I am very concerned about current gender theory rhetoric that convinces young people that if they feel uneasy about or alienated from their assignment to one sex, then they must take concrete steps, from hormone therapy to alarmingly irreversible surgery, to become the other sex. I find this an oddly simplistic and indeed reactionary response to what should be regarded as a golden opportunity for flexibility and fluidity.

While Paglia might sound shockingly conservative for someone who has always lived her life in a way that has been true to her own sexual identity and politics, she's actually being consistently liberal: she's saying, in other words, feel free to live as a girl with a penis or as a boy with a vagina, or as a gay girl with a vagina or a lesbian boy with a penis, or whatever, but don't get bogged down with trying to fit your parts into a binary identity of boxers or bikinis.

My friend "Mike" doesn't agree. Mike is living his life as a male while identifying as a female. He's heterosexual (i.e., he is attracted to women. Or, I ask, perhaps he's a lesbian? "Maybe," he says, after a pause), he's married, and he has a daughter whom he adores. Yet for him, the feeling of being trapped in a male body has been brutal. It's led to breakdowns and a psychiatric hospitalization. "If there's anything I can do to help someone—child or adult—going through this pain, I'd do it," he tells me.

When I first met Mike at a writing seminar almost ten years ago, I had no idea he was in such pain. He was inspired to come out of the closet by Caitlyn Jenner. If someone as high profile as Bruce Jenner could do it, and at an advanced age, so could he. (Of course, age is relative; Mike is only 40 compared to Jenner's 67.)

Mike still lives as a man without using hormones or having any genital reconstruction surgery. He currently has a beard for an acting role and he prefers to use masculine pronouns when referring to himself. But he's most comfortable and at ease with his sexual identity when he's clean-shaven, dressed in traditionally female clothes, and presenting himself as a woman. At these times Mike would like to be able to use female bathrooms. "The real intent of 'bathroom bills,'" he says, "is to get people who want to protect women and children to support laws that won't do anything in that area, but will actually have the effect of marginalizing trans people by making them feel unsafe in society because they won't be able to use the bathroom in a public place." Mike feels that as long as we have gender-specific bathrooms we should be able to use the one that matches the presented gender.

Some might scoff and say that makes Mike a cisgender White male who just likes to put on women's clothing. Why can't he just do that? Mike says it's not the same. Living with gender dysphoria—a general state of unease about one's biological sex—is agonizing for him. Growing up, he didn't realize it was something he could change. And if he were 18 now instead of 40, would he change? He says perhaps, but it's a moot point and he wouldn't want to erase the joy of being married and having a child. From now on out, however, he intends to live his life in the most authentic way possible. Transitioning might be a challenge to his relationship because his wife is cisgender, but that's something they have to work on together—or apart—if it should come to that.

Transgender identity is not new. While it is well-known that many cis women in history have hidden their sexual assignment in the hopes of getting an education, professional acknowledgement, and even to go to war as soldiers, there are also documented cases of men and women who transitioned because of their gender identity. Judging from her self-portraits and family photographs, it's possible that artist Freda Kahlo had a fluid gender identity even though she was married and had hoped to have children.

In the eighteenth and nineteenth centuries in Italy, the castrati were young boys who had voices that were deemed perfect, pure, angelic—and fleeting. Given all they'd put in to becoming great singers, it was a great honor for young boys on the verge of puberty to be chosen for castration, thereby preserving their pure, prepuberty singing voices. Some were eager to submit to the knife. Losing human desire for love, sexuality, marriage, and fatherhood was nothing compared to the purity of protecting God's voice personified. Sometimes they died, and sometimes the reverse metamorphosis didn't take. What then for the neutered and deep-voiced man? There was always the priesthood to fall back on. After all, they were still men, and the church appreciated their chaste lifestyle.

While early castration is no longer considered moral or desirable, the transition from one's assigned sex to one's sexual identity is more controversial and is a complex process not everyone follows in the same order. Mike says that just because you haven't undergone surgery or taken hormones, doesn't mean you're faking it.

For young people, the first step in transitioning to a different gender is made far easier if their family is understanding and allows them to live as their preferred identity with undeveloped sexual organs intact. This is known as socially transitioning and also requires a liberal school and state which will allow these children to use their preferred gender toilets and locker rooms, play in coed sports teams, and will educate the other children in the classroom about transgender rights and issues, as was done in Jan's school. In the United States, the Transgender Law Center ranks 14 states plus DC as having a high gender-identity policy ranking, meaning they are tolerant of gender-identity issues, and 23 states as having negative gender-identity policies.

During puberty, the treatment becomes more difficult because this is when the secondary sex characteristics appear. Endocrinologists recommend the use of puberty blocking hormones, such as Lupron (leuprolide), in order to protect voice quality and other gender-specific secondary sex characteristics until patients can become old enough to make an informed decision.

The so-called "pausing" of puberty is helpful and reversible but the benefits come with potentially serious risks—they are, after all, synthetic hormones. In the *Washington Free Beacon* article, Paglia issued a strong warning against the use of hormone blockers:

> Because of my own personal odyssey, I am horrified by the escalating prescription of puberty-blockers to children with gender dysphoria like my own: I consider this practice to be a criminal violation of human rights. Have the adults gone mad? Children are now being callously used for fashionable medical experiments with unknown long-term results.

Some psychologists are also concerned that the use of puberty blockers can make transgender children feel left behind and even more isolated and different as their peers develop into young women or men.

There is another issue: according to several studies, a majority of gender-fluid children outgrow the need to transition. Their sexual preference may be gay or lesbian or bi or queer or cis, but ultimately their gender identity matches their assigned sex and they want their breasts or penises or hairy chests to stay put as chromosomes intended.

Doctors worry that the use of synthetic hormones to medically treat a gender-fluid identity can be harmful. There have been quite a few well-publicized misdiagnoses of gender dysmorphia that have fallen into the "first do no harm" category, leaving transsexuals feeling mutilated and desperately unhappy with the sex they have become. Indeed, the criteria for a gender dysmorphia diagnosis appears quite arbitrary and can be true for any number of LGBTQ+ or cisgender children, for example avoiding the assigned sex roles in play and showing a preference for the clothing, toys, and playmates of the opposite identified gender. A more telling criterion is when a transgender child insists from an early age that he/she *is* the identified sex, rather than *wants to be* the identified sex.

Beyond the possibility of a child reverting to their assigned gender, there's another issue that terrifies parents like my humanist friend: according to the National Transgender Discrimination Survey, 41 percent of transgender adults have attempted suicide. It's clear that the pain of gender dysmorphia is life-threatening and doctors realize the stakes. Using puberty blockers to help ease the transition into the third stage of gender reassignment is very helpful for a successful transition. And this is the path my humanist friend is allowing her daughter to pursue. Now that Pat is 10 years old, she's taking hormones prescribed by her doctor to postpone puberty and is living as a tween girl, wearing traditionally feminine clothes, using the girls' locker room and bathroom at school, and playing on coed sports teams. The hormone treatment is paid for by their medical insurance.

The third stage of gender reassignment happens after age 16 when patients are given lifelong cross-gender hormones. These are serious drugs with serious and permanent side effects but they are also lifesaving for many transgender individuals, and many have made the informed decision to use them.

Gender reassignment surgery is the next stage, whereby surgeons are able to create a sexually satisfying penis or vagina for a patient. In 2016, the Johns Hopkins University School of Medicine announced it would resume gender reassignment surgery after refusing to do so for 35 years. This is considered a major victory for transgender-rights activists. Other surgical options include facial surgery, breast removal or augmentation, and a new procedure where the vocal cords are operated on to raise the pitch of the voice for transwomen.

With or without surgery, high-profile celebrities like Chaz Bono, Caitlyn Jenner, and Laverne Cox have shown the joy of living in a body that matches their true sexual identity. They and others like them are inspiring many people, from fellow transgender people to cisgender me.

Critical Thinking

1. At what age should children or adolescents be legally able to choose gender reassignment surgery?
2. What are the "bathroom bills" and what are they for?

Internet References

Gender Identity Development in Children

https://www.healthychildren.org/English/ages-stages/gradeschool/Pages/Gender-Identity-and-Gender-Confusion-In-Children.aspx

Sex-change Treatment for Kids on the Rise

https://www.cbsnews.com/news/sex-change-treatment-for-kids-on-the-rise/

Transgender Children: The Parents and Doctors on the Frontline

https://www.theguardian.com/society/2016/nov/13/transgender-children-the-parents-and-doctors-on-the-frontline

When Transgender Kids Transition, Medical Risks Are Both Known and Unknown

http://www.pbs.org/wgbh/frontline/article/when-transgender-kids-transition-medical-risks-are-both-known-and-unknown/

DEBORAH JUNE GOEMANS has lived in four countries on three continents and considers herself a world citizen. She is a mother, wife, humanist, writer, editor, and acrobat. Her book, *The Amaranth Bloom*, is a humanistic novel set in South Africa during apartheid.

Article   Prepared by: Claire N. Rubman, *Suffolk County Community College, Selden, NY*

The Drugging of the American Boy

RYAN D'AGOSTINO

Learning Outcomes

After reading this article, you will be able to:

- Discuss the implications of 6.4 million children with an ADHD diagnosis.

- Explain what the author means when he says "we are pathologizing boyhood."

- Explain the effect of Methylphenidate on the brain.

By the time they reach high school, nearly 20 percent of all American boys will be diagnosed with ADHD. Millions of those boys will be prescribed a powerful stimulant to "normalize" them. A great many of those boys will suffer serious side effects from those drugs. The shocking truth is that many of those diagnoses are wrong, and that most of those boys are being drugged for no good reason—simply for being boys. It's time we recognize this as a crisis.

If you have a son, you have a one-in-seven chance that he has been diagnosed with ADHD. If you have a son who has been diagnosed, it's more than likely that he has been prescribed a stimulant—the most famous brand names are Ritalin and Adderall; newer ones include Vyvanse and Concerta—to deal with the symptoms of that psychiatric condition.

The Drug Enforcement Administration classifies stimulants as Schedule II drugs, defined as having a "high potential for abuse" and "with use potentially leading to severe psychological or physical dependence." (According to a University of Michigan study, Adderall is the most abused brand-name drug among high school seniors.) In addition to stimulants like Ritalin, Adderall, Vyvanse, and Concerta, Schedule II drugs include cocaine, methamphetamine, Demerol, and OxyContin.

According to manufacturers of ADHD stimulants, they are associated with sudden death in children who have heart problems, whether those heart problems have been previously detected or not. They can bring on a bipolar condition in a child who didn't exhibit any symptoms of such a disorder before taking stimulants. They are associated with "new or worse aggressive behavior or hostility." They can cause "new psychotic symptoms (such as hearing voices and believing things that are not true) or new manic symptoms." They commonly cause noticeable weight loss and trouble sleeping. In some children, some stimulants can cause the paranoid feeling that bugs are crawling on them. Facial tics. They can cause children's eyes to glaze over, their spirits to dampen. One study reported fears of being harmed by other children and thoughts of suicide.

Imagine you have a six-year-old son. A little boy for whom you are responsible. A little boy you would take a bullet for, a little boy in whom you search for glimpses of yourself, and hope every day that he will turn out just like you, only better. A little boy who would do anything to make you happy. Now imagine that little boy—your little boy—alone in his bed in the night, eyes wide with fear, afraid to move, a frightening and unfamiliar voice echoing in his head, afraid to call for you. Imagine him shivering because he hasn't eaten all day because he isn't hungry. His head is pounding. He doesn't know why any of this is happening.

Now imagine that he is suffering like this because of a mistake. Because a doctor examined him for twelve minutes, looked at a questionnaire on which you had checked some boxes, listened to your brief and vague report that he seemed to have trouble sitting still in kindergarten, made a diagnosis for a disorder the boy doesn't have, and wrote a prescription for a powerful drug he doesn't need.

If you have a son in America, there is an alarming probability that this has happened or will happen to you.

The Diagnosis

6.4 Million children between the ages of four and seventeen have been diagnosed with ADHD. By high school, nearly 20% of all boys will have been diagnosed with ADHD—a 37% increase since 2003.

On this everyone agrees: The numbers are big. The number of children who have been diagnosed with attention-deficit/hyperactivity disorder—overwhelmingly boys—in the United States has climbed at an astonishing rate over a relatively short period of time. The Centers for Disease Control first attempted to tally ADHD cases in 1997 and found that about 3 percent of American schoolchildren had received the diagnosis, a number that seemed roughly in line with past estimates. But after that year, the number of diagnosed cases began to increase by at least 3 percent every year. Then, between 2003 and 2007, cases increased at a rate of 5.5 percent each year. In 2013, the CDC released data revealing that 11 percent of American schoolchildren had been diagnosed with ADHD, which amounts to 6.4 million children between the ages of four and seventeen—a 16 percent increase since 2007 and a 42 percent increase since 2003. Boys are more than twice as likely to be diagnosed as girls—15.1 percent to 6.7 percent. By high school, even more boys are diagnosed—nearly one in five.

Almost 20 percent.

And overall, of the children in this country who are told they suffer from attention deficit/hyperactivity disorder, two-thirds are on prescription drugs.

And on this, too, everyone agrees: That among those millions of diagnoses, there are false ones. That there are high-energy kids-normal boys, most likely—who had the misfortune of seeing a doctor who had scant (if any) training in psychiatric disorders during his long-ago residency but had heard about all these new cases and determined that a hyper kid whose teacher said he has trouble sitting still in class must have ADHD. That among the 6.4 million are a significant percentage of boys who are swallowing pills every day for a disorder they don't have.

On this, too, everyone with standing in this fight seems to agree.

But on the subject of attention-deficit/hyperactivity disorder, that is where the agreement ends.

For example: Doctors, parents, and therapists give a lot of different explanations for the sharp rise. Increased awareness—that's a big one. *We know more now.* Other possibilities put forth: Too many video games. Too much refined sugar. Pharmaceutical companies pushing ADHD drugs. Lack of gym classes at schools. All of these factors are cited. And people have a lot of different ideas about what to do for the children who receive these diagnoses. Many believe that medicine should be the first treatment, either combined with behavioral therapy or not. Others feel that drugs should be a last resort after making every other alleviative effort you can find or think of, from hypnosis to herbal treatments to neurofeedback.

Given today's prevailing pharmaceutical culture, clinicians who believe that drugs should never be used to treat ADHD in children are very much in the minority. Marketing is powerful, and blockbuster drugs like Ritalin are big business. Business booms, market share grows when scripts are written, and countercultural doctors and therapists who advocate caution and who believe that diagnoses are made too easily—doctors and therapists who preach alternatives to drugs—are finding themselves the butt of jokes.

But more about them shortly.

The United States government first collected information on mental disorders in 1840, when the national census listed two generally accepted conditions: idiocy and insanity. A century later, psychiatrists knew more. They had options when making diagnoses, and by the 1940s difficult kids were classified as "hyperkinetic." Other terms would follow, like minimal brain dysfunction. In 1955, there came a pill doctors could prescribe for these children to temper their hyperactivity and make them behave more like "normal" children. It was a stimulant, so called because it heightened the brain's utilization of dopamine, which can improve attention and concentration. The active ingredient was a highly addictive compound called methylphenidate. The drug was called Ritalin.

By 1987, the American Psychiatric Association (APA) had settled on a more refined name for a disorder among children who exhibited the same set of symptoms, including trouble concentrating and impulsive behavior: attention-deficit/hyperactivity disorder. ADHD. At the time, in American schools, it was still considered unusual for a child to take Ritalin. It was, frankly, considered weird.

Today, it has simply become a default method for dealing with a "difficult" child.

"We are pathologizing boyhood," says Ned Hallowell, a psychiatrist who has been diagnosed with ADHD himself and has cowritten two books about it, *Driven to Distraction* and *Delivered from Distraction*. "God bless the women's movement—we needed it—but what's happened is, particularly in schools where most of the teachers are women, there's been a general girlification of elementary school, where any kind of disruptive behavior is sinful. What I call the 'moral diagnosis' gets made: *You're bad. Now go get a doctor and get on medication so you'll be good.* And that's a real perversion of what ought to happen. Most boys are naturally more restless than most girls, and I would say that's good. But schools want these little goody-goodies who sit still and do what they're told—these robots—and that's just not who boys are."

Especially when they're young. One of the most shocking studies of the rise in ADHD diagnoses was published in 2012 in the *Canadian Medical Association Journal*. It was called "Influence of Relative Age on Diagnosis and Treatment of Attention-Deficit/Hyperactivity Disorder in Children." Nearly one million children between the ages of six and twelve took part, making it the largest study of its kind ever. The researchers found that "boys who were born in December"—typically the youngest students in their class—"were 30 percent more likely to receive a diagnosis of ADHD than boys born in January," who were a full year older. And "boys were 41 percent more likely to be given a prescription for a medication to treat ADHD if they were born in December than if they were born in January." These findings suggest, of course, that an errant diagnosis can sometimes result from a developmental period that a boy can grow out of.

And there are other underlying reasons for the recent explosion in diagnoses. Stephen Hinshaw, a professor of psychology at the University of California, Berkeley, and the editor of *Psychological Bulletin,* the research publication of the American Psychological Association, presents evidence in a new book that ADHD diagnoses can vary widely according to demographics and even education policy, which could account for why some states see a rate of 4 percent of schoolchildren with ADHD while others see a rate of almost 15 percent. Most shocking is Hinshaw's examination of the implications of the No Child Left Behind Act of 2001, which gave incentives to states whose students scored well on standardized tests. The result: "Such laws provide real incentive to have children diagnosed and treated." Children with ADHD often get more time to take tests, and in some school districts, tests taken by ADHD kids do not even have to be included in the overall average. "That is, an ADHD diagnosis might exempt a low-achieving youth from lowering the district's overall achievement ranking"— thus ensuring that the district not incur federal sanctions for low scores.

In a study of the years between 2003 and 2007, the years in which the policy was rolled out, the authors looked at children between ages eight and thirteen. They found that among children in many low-income areas (the districts most "targeted" by the bill), ADHD diagnoses increased from 10 percent to 15.3 percent—"a huge rise of 53 percent" in just four years.

The Consequences

48% of subjects of one study who took ADHD medications experienced side effects like sleep problems and "mood disturbances." In another, 6% of children suffered psychotic symptoms, including thoughts of suicide.

Source: *Psychiatry,* April 2010; *The Canadian Journal of Psychiatry,* October 1999.

And yet among many of the people interviewed for this story, the most common explanation for the staggering increase in diagnoses is that doctors know more now. *Great strides have been made.* "I don't think there's an epidemic of new cases," says Mario Saltarelli, a neurologist and the senior vice-president of clinical development at Shire, which manufactures Adderall and Vyvanse. (Since our interview, he has left the company.) "It's always been there. It's now more appropriately understood and recognized." Instead of lumping together all the kids with high energy and bad behavior and calling them hyper, many experts say, doctors can identify the children who exhibit the symptoms specific to ADHD and treat them accordingly. "We were paying attention," says Jeffrey Lieberman, the president of the American Psychiatric Association and chairman of psychiatry at Columbia University Medical Center. "We [now] have reliable descriptions and the means of diagnosing."

Every 15 years or so, the APA publishes a book called the *Diagnostic and Statistical Manual of Mental Disorders,* which doctors around the world use as a guide for diagnosing mental disorders in their patients. Known as the DSM, it has been published seven times, first in 1952 and most recently in 2013. For each revision, a new task force of psychiatrists tweaks, refines, and often expands the descriptions, definitions, and symptoms of hundreds of psychiatric disorders. It's not uncommon for definitions to be written more broadly, thus broadening the universe of people who might be diagnosed with a given disorder.

In the *DSM-5,* the 916-page version that came out last year, there was one important change made to the section on ADHD. The age at which a child can be diagnosed with ADHD was raised from seven to twelve. In the previous edition of the *DSM,* in order to meet the criteria for diagnosis, several symptoms of ADHD had to be present by age seven. Citing "substantial research published since 1994," the authors increased the window for diagnosis by five years, meaning that 20 million more children are now eligible to be told they have ADHD.

And so if a child is deemed to meet the criteria for ADHD as defined in the *DSM*, even by a rushed pediatrician after a cursory twelve-minute examination, the clinical-practice guidelines strongly recommend medication as part of the first step in treating kids starting at age six. (Behavior therapy is recommended as a first step for four- and five-year-olds, followed by methylphenidate, or stimulants, if the behavior therapies "do not provide significant improvement and there is moderate-to-severe continuing disturbance in the child's function.")

A cynical person might wonder whether the task forces who write the *DSM* are influenced by pharmaceutical companies, seeing that with each new disorder they add and each new symptom they deem valid, more people can get expensive prescriptions. ADHD drugs alone were a $10.4 billion business in 2012, a 13 percent increase over the year before.

"I think it happens in an indirect but nonetheless powerful way," says Lisa Cosgrove, a clinical psychologist who is an associate professor at the University of Massachusetts, Boston, and a fellow at the Center for Ethics at Harvard. In a study of the *DSM-5,* she found that 69 percent of the task force acknowledged ties to the pharmaceutical industry. Many of these were likely indirect affiliations, but Cosgrove says that doesn't matter. "It's not that I think there's this quid pro quo kind of corruption going on. But when the individuals who are charged with the responsibility of developing criteria or with changing the symptom criteria—I don't think they are consciously aware of the way in which industry affiliations create pro-industry habits of thought." Cosgrove points to what she calls a "major gap" in the APA's disclosure policy for doctors who worked on the *DSM-5:* It allows unrestricted research grants from drug companies. "'Now, unrestricted' means that the pharmaceutical company cannot in-house analyze the data . . . but there's a wealth of social-psych research that shows that when you are paid even small amounts—and there's the potential for future payment—it affects your behavior. If I get an unrestricted research grant from Pfizer for $500,000, and I'm hoping to get a $2 million grant, at some level I'm going to be aware of how I talk about the results."

The journal *Accountability in Research* chose Cosgrove's paper "Commentary: The Public Health Consequences of an Industry-Influenced Psychiatric Taxonomy" for publication in 2010, when a first draft of the *DSM-5* was made public. In the paper, Cosgrove and her coauthors lambasted the psychiatric community for supporting a manual that largely ignores side effects and promotes diagnosis by constantly adding symptoms and disorders. "A psychiatric taxonomy [i.e., the *DSM*] which touts indication for medications, but is effectively silent about their associated risks, is evidently unbalanced and raises questions about undue influence," they wrote. "The time has come

to seriously reconsider whether the heavily pharmaceutically funded APA should continue to be entrusted with the revision of the *DSM.*"

Dr. Allen Frances, professor emeritus at Duke University School of Medicine, the former chairman of its psychiatry department, and the chairman of the *DSM-IV* (1994) task force, feels the problem is not corruption but the slow creep of misinformation. "I know the people. They're not doing it for the drug companies—they really believe what they're doing is right. They really believe ADHD is underdiagnosed, and they want to help people who should be getting medication. I just think they're dead wrong."

Frances points to the fact that in August 1997—the same year the CDC first started tallying ADHD cases in the United States—the Food and Drug Administration made it easier for pharmaceutical companies to advertise their drugs to consumers. Spending on direct-to-consumer drug advertising increased from $220 million in 1997 to more than $2.8 billion by 2002.

It's not that Frances believes ADHD is not a real and valid diagnosis; he just believes that these days it's made so frequently it has been rendered meaningless. "It's been watered down so much in the way it's applied that it now includes many kids who are just developmentally different or are immature," he says. "It's a disease called childhood."

Falsely diagnosing a psychiatric disorder in a boy's developing brain is a terrifying prospect. You don't have to be a parent to understand that. And yet it apparently happens all the time. "Kids who don't meet our criteria for our ADHD research studies have the diagnosis—and are being treated for it," says Dr. Steven Cuffe, chairman of the psychiatry department at the University of Florida College of Medicine, Jacksonville, and vice-chair of the child and adolescent psychiatry steering committee for the American Board of Psychiatry and Neurology.

The ADHD clinical-practice guidelines published by the American Academy of Pediatrics—the document doctors are supposed to follow when diagnosing a disorder—state only that doctors should determine whether a patient's symptoms are in line with the definition of ADHD in the *DSM*. To do this accurately requires days or even weeks of work, including multiple interviews with the child and his parents and reports from teachers, plus significant observation. And yet a 2011 study by the American Academy of Pediatrics found that one-third of pediatrician visits last less than 10 minutes. (Visits for the specific purpose of a psychosocial evaluation are around 20 minutes.) "A proper, well-done assessment cannot be done in ten or fifteen minutes," says Ruth Hughes, a psychologist who is the CEO of Children and Adults with ADHD (CHADD), an advocacy group.

Only one significant study has ever been done to try to determine how many kids have been misdiagnosed with ADHD, and it was done more than 20 years ago. It was led by Peter Jensen, now the vice-chair for psychiatry and psychology research at the Mayo Clinic, but at the time a researcher for the National Institute of Mental Health. After a study of 1,285 children, Jensen estimated that even way back then—before ADHD became a knee-jerk diagnosis in America, before one in seven boys had been given the diagnosis—between 20 and 25 percent were misdiagnosed. They had been told they had the disorder when in fact they did not.

Part of the problem is subjectivity, and the power of a culture that has settled on a drug-based solution. Decades of research have gone into trying to define the disorder in a clinical way, and yet the ultimate diagnosis—Your son has ADHD—is inherently subjective. And insurance companies don't reimburse or reward doctors for time spent doing the diligent work involved in giving a proper opinion. "You have to observe the behavior of the child over different environments. You have to talk to the parents. You have to talk to the teachers. I don't know an insurance company out there that pays for a pediatrician to call and talk to the teachers. They just don't," says Hughes.

Ned Hallowell does not accept insurance in his private psychiatry practice, which he says allows him to spend more time with patients. "But for the average person, it's the luck of the draw," he says. "Do they have a good, savvy pediatrician who can be careful about the diagnosis, or do they have somebody who just hears 'ADD' and writes a prescription?"

Lieberman, the APA president, says most doctors try to get it right. "Are there pressures that are packed on clinicians that make them less than optimally rigorous [in making a diagnosis]? Unfortunately, there are," he says. "But I mean, you have our healthcare financing system that's quite dysfunctional, and it's created a situation where doctors have to spend a certain amount of time with bureaucratic, administrative paperwork and regulatory-compliance stuff. . . . We also have a culture where there's pressure, both from schools as well as from parents, to do something—to alleviate the problem and enhance the performance of the child. That's no excuse, and doctors shouldn't succumb to that. But, you know, doctors are human. . . . We'd like everybody to be these heroic figures who fulfill the virtues of the Hippocratic oath. I think most doctors aspire to try to do that. But human limitations being what they are . . . *caveat emptor.*"

One man believes that drugging children's brains is too risky. That until we get a lot closer to achieving a foolproof diagnosis for ADHD, we need to think twice about giving a single pill to a single child. He believes that what is called attention-deficit/ hyperactivity disorder might in fact be a boy's greatest gift, the gift of energy. And that the best way to treat it is to first teach the boy to control the energy all by himself, because by learning to control it all by himself, a boy can channel that energy to help him succeed. That the responsible thing to do is first to see if there is some problem with the boy's heart—not with the way it pumps blood, but with its

ability to show and accept love. The man's name is Howard Glasser, and he is one of those countercultural clinicians who, as American society has become inured to giving psychotropic drugs to kids, has built a practice predicated on opposing the very idea.

If he were a child today, Glasser would be given a prescription for a stimulant in about five minutes. Little Howie was a wired kid. Obstreperous. But good. A good kid. And when he grew up and became a family therapist—he has applied to earn his doctorate in education from Harvard starting this fall—he created a way of dealing with wired, obstreperous, uncontrollable kids who are, beneath all that, good. And he believes all of them are good.

He calls the method the Nurtured Heart Approach, and it seems simple on the surface: You nurture the child's heart. If a child is hyperactive and defiant and has trouble listening and concentrating, Glasser feels it is our responsibility as a society— as grown-ups—to do everything we can for a child's heart before we start adding chemicals to his brain, because what if his brain is fine? What if the diagnosis isn't right? And even if it is, what if something else works?

Hyperactive, defiant—he was all those things. At home—the apartment his parents rented in Kew Gardens, a leafy, almost suburban corner of Queens—he was sometimes so defiant that his mother would shout into the air, asking what she had done to deserve this, her face brightening with incarnadine helplessness. His father was a salesman of electrical supplies, and he and Howie used to go at it pretty good. Sometimes, when it was his turn to teach Howie a lesson, his father would reach for the rubber machine belt. Howie took that punishment laughing. Heartbreaking laughter.

At school he would sit in the back of the class, cracking jokes until his teachers were overcome with that unique kind of exasperation that results from feeling outrage and disappointment at the same time. Outrage because you wouldn't believe the mouth on this kid. Disappointment because he was so smart. Because he had so much potential.

Man, was Howie Glasser smart. That was the problem nobody saw: He was a funny, clever kid who scored high in both English and math without much studying. School bored him. The teachers, though, had to teach to every student in the class, and Howie felt forgotten. He didn't need to listen, so he sat in the back of the room and goofed off, his gangly frame folded awkwardly into a too-small wooden chair. Kids would laugh, and he'd do it more. And every time the teachers got angry and pointed their fingers toward the principal's office, struggling to keep from screaming at Howie—to keep from smacking him, probably—they were only feeding his recalcitrance. Finally, someone was paying attention to him! Deep down Howie didn't like the negative attention, but it was better than no attention at all.

In junior high school, they wanted to hold him back. He couldn't handle the next grade, they said—he couldn't concentrate, he was hanging around with the wrong kids, he just wasn't ready. But then Howie took a test, and his score surprised even the teachers who knew he was smarter than he let on. He scored high enough to skip ahead and graduated high school at sixteen.

Glasser graduated from City College with a degree in psychology, then got a master's in counseling at New York University. He had started work on a PhD, also at NYU, but after a year or so he dropped out to do the thing he loved most, the thing that made all the noise go away, all the trouble, all the teachers who couldn't figure out how to harness and channel his energy, his hollering parents who didn't understand why he couldn't be more like his older brother: He worked with wood.

Howie's Woodworking opened on Third Avenue and East Twelfth Street in New York in 1980. He collected wood around the city—old floorboards from gutted townhouses, planks, pallets, scraps. He made planters and mosaics and odd pieces of furniture. People would see the sign and come in and ask if he could do bigger jobs—cabinetry, fine furniture, storefronts. Glasser would always tell them he could do it, even though he had no idea how. Then he'd hire people who could show him.

After a few years, Glasser moved out west, far from the overdrive of New York, to the Arizona desert. On his way out, in Boulder, Colorado, he got to know a man named Michael Davis, who, with his wife, Anita, was raising four sons, two of whom were adolescents at the time. The first time Glasser visited Davis's house, there was some kind of minor drama unfolding that day, the kind of argument that periodically bubbles up in a house where teenagers live.

And the way the Davises handled it made Glasser weep.

"Michael and Anita were talking to their kids in the most loving way. I had never until that day—ever—encountered anybody who talked to their kids that way. I had tears streaming down my face," he says. "In my world, in my circumscribed world, it was not the culture. It's kind of breathtaking to me now." Even as he tells this story almost 30 years later, Glasser has to pause, swallow hard, and clear his throat.

He eventually moved to Tucson with the woman who would be the mother of his only child, a daughter. Almost as soon as he arrived, he found a job at a family-therapy institute where he could use his psychology training. "It was like the sea parted," he says. He felt as if he was doing what he needed to be doing. He got a second job at a clinic that was known for helping kids with behavior problems. Many of them had been diagnosed with ADHD.

"I had been one of these kids," he says. "And here I am with twelve preadolescent kids who aren't on their meds on the weekends—I would meet with them on Saturday mornings. So you get to see: These are very interesting human beings. I got to experience the truth of these kids off medication."

Glasser would open up group discussions by asking what the rules should be. The children half-raised their hands and called out predictable answers: no hitting, no yelling, no bad words, no this, no that. The first time it happened, Glasser was seized with memories, a darkness moving over his brain like a shadow. "It was PTSD for me. I grew up with rules that start with *no,* and I hated rules that start with *no.* They always led to me getting in trouble, and ultimately getting hit," he says. "It got my attention that kids saw rules that way."

The clinic and the therapy institute both employed other bright young therapists, and they all called on their state-of-the-art psychology training to try to help the troubled families in their care. They used positive reinforcement. Instead of rules that started with no, they set rules like "Be respectful" and "Use nice words." This was all fine and hewed closely to the education and therapy trends of the day. Kids behaved better. Families improved. But they didn't change. Positive reinforcement is great, but there was only so far it could go with a difficult child. Glasser knew he hadn't truly scraped away the artifice of defiant behavior to get at whatever pain was festering inside these kids. He wasn't finding whatever it was that stirred them to yell and swear and make the grown-ups think they needed medication.

The problem with the positive rules was that there didn't seem to be a very good way to teach them. The old rules were mostly taught when children broke them. If the rule is "No hitting" and one kid hits another, you'd teach the child the rule in that moment. "What you just did was wrong." You'd tell him to go sit in the corner, or go to his room, or apologize. But in those moments, everyone's upset. The kid who got hit is crying, the hitter is angry and scared, and the grown-up is amping up the authority. The offending child gets all the attention. The rule doesn't stick.

Still, Glasser saw that kids seemed to like "no" rules because they're clear. The line of transgression was definite. He had an idea: What if he told the children how great they were when they didn't break a rule? It would be like a video game. When you do something great while playing a video game—when you simply do what the game expects—you get points and you get to keep going. When you go out of bounds or break one of the game's rules, no one yells at you or reminds you what rule you've broken. You simply miss a turn or lose points. And there is no grudge once you pay the fine. As Glasser wrote in his first book in 1999, *Transforming the Difficult Child,* "When the consequence is over, it's right back to scoring."

Kids love video games. "They don't need us to figure out a video game for them," he says. "They figure it out in three minutes, and then they become stars. The beauty of those games is the energy of success is so strong, consistent, reliable, available. If they break a rule in the next two seconds, the game unplugs momentarily. Grown-ups look at the consequences in these games and we don't always see the truth of what's going on. It looks to us like, Oh my God, huge consequence—blood spurting, heads rolling. But actually, the kid's out of the game for two seconds but it feels like an eternity to them because they've become such a devotee of being plugged in to success, and they vividly feel the energy of missing out. When the consequence is over, they don't just come back into the game, they come back ever more determined: I'm not gonna break another rule."

And so he thought, What if a child was sitting quietly, not bothering anyone, and you went out of your way to congratulate him on that, very specifically, by telling him how proud you are that he's not hitting anyone, not screaming, not throwing toys, but just sitting quietly? What if you gave a child the equivalent of points—what if you thanked him or hugged him—for not putting his feet on the couch? How would he respond to that?

He'll like it, it turns out.

"I started accusing kids of being successful for not breaking rules. Nobody ever in my professional career had done that," he says. "All of a sudden—and it was as weird as it could be—I knew I was speaking to some level of a kid's soul. I knew it was nourishing them in some way. It was like me weeping at Michael Davis's house. In my professional career, no kid had ever been told they were successful when it came to rules."

Many of the people I interviewed who have had direct experience with ADHD—parents of children who'd been diagnosed, psychiatrists, adult ADHD patients—assured me, within the first minute of our conversation, that ADHD is a real disorder, not some made-up condition.

"It's important to understand that ADHD is a very real, serious, neurobiological disorder," said Saltarelli, the neurologist who was formerly senior vice-president of clinical development at Shire, maker of Adderall and Vyvanse, which is now the most common brand of stimulant prescribed for ADHD. He repeated this point several times during our hour-long conversation.

"I don't think in the medical community or in the research community there is any question that this is a brain disorder. I really don't think that is in question," Ruth Hughes, the CHADD CEO, told me after I asked her about the validity of brain scans that purport to show ADHD, which have been disputed by other scientists.

"There is no doubt in my mind that I really believe this is a disorder, disease, condition, whatever you do—like, it is for real," said Tracie Giles, a parent of four children, two of whom have been diagnosed. She is the coordinator of the local CHADD chapter in Wayne County, Michigan.

The interesting thing is I never asked any of these people whether ADHD is real. But their defensiveness is understandable. ADHD isn't strep throat—there's no culture, no test. To find out if you have it, or if your son has it, or if your daughter has it, you just need a human being to say so—a physician or a psychiatrist—and that makes some people skeptical. Google "Does ADHD exist?" Up pop the detractors who call the very disorder into question.

ADHD has become the most controversial medical topic in America when it comes to children. In 2000, Bob Schaffer, then a Colorado congressman, called a hearing about ADHD medication before the House Committee on Education and the Workforce. "I had been in politics a long time even before I had this hearing," he says. "And you would think that with issues of national missile defense, the space program, the billions we spend on public education, the China trade bill I voted on—that something else would have resulted in more blowback, but I can't think of anything else that did. It inspired more personal hostility and defensiveness than anything else I'd ever been involved in."

The biggest reason: Managing ADHD, for most people who receive the diagnosis, includes taking medication. If the diagnosis is real, a prescription can turn around a child's life in an instant, improving his ability to concentrate and jacking up his self-esteem. Denying a child who needs the medicine is as cruel as forcing it on a kid who doesn't. Even Howard Glasser is not anti-medication—not entirely. He believes that in rare cases it can be effective as a temporary measure. But it's a terrifying choice to make for many parents.

Ned Hallowell once famously said that stimulants were "safer than aspirin," a statement he has since backed off of. ("That's almost a preposterous statement for anyone to say," says Saltarelli.) "I think that was misleading," Hallowell says now. "I was dealing with people who thought these medications were extremely dangerous, and if they're used properly, they are not. But now I don't say that anymore because I'm worried about high school students taking them without any medical evaluation." But Hallowell stands by his assertion—widely corroborated—that it's silly to try to treat ADHD without medicine. "I certainly am not gonna try to persuade you to use medication, but once you learn the facts, chances are you will want to. Because doing a year, say, of non-medication is sort of like saying, Why don't we do a year of squinting before we try eyeglasses."

The Epidemic

2003: The No Child Left Behind Act rewards schools for higher test scores. Kids with ADHD get more time to take tests, and sometimes their scores aren't counted in the overall average. As the law rolls out, ADHD diagnoses increase 53% in poor areas.

In 1999 the National Institute of Mental Health published its landmark study "Multimodal Treatment of ADHD," which was led by Peter Jensen; 579 children ages seven to nine took part. The study declared that the best treatment, across the board, is medication combined with behavioral therapy—but that the combination works only marginally better than medication on its own, with no behavioral component. This made a lot of parents feel better about accepting a prescription for their children, and the study is frequently cited by pharmaceutical companies, psychiatrists, and organizations like CHADD.

Research published since the multimodal study, however, suggests that treating kids who have ADHD with cognitive behavioral therapy can have the same positive effect as stimulants. A new study in the *Journal of Abnormal Child Psychology* shows that behavioral therapy, alone or in combination with stimulants, is far more effective than medication alone. The children in the study—forty-four boys, four girls, all diagnosed with ADHD—were given varying doses of medication and behavioral therapy, and researchers monitored their episodes of "noncompliance" each day. The worst-behaved children were the ones receiving only drugs and no behavioral therapy. Even kids given a placebo while also receiving some behavioral therapy behaved far better than kids being treated with drugs alone. The sweet spot was a low dose of medication plus behavioral therapy.

William Pelham of Florida International University, the lead author of the study and one of the original investigators on the multimodal study, says that these findings show that psychosocial treatments "are the key to long-term success. Medication alone is not the solution to the long term."

I wanted to talk to an actual person at a drug company about the difficult choice. I called Novartis, which manufactures Ritalin and Focalin XR. A media-relations specialist, Julie Masow, declined to make anyone from the company available to me for an interview, citing the fact that it was summer and people were traveling, and instead provided me with a vague written statement. But eventually Masow agreed to provide written answers

to any questions I wished to send her via e-mail. It was a fairly fruitless exercise—a lot of anodyne corporatespeak about how "ultimately, the decision to prescribe an ADHD treatment for a child with ADHD is between the physician and the patient's parent/guardian" and "Patients and parents/guardians also receive a copy of the medication guide included in the drug package insert."

Novartis is right, to a point—pharmaceutical companies do not prescribe the drugs they manufacture. So do they care what happens once the drugs leave the factory? When I asked Saltarelli of Shire whether drug companies should do anything to make sure their products are used correctly, he said, "It is our responsibility to make sure that the drugs are being appropriately utilized. It's obviously impossible for us to be in any way involved in diagnosis, let alone in every doctor's office where diagnoses are being made. But we do feel an ethical obligation—and we've actually invested quite a bit to do whatever we possibly can through educational efforts to make sure that these drugs are being used appropriately." When I asked the same question of Novartis, the answer (via e-mail) was "Novartis supports only the appropriate use of ADHD medicines as indicated and prescribed by qualified, licensed health-care providers. Novartis does not participate in the diagnosis of patients with ADHD, as the diagnostic criteria. . ."

Karen Lowry, a nurse in Medford, New Jersey, helps run a local CHADD chapter. She has four children, the youngest of whom has ADHD. "When he was first diagnosed, we were adamantly against medication. *No, it might prevent his brain growth. We'll deal with behavioral programs. It's not happening,*" she says. "But as first grade progressed and we saw our child with an ADHD diagnosis experiencing hyperactivity, impulsivity, and inattentiveness in a classroom setting with a teacher who was really not very understanding, we saw a kid who was falling through the cracks. We saw a kid who was not developing friendships, peers who were always blaming him for everything that was going on around him. So my husband and I looked at each other again and said, Oh my gosh, we need to rethink this. Are we not being fair to him? What's worse? Not fully understanding the medication and what can happen in a positive way, or just standing our ground saying, We're unsure about this?"

Lowry and her husband ended up putting their youngest son on a stimulant. His behavior improved vastly, and the ADHD seemed to be under control. But toward the end of the school year, he developed severe facial tics, a side effect of some ADHD medications. They took him off the medication for the summer, a decision many parents make at some point. "He's adjusted pretty much," she says. "He's on a very low dose because he does get the headaches. It's sometimes hard to balance, you know, the side effect with the effects of the drug."

Overall, Lowry thinks they made the right call. It's a question she gets a lot from other parents of children with ADHD. "I would never tell anyone to put their kid on medication. All I will say is look at the results. And I always commend the parents who come to our classes, even if they're frantic: Your kid will be okay because you're here."

Ruth Hughes, CHADD's CEO, finds herself defending—or justifying—ADHD as a diagnosis regularly. More than 12,000 people are members of the organization. Its annual budget is about $3.5 million, of which up to 30 percent can come from the pharmaceutical companies that manufacture ADHD drugs, according to Hughes.

During our phone interview, I asked Hughes whether CHADD could be classified as pro-medication. "Well, I'm going to reframe this a little bit," she said. "We are pro-science, pro-research. Our issue is to make parents or adults who potentially have ADHD to be very well informed consumers of medical services."

I told her I was asking because while there are lots of books and articles out there about how to treat ADHD without medication, you hardly ever see anything about that on CHADD's website or in its bimonthly magazine, *Attention.*

"You don't," she said.

If we don't know what we're doing, maybe we shouldn't be doing it. Putting a child on highly addictive psychotropic drugs ought to be very difficult, not shockingly easy. And yet even if Peter Jensen's 20-year-old estimates about misdiagnosis are still correct, an astonishing 25 percent of today's 6.4 million kids, overwhelmingly boys with developing brains, might be experiencing side effects for no reason. Because he made that assumption long before ADHD became such a popular diagnosis, the number could be far higher now.

Yes, the drugs these children consume may work. They help them focus for longer periods of time. They help them do better in school. But consider this: Stimulants work on just about anyone. "These are powerful drugs," says Bob Schaffer, the former Colorado congressman. "They would work on me. They would make anyone more focused. And everyone's happy because the kid is now under control." The fact that the drugs would help you perform better at work doesn't mean you should take them. And it certainly doesn't mean a seven-year-old boy who doesn't suffer from a psychiatric disorder should be taking them.

Why not, if they help him do better? Because, for one thing, an important study of 4,000 children published last year concluded that children who took stimulants didn't do any better in school than kids who didn't. But also, and perhaps more important, because he might not be the same seven-year-old boy once he starts, and he may never be the same boy again.

Another little-examined feature of these drugs is the global changes in personality that they can cause. Jim Forgan is a

psychologist in Jupiter, Florida. The first thing you see on his website is an ad:

"Dr. Jim Forgan's Parent Support System
10 Easy to Use Modules
Over 80 Educational Videos
Downloadable Resources
Online Access 24/7
And Much More!"

The video support system is available for a one-time fee of $49.97. Forgan is the coauthor of a book called *Raising Boys with ADHD,* also available for purchase. He speaks from experience. His son has been diagnosed with ADHD. Forgan knows all the warning signs, and he tells parents about them. He's in favor of drugs when they're administered correctly—starting with low doses, watching vigilantly for side effects, stopping use if the side effects outweigh the benefits.

How do you know if the side effects outweigh the benefits?

"Careful monitoring," says Forgan. "And for me personally, with my son being on the stimulant medications, those are medications you don't have to take every day, so we would give him the holiday breaks on the weekends and spring break and summertime, just so that he didn't have the medication all the time. And yeah, there's a difference, he has more energy. My son doesn't like to take the medications because he feels like it makes him feel flat, and he doesn't like what it does to his personality. And he says he's not the same fun person that he is when he's not on the medication. And some of that fun gets him in trouble at school, because he's funny and knows how to entertain people. But at the same time, he likes that characteristic about himself—that he is fun and knows how to get people laughing and working together and bring energy into a room. Kinda like the life of the party."

I tell Forgan that there is something heartbreaking about the fact that such a lively part of his son's personality disappears when he's on medication, and that his son knows it disappears. "Is it just that he was getting into too much trouble?" I ask.

Forgan pauses and says, "Right. Yup, it gets him in trouble and he hasn't—when he was in elementary school, he didn't have his own ability to have the self-control not to say impulsive things and do impulsive things that other people find funny but the teacher finds very annoying."

"And you see the fun part of him reemerge during breaks from the medicine?"

"Right."

Howard Glasser's biggest fear in life is that a child might grow up not knowing how great a person he is. It keeps Glasser awake at night sometimes, this image of a kid thinking he's no good. It lodges a pit in his throat.

Ned Hallowell, the ADHD expert who has the disorder, writes books about it, has talked about it on *Dr. Oz,* and thinks medication usually gets good results, feels the same. "The medical model is so slanted toward deficits that it excludes strengths—and it also reinforces stigma, that this is shameful, this is bad, this means you're a loser. And that becomes a self-fulfilling prophecy. It's the old line of whether you think you can or you think you can't, you're right. And what breaks my heart is how these kids, and the parents along with them, get broken in school, and they come out of twelfth grade believing that they're stupid. Believing that they're defective. But this trait, these are the people who colonized this country! Just think of it: Who in the world would get on a boat in 1600 and come over here? You had to be some kind of a nut. You had to be a visionary, a dreamer, an entrepreneur—you know, a risk-taker. That's our gene pool. So this country is absolutely full of ADD."

So there is something great about having ADHD. The question is how to treat the difficult parts in a way that pushes the greatness forward.

"I confront kids with their own greatness," Glasser says. "Because that's what I think allows a kid to go from an ordinary life to a purposeful life. To see who they really are. The worst-case scenario in life is that a boy grows up thinking: Who I really am is a kid who annoys everybody."

In 1994 Glasser opened the Center for the Difficult Child in Tucson, his first effort to teach therapists his Nurtured Heart Approach. In 1999 he published *Transforming the Difficult Child*, which has quietly sold nearly 250,000 copies. Today he runs an organization he named the Children's Success Foundation, which is an expanded effort to teach educators and therapists around the United States how to use what he has found from 20 years of practicing the Nurtured Heart Approach.

"It's much more about reaction than attention." That sentence appears on page 10 of *Transforming the Difficult Child*. It's a profound distinction, and there is no deeper nor more simple understanding of a child's needs. Parents of intense boys can shower their children with love and attention, and still the boys might be difficult boys. What's important is how you react to what a child does, good or bad, Glasser says. Mostly, we get animated when our kids do something bad. We get worked up, and we give them energy—negative energy, but energy nonetheless. But when a difficult child is sitting quietly, playing or writing or drawing, not disturbing anyone, not throwing food, not picking on a sibling—we do nothing. We don't acknowledge it at all. The way a difficult child gets a parent's energy, then, is to do something bad.

"Most parenting approaches have you giving a strong punitive consequence that's all energy and that confirms that, as a parent, you're highly available through negativity—you're a toy that works when they push buttons," he says. "And you work if and only if they act out bigger."

Watching Glasser work with a child is a marvel.

He is sitting on the carpeted floor of a family's basement playroom, his lanky frame contorted into what passes for comfort for a 63-year-old man sitting on the floor. He is watching a sandy-haired boy of seven play with his toys. A few minutes before, the boy had been hitting his younger brother, and he had been scolded, hit his brother again, and been banished from the kitchen. Now he plays peacefully.

"I see that you are very calmly building with your Legos," Glasser says to the boy, in a smooth and even voice, as if he were commenting on clouds moving across the sky. "That's really great to see. It shows that you respect your mom and dad, because they love it when you play nicely."

The boy just nods without looking up, like, Sure, thanks mister. So Glasser keeps at it.

"So I assume you heard what I said. And I just want to elaborate a little more. Because here's what's great: You have this wonderful quiet way of thinking things through. I can tell that you're thinking about what it means to be calm. And maybe you don't quite know what calm means. Let me tell you how great calm is. What does it take to be calm?"

The boy looks up now. Words are starting to register with him. His face is blank, but he's thinking. This is unusual for him—getting attention, getting a reaction, for being so good.

"Well, while you're thinking about it, let me tell you. It takes wisdom, for one thing, because you could be yelling. You could be annoying people. Have you ever been annoying? Well, you're not being annoying. You're not running around the lunch table. You're not throwing your food or hitting your brother. All these things that kids your age could do, you're not doing. That's being calm. That shows me you're being thoughtful. That you care about other people, and that you're in control of your body. Being in control takes a lot of concentration and effort. Doesn't it?"

The boy nods, just barely. He is looking right into Glasser's eyes. For years, since he was two, the boy has had trouble controlling his body sometimes. Sometimes the energy inside him is just too much, and it builds like gas trapped in rock until it bursts forth in a violent, painful mess. At times he has driven his parents to a crisis of helplessness. The heartbreaking part is the boy has tried so hard to control his energy, and he's gotten better at it. But sometimes he still just can't. Once, in the middle of the night, when he was four, he wouldn't go to sleep and kept throwing toys at the door until his mother cried and his father yelled, and then through the tears streaming down his tiny cheeks he looked up at his father over the plastic gate that was jammed in his bedroom door and, in a moment of astonishing self-awareness, pleaded, "I need to calm my body down!" When he started school, his parents mentioned to the school psychologist that their son sometimes had an issue with impulsive behavior. The psychologist, who had never met him—who had never met the boy—told the parents that it sounded like he probably had ADHD. The parents had had their son evaluated by child psychologists, pediatricians, teachers, and independent therapists, and not one person had ever suggested ADHD, and in fact, the boy's pediatrician and the rest of the school's counseling, teaching, and professional staff said resolutely the boy showed no signs of it. (When he heard that a school psychologist had said this, Glasser wasn't surprised. "Sure. Your son is intense. If you wanted to go out and get him a prescription for ADHD medication, you could do it tomorrow," he told the parents.)

"That's right," Glasser says to the boy. "It does take a lot of effort. And I want to tell you something: A few minutes ago, you hit your brother. And he started crying, and then you got really upset when your parents told you to stop. You were really mad at him and at them. But look at you now. Look at yourself! You calmed yourself down so beautifully. And that was an amazing, amazing thing to do, because it's hard to calm yourself down when you're so upset. But you figured out how to control your body in a really bad moment. You did that yourself. No one did it for you. And that shows greatness. That shows me and everybody else that you have greatness inside you."

The boy is looking at him still, locked in.

And, slowly at first, the boy begins to smile. And then the smile spreads across his whole, beautiful seven-year-old face. His teeth, missing here and there and sticking out in gaps where he used to suck his thumb, shine across the room, and he lets out a giggle, and the giggle turns into the kind of proud, embarrassed laugh kids do when they haven't learned how to take a compliment. His face is lit up—he is shocked by what he has just heard, and shocked by his own joyful reaction. He's laughing, looking at this man who has just told him that he has greatness within his soul, and the kid slaps the floor, then crosses his skinny arms on top of his head, and smiles with pride. He is euphoric.

It is almost as if he has been drugged.

Critical Thinking

1. How can a parent differentiate between an energetic son and a possible ADHD diagnosis?

2. How do educational policies such as " The No Child Left Behind Act" of 2001 or the recent "Common Core" standards impact rates of ADHD diagnosis and treatment?

3. Are the known side effects of ADHD medications such as Ritalin, Adderall, or Concerta worth the risk to the child?

Internet References

Boys with ADHD may face tougher times as men
http://www.cbsnews.com/news/boys-with-adhd-may-face-tougher-times-as-men

Gender Differences in ADHD Symptoms
http://www.healthline.com/health/adhd/adhd-symptoms-in-girls-and-boys

The Ritalin Explosion
http://www.pbs.org/wgbh/pages/frontline/shows/medicating/experts/explosion.html

Why Boys with ADHD Need Their Dads
http://www.additudemag.com/adhd/article/707.html

Article Prepared by: Claire N. Rubman, *Suffolk County Community College, Selden, NY*

Responding to Defiance in the Moment

EDUCATION DIGEST

Learning Outcomes

After reading this article, you will be able to:

- Discuss the root cause of defiance.

- Explain how fear of failure, lack of attention or toxic stress contribute to defiance.

- Describe five possible ways that a parent can respond to de-escalate a situation with a defiant child.

Why Do Children Defy Authority?

At certain ages, children are more likely to defy us and take active steps to test limits. At other ages, children are tuned in to issues of fairness and may push back when they sense an adult is being unjust. Picture Amelia, a sixth grader. Whenever presented with an assignment that she found less than engaging, she'd say, "I'm not going to do that. It's a waste of my time." One day, when a teacher asked her to go to the back of the line as a consequence for a rulebreaking behavior, Amelia sat down and refused to move.

With students like Amelia, it's easy to get enmeshed in a power struggle. We may think that students use defiant behavior to annoy us or ruin our day. But their acts of defiance rarely have much to do with us. The main reasons why students act defiantly include:

Unmet physical needs—When students are hungry or tired, they have less energy and it's harder for them to regulate their behavior.

Academic challenges—Some students refuse to do assignments to hide their fear or inability to do what's being asked, such as solving a math problem. They would rather be seen as defiant than incapable, especially in front of their peers.

A sense of belonging and significance—Children who struggle academically or socially may believe that they're "bad" students and thus are not valued. They may use defiance as a way to gain a sense of personal importance.

A need for more control—Sometimes what we say and do unintentionally diminishes a child's feelings of significance. If we find ourselves being too controlling with children who defy us, they may rebel even more—starting a frustrating cycle of our trying to impose more control and receiving back more defiance.

A need for more attention—Some children have learned that defiance can bring them extra attention from teachers and classmates—even if that attention is negative.

Testing limits—Testing limits is a natural part of childhood; some children may thoroughly test adults to find out where the limits are and whether we will keep our word.

Experiencing toxic stress—Children who experience toxic stress come to school on high alert. (In brief, toxic stress is when a child experiences strong, frequent, and/or prolonged adversity, such as physical or emotional abuse or chronic neglect.) These children quickly react when they sense that trouble is coming; they may talk back to teachers, fight, and argue with peers.

The more we can focus on the underlying reasons students engage in defiance, the more we'll be able to maintain our cool in the moment when students act defiantly.

Early Signs of Distress

Children who are defiant usually give clues that they're feeling distressed. If you can watch for these early signs, you can often tell when they may be headed toward a confrontation. Here are some typical warning signs:

- Shifting in seat,
- Opening and closing fists,
- Drumming on desk with fists,
- Slumping shoulders,
- Crossing arms against chest, and
- Trouble making eye contact.

De-escalating Defiance in the Moment

The key to responding effectively to a child who's being defiant is straightforward: Keep the child (and classmates) safe while giving the defiant child a chance to cool down. When a child is behaving defiantly, avoid responses that will heighten stress and invite more resistance. Don't expect that you can reason with the child or make an emotional appeal to get them to behave.

In the moment:

Avoid public confrontations: When you publicly give redirections or consequences to a student who's challenging you, the stakes become higher for both of you. Public disagreements between you and the student can also harm a student's relationship with peers; classmates may label them as "bad" and avoid them as a result. Whenever possible, give reminders, redirections, and consequences privately. Doing so will help preserve your relationship with the student and their relationship with classmates.

Stay calm: When you notice that a child is getting upset or refusing to do what you asked, first tell yourself to slow down. Don't rush to respond (unless to take immediate action for safety's sake). If you stay calm, you give the child more of an opportunity to calm down, too. Allow yourself a few seconds to pause or take a few deep breaths. This will give you time to assess the situation calmly and objectively.

Respectfully remind or redirect: Students who have difficulty cooperating can be especially sensitive to being "bossed around." Whether you're responding to early warning signs or full-blown defiance, use respectful words and an even tone. For example, to a child who's challenging your directions, you might say, "Morgan, take a seat. You can read or draw for now." Here are some more tips:

- Be brief. Avoid lectures and sarcasm.
- Speak in a calm, matter-of-fact tone.

- Use short, direct statements.
- Don't ask questions (unless you will accept any answer).
- Keep your body language neutral.

Intervene as early as possible: As soon as you notice early warning signs, respond to them with respectful reminders or redirections. If you wait until a student acts defiantly, they will be less capable of responding rationally to your directions.

Offer limited choices when possible: Because children who struggle with defiance are often seeking power, it can help to offer them two options. By offering two options—not one "do this"—the child can hold on to a sense of significance while you remain consistent. This teaches the child (and the class) that he is still being held accountable for his behavior. However, don't expect immediate compliance. The child will likely need a minute or two to decide what to do.

Avoid negotiating in the moment: Negotiating during an incident will invite further testing. It also sends the message that children can avoid a consequence or redirection by resisting. If you find yourself in a power struggle, take a deep breath and disengage. Let the child (and the whole class, if they're watching) know that you're finished talking for now and will address the issue after the child calms down. For instance: "Max, we're done talking for now. Everyone else, get your writing journals and start on your stories."

Give children time and space to cool down: Once children start to refuse directions or speak angrily to adults, they're likely in the "fight-or-flight" mindset and can't think rationally. Whenever possible, avoid any discussion until the child has completely calmed down. Consider ways to help the child regain self-control. For example, gross motor movement, such as taking a walk or getting a drink of water, may help more than having the child sit still.

Reflect on What's Working and What's not

It's worth taking some time after an incident of defiance to take a step back and reflect: Are your expectations for yourself or the child simply too high? Is there another approach you haven't tried that might help?

Remember that your main objective in responding in the moment is to keep the child and other students safe. However, in-the-moment responses play a limited role in helping children develop prosocial skills such as cooperation, empathy, and self-control. Helping a child develop these prosocial skills can go a long way toward reducing acts of defiance. After all, the ultimate goal of discipline is to help a child develop these and other social–emotional skills that are essential to their success in school—and in life.

Note

Condensed, with permission, from a November 7, 2016 article on the Responsive Classroom *website. Read the entire article at* https://www.responsiveclassroom.org/responding-defiance-moment.

Critical Thinking

1. What can parents do differently when raising children to prevent some of the insecurities that lead to defiance from developing?

2. What can we do to encourage the development of prosocial skills in children?

Internet References

8 Strategies for Dealing with a Defiant Child
   http://www.quickanddirtytips.com/parenting/behavior/8-strategies-for-dealing-with-a-defiant-child

Dealing with Defiance
   http://www.parenting.com/article/disobedience-and-defiance

Parent Acts: How to Deal with a Defiant Child
   http://www.cnn.com/2016/08/30/health/parent-acts-defiant-children/index.html

Why Is My Child So Angry and Defiant? An Overview of Oppositional Defiant Disorder
   https://www.additudemag.com/parenting-a-defiant-adhd-child/

Article   Prepared by: Claire N. Rubman, *Suffolk County Community College, Selden, NY*

Time to Lower the Drinking Age

A lower age would discourage binge drinking and may help combat sexual assault.

MARY KATE CARY

Learning Outcomes

After reading this article, you will be able to:

- Discuss when and why the laws regarding the legal drinking age were changed.

- Talk about the increase in illegal drug (such as OxyContin, Vicodin, Xanax, and Valium) use since the drinking age was raised.

- Articulate why the author reports that it is time to lower the drinking age.

I was telling my college-age daughter recently that back in the olden days when I went to college, you could fill a red Solo cup with beer at a fraternity party and sip it all night long. No one knew if it was your first beer or your 10th. There was no need for "pregaming"—binge drinking in private apartments or dorms before heading out in public. And unlike today, college kids didn't tend to use fake IDs as much.

That's because when I was an undergrad, the drinking age was 18. Fraternities had kegs out in the open on university property, and student gatherings on campus often included beer. I remember university police regularly strolling through the fraternity parties, making sure everything was under control. That tended to keep a lid on things.

Then, 30 years ago this summer, President Ronald Reagan signed into law the Federal Uniform Drinking Age Act of 1984, which mandated that all states adopt 21 as the legal drinking age over the next five years. States that did not comply faced a cut in their federal highway funds; by 1988, all 50 states had moved the minimum drinking age to 21.

The well-intentioned leaders of Mothers Against Drunk Driving were able to convince politicians that a vote against the bill was a vote in favor of drunken driving, and they succeeded in gaining unanimous passage in both the House and the Senate. According to the MADD website, the National Highway Traffic Safety Administration estimates that the law has saved about 900 lives a year.

Drunken driving deaths have decreased over the last three decades in large part because we now throw the book at drunken drivers in this country: All 50 states currently define a driver's having a blood-alcohol concentration of 0.08 or higher as a crime; 42 states suspend drivers' licenses on the first offense. Every state also now has some type of ignition interlock law, requiring devices to be installed in the vehicles of convicted drunken drivers that prevent a vehicle from starting if the driver breathes into the device and produces a breath-alcohol level above a preset limit. Thanks to MADD, drunken driving isn't the problem it used to be.

The Centers for Disease Control and Prevention reports that in 2010 drug overdoses caused more deaths than motor vehicle crashes among people 25 to 64 years old. The CDC estimates that from 1999 to 2010 drug overdose death rates jumped 102 percent. While first-time use of illegal street drugs such as heroin by young people increased from 90,000 users in 2006 to 156,000 in 2012, it's abuse of prescription drugs that has really skyrocketed. One recent report cited by the Department of Justice says that between 1993 and 2005, the proportion of college students abusing opioids like Vicodin and OxyContin jumped 343 percent and 450 percent for tranquilizers like Xanax and Valium.

Prescription drug use among young people at colleges is, along with binge drinking, part of the epidemic of pregaming. The CDC reported that alcohol is responsible for more than 4,300 deaths annually among underage youth. The CDC also found that young people between the ages of 12 and 20 drink 11 percent of all the alcohol consumed in the U.S., and more than 90 percent of this alcohol is consumed during binge drinking.

Here's the problem with both binge drinking and drug abuse: When you're that impaired, you do things you wouldn't normally do. In an April speech, Dartmouth College's president listed the outrages he now witnesses regularly: "From sexual assaults on campus . . . to a culture where dangerous drinking has become the rule and not the exception . . . to a general disregard for human dignity as exemplified by hazing, parties with racist and sexist undertones, disgusting and sometimes threatening insults hurled on the Internet . . . to a social scene that is too often at odds with the practices of inclusion that students are right to expect on a college campus in 2014." I doubt that list is unique to just one Ivy League school.

President Obama recently announced the creation of the White House Task Force to Protect Students from Sexual Assault, after stating that "1 in 5 women on college campuses has been sexually assaulted during their time there." (If that were true, as one critic pointed out, the crime rates on college campuses would be astronomically higher than America's most violent cities.)

Despite the hyperbole from the White House, we can all agree that sexual assault as a result of alcohol and drug abuse is a very serious problem on America's college campuses. But forming a task force in Washington probably won't help. Allowing states to lower the legal drinking age would. The U.S. is one of only seven nations in the entire world with a drinking age of 21. Most Western democracies allow their citizens to fight in wars, vote in elections and drink alcohol at age 18—as do even China and North Korea.

I'd rather see my kids sipping beer out of a red Solo cup at a well-patrolled fraternity party than drinking shots and popping a Vicodin in someone's basement off campus. Lowering the drinking age will help slow the need for pregaming and bring the college fake ID business to a dead stop. It can't help but reduce the binge drinking, drug overdoses and sexual assaults.

Thirty years ago, drunken driving was the problem. Now that is less true. Let's take a lesson from MADD and make a vote against lowering the drinking age to 18 a vote for drug overdoses and sexual assaults against young women. Times have changed.

Critical Thinking

1. Were women safer on college campuses when the drinking age was lower?
2. Would lowering the drinking age decrease binge drinking episodes?
3. If the drinking age was lowered, would adolescents seek out other thrills instead of alcohol?

Internet References

A Rising Epidemic on College Campuses: Prescription Drug Abuse
   https://www.clintonfoundation.org/blog/2014/01/12/rising-epidemic-college-campuses-prescription-drug-abuse

College Drinking
   http://www.niaaa.nih.gov/alcohol-health/special-populations-co-occurring-disorders/college-drinking

MADD
   http://www.madd.org

Should the Drinking Age Be Lowered from 21 to a Younger Age?
   http://drinkingage.procon.org

The Missing Key to Fighting Sexual Assault on Campus
   http://www.slate.com/articles/news_and_politics/jurisprudence/2014/05/drinking_and_sexual_assault_on_campus_universities_must_define_when_sex.html

---

MARY KATE CARY is a former White House speechwriter for President George H.W. Bush. She currently writes speeches for political and business leaders, and is a contributing editor for *U.S. News & World Report*.

Article   Prepared by: Claire N. Rubman, *Suffolk County Community College, Selden, NY*

When to Worry about Your Child's Aggression

JORDANA MANSBACHER

Learning Outcomes

After reading this article, you will be able to:

- Define aggressive behavior in children.

- Articulate when a child's aggressive behavior might warrant professional help.

- Discuss the possible underlying causes of aggressive behavior in children.

Hearing that your child has caused physical harm to anyone can elicit an emotional tailspin. The immediate onslaught of panic, denial, shock, anger, fear, disappointment, shame, and guilt—mixed with thoughts about injuries, possible thoughts about injuries, possible legal or financial repercussions, and so forth—can be dizzying, albeit normal.

But before you over analyze the meaning and implications of your child's aggressive outburst and worry about how others will judge your parenting skills, take a deep breath or two and center yourself for this next bit of news. Your child is not the only one with aggressive tendencies. You have them, too. In fact, we all do.

Statistical data show:

- 45 percent of us regularly lose our temper at work.
- 66 percent of all annual traffic fatalities are caused by aggressive driving actions, such as passing on the right, running red lights, and tailgating.
- one in five adults in the U.S. workforce has experience a workplace bully; that's 28 million of us.
- 41 percent of us reported workplace incidents cause such severe trauma that a clinical diagnosis of depression is warranted.

- Nearly one in four of all employees suffer chronic anger on the job.
- 1 in 20 of us has had a fight with the person living next door.
- 71 percent of Internet users admit to having suffered 'net rage because of severe frustration from surging online.
- 50 percent of us have reacted to computer problems by hitting our PC, hurling parts of it around, screaming, or demonstrating other extreme behaviors.
- Depression and anxiety have overtaken physical ailments as the chief cause of long-term sickness.

A once or twice angry outburst in life is not outside the realm of what is considered normal behavior. Haven't you ever lost your cool (without causing bodily harm) and also felt a bit guilty about how energized you felt afterward? When aggressive behavior becomes more than an infrequent occurrence, however, it is time to consult with a professional.

According to the American Academy of Pediatrics, if your child has exhibited any one of the following criteria, it is time for professional intervention:

- Aggression that has caused physical injury to self or others.
- Aggression that has lasted longer than a few weeks, and you are unable to change or manage this situation.
- Your child attacks you or someone else.
- Your child has been sent home from school or is barred from playtime as a result of aggression.
- You feel afraid for your safety.

Aggressive behavior is not just a stronger form of assertiveness. It is the acting out of deeper emotional experiences that your child does not have the maturity to process, cope, or integrate in a healthy manner.

Anger, pain, disappointment, abuse, neglect, sadness, fear, and embarrassment are often at the core of aggressive behavior. Children often lack awareness and insight as to why they behave a certain way, and they lack the verbal skills to adequately express all that they feel inside. Yet, they do know that something does not feel right. Targeting harmful behavior sends a message to your child that you not only notice and hear they are struggling internally, but you will take action to try and alleviate that discomfort.

Critical Thinking

1. How do parents gauge if their children's behavior falls within the normal range?

2. How does social media impact aggressive behavior in children?

Internet References

Aggressive Behavior
https://www.healthychildren.org/English/ages-stages/toddler/Pages/Aggressive-Behavior.aspx

Children Learn Aggression from Parents
https://www.psychologytoday.com/blog/the-big-questions/201111/children-learn-aggression-parents

Covert Anger in Your Child: Why You Should Worry about Passive Aggression
http://www.focusonthefamily.ca/parenting/school-age/covert-anger-in-your-child-why-you-should-worry-about-passive-aggression

What Are Some of the Causes of Aggression in Children?
http://childmind.org/article/aggression-in-children-causes/

DR. JORDANA MANSBACHER is a licensed psychotherapist and human behavior expert specializing in the treatment of eating disorders, depression, anxiety, and relationship issues. She provides service from her practice in Los Angeles, California and globally, via Skype. Dr. Mansbacher is sought out for her expertise in a variety of professional arenas as a speaker, mentor, and psychological commentator for various radio and television news programs.

Article   Prepared by: Claire N. Rubman, *Suffolk County Community College, Selden, NY*

Displacement Crisis Grows as Boko Haram Increases Exploitation of Girls

Fredrick Nzwili

Learning Outcomes

After reading this article, you will be able to:

- Articulate why Boko Haram focuses its attention specifically on young girls.

- Develop a deeper appreciation for the breadth and scope of the abuse in Nigeria, Cameroon, and Chad.

- Better articulate the tragic plight of the 300 Chibok schoolgirls since 2014.

Two years after the abduction of nearly 300 schoolgirls by Boko Haram militants in Chibok, in northeast Nigeria, parents are still hoping their daughters will return home.

The same week as the anniversary of the kidnapping, UNICEF released a report titled *Beyond Chibok*, which called the conflict with Boko Haram "one of the fastest growing displacement crises in Africa," with more than 1.3 million children displaced, 1,800 school closures, and 5,000 children separated from their parents.

The report states that suicide attacks involving children have increased in Cameroon, Chad, and Nigeria and that girls were most often the attackers. Thousands of children have disappeared in those countries, the report states.

In Nigeria, some church leaders are concerned that the authorities have not done enough to rescue the Chibok schoolgirls, who were ages 16 to 18 when they were kidnapped on April 14, 2014.

[Most of the girls' families are part of the Ekklesiyar Yan'uwa a Nigeria (the Church of the Brethren in Nigeria). Many of the girls' parents were killed, according to Rebecca Dali, executive director of a nongovernmental organization providing care alongside EYN. The Church of the Brethren, United States reported that 57 of the girls have escaped. However, 219 girls remain missing.]

"The whole nation has failed these children, and we must repent," said Tunde Bakare, a prominent Nigerian evangelical pastor, during a sermon to mark a global action week for the abduction's second anniversary.

According to the UNICEF report, Boko Haram sent 44 children on suicide missions last year against civilians in Nigeria, Cameroon, Chad, and Niger. That represented an 11-fold increase from 2014. The overall number of attacks across those countries rose from 32 to 151 in the same period.

Since Nigerian president Muhammadu Buhari took office in March 2015, his forces have had some success in recapturing territory from Boko Haram and rescuing abducted girls and women. In December he announced that Boko Haram had been "technically defeated," but that claim was followed by an escalation in suicide attacks.

"When these groups are losing—when they're losing territory in particular—one of the ways to project that they're relevant, they're strong, they're still a force with which to be reckoned, is to have these attacks," said Mia Bloom, a professor of communication at Georgia State University and author of multiple books on terrorism, including *Bombshell: Women and Terrorism*. "Boko has been targeting cellphone markets, chicken markets, places where civilians congregate . . . the idea being that using the children against these targets is ideal because they fall under the radar screen. Nobody is going to be suspicious of an eight-year-old girl, a ten-year-old girl."

Boko Haram's exploitation of girls is precise, according to research by Bloom and her colleagues. Girls who are too young to bear children, and women who are too old, carry out many suicide attacks. Those in their teens to early twenties are most often sexually exploited by Boko Haram fighters; 91 percent who are released are pregnant.

But even if the girls are released or escape, they face challenges, according to the UNICEF report. They are often seen as security threats, which has proven justified on some occasions. The children born to women who've been impregnated by militants also face stigma when they return home and in the places they live after being displaced.

Manuel Fontaine, UNICEF's regional director for West and Central Africa, said this is unjust.

"Let us be clear: these children are victims, not perpetrators," Fontaine said in the statement accompanying the release of the report. "Deceiving children and forcing them to carry out deadly acts has been one of the most horrific aspects of the violence in Nigeria and in neighboring countries."

There have been instances of girls halting suicide operations. The *New York Times* reported that a girl sent to bomb a village in northern Cameroon dropped her explosives at the last moment and instead ran to authorities and provided information that led to a raid on Boko Haram.

On another occasion, three girls were sent to bomb an internally displaced persons camp in northeastern Nigeria. Two detonated their explosives, killing 60 people, but the third, after glimpsing her parents among those fleeing, threw her explosives in the bush.

Critical Thinking

1. What can be done to protect girls and young women from abuse among terrorist groups?
2. Should countries meet terrorist's demands for the safe return of children or other captives?

Internet References

10 Tips for Keeping Children Safe from Terrorism
http://www.savethechildren.org/atf/cf/%7B9def2ebe-10ae-432c-9bd0-df91d2eba74a%7D/10TIPS_TERRORISM.PDF

Boko Haram Releases 21 Chibok Girls to Nigerian Government
http://www.cnn.com/2016/10/13/africa/nigeria-chibok-girls-released/

Who Are Nigeria's Boko Haram Islamists?
http://www.bbc.com/news/world-africa-13809501

Unit 5

UNIT

Prepared by: Claire N. Rubman, *Suffolk County Community College, Selden, NY*

Development during Adolescence

The period of development between childhood and adulthood appears to be evolving and expanding. What is causing those changes and how do they impact early adulthood. Is it possible that we are becoming more self-centered and more self-indulged than ever before? How do these potential changes impact our careers, our marriage and our lives? This unit looks at a diverse range of topics from the adolescent allure of e-cigarettes, prescription medications and heroin to cyberbullies, antiquated high school paradigms, and sexting.

Adolescent brains go through many changes with the onset of puberty. One change in particular seems to account for the need to "sensation seek" and find new and more stimulating interactions. This is caused in part by the increased rates of the neurotransmitter Dopamine that floods the adolescent brain. This causes teens to seek out more rewarding and pleasurable behaviors while compromising their judgement. This may begin to account for the increased use of e-cigarettes, heroin, prescription pills, and so on. Read about each of these in "Dangers of E-Cigarettes and Liquid Nicotine among Children" (2017) and "Substance Abuse Concerns: Heroin & Prescription Drug Use on the Rise Among Teens" (2016). Read more about the hormonal changes that can lead to chaos in our teenager's life in "Secrets of our Modern Youth" by Piniewski (2016).

As the adolescent brain myelinates, grows, and evolves, the prefrontal cortex and the executive function allow adolescents to think in new ways. Unfortunately, these changes do not always lead to good behavioral outcomes. Consider the social issues of sexting and cyberbullying. In her article "High-Tech Bullies," Ingrid Sturgis discusses bullying at the college level. Problems on college campuses include cyberstalking, gossiping, and masquerading as another person. Tyler Clemente's tragic cyberbullying case brought this issue to light in 2010 as his Rutger's roommate videotaped him in a sexual encounter that he played on the Internet for all to witness. Unable to withstand the humiliation, Clemente committed suicide by jumping off the George Washington Bridge in NY. Sturgis explores why college students use this perceived anonymity to bully and humiliate their peers. She also explores what college campuses are doing to combat this high-tech bullying. Read about preventive measures that parents can take to combat poor adolescent decision-making in "Pediatricians Primer on Sexting" by Bass (2016).

Our discussion ends on a more positive note—how to create positive interactions with adolescents, how to maximize our understanding of the adolescent brain, and how to promote leadership and better decision-making skills in our adolescent population. Read Groller's article on how to interact with adolescents titled "Twenty Insider Tips for Working with Adolescents at Camp" (2016).

Article Prepared by: Claire N. Rubman, *Suffolk County Community College, Selden, NY*

Dangers of E-cigarettes and Liquid Nicotine among Children

LAURA FRIEDENBERG AND GARY A. SMITH

Learning Outcomes

After reading this article, you will be able to:

- Discuss six suggestions in the 2016 report by the new Surgeon General.

- Describe why e-cigarettes have so much potential appeal to adolescents.

Since e-cigarettes, vape pens, and other similar devices hit the U.S. market several years ago, their popularity has skyrocketed. While we don't know a lot about the long-term effects of using e-cigarettes or the effects of secondhand vapor, we do know that liquid nicotine is a dangerous poison for children. Liquid nicotine is the fluid used to fill e-cigarettes and is increasingly found in homes with young children across the country.

A new study conducted by the Center for Injury Research and Policy of The Research Institute and the Central Ohio Poison Center, both at Nationwide Children's Hospital, investigated exposure to e-cigarettes, liquid nicotine, and other tobacco products among U.S. children younger than six years of age during a 40-month period from January 2012 to April 2015.

Calls to U.S. poison control centers related to e-cigarette and liquid nicotine exposure saw a remarkable 1,500 percent increase during the study period. Data from April 2015 show that on average, every three hours a poison center received a call about a young child exposed to an e-cigarette or liquid nicotine—that's more than seven children each day. Although liquid nicotine can be absorbed through the skin, more than 90 percent of children were exposed through ingestion (swallowing it).

After even small doses, liquid nicotine can cause serious poisoning, and even death, among young children. In the recent study, children exposed to e-cigarettes and liquid nicotine were more than five times more likely to be admitted to the hospital and two-and-one-half times more likely to have a severe medical outcome than children exposed to traditional cigarettes. There was one child death during the study period associated with exposure to liquid nicotine.

Children younger than three years of age are the most vulnerable age group. Children in this age group are curious, have newfound mobility, explore their environment by putting things in their mouth, and do not recognize danger.

It is of great concern that liquid nicotine is sold in bottles with non-child-resistant closures and comes in attractive colors and flavors like chocolate cake, gummy bear, and cotton candy. Flavoring in cigarettes (other than menthol) has been prohibited since 2009; the same should be done for e-cigarettes and liquid nicotine. E-cigarettes and liquid nicotine refill containers should be child-resistant and labeling should not display images attractive to children.

E-cigarettes and their refill bottles often end up in purses and backpacks, which get thrown on a floor or couch. Sometimes people leave e-cigarettes and liquid nicotine bottles in their car or just out on a coffee table. This practice is dangerous because young children are curious and want to check out everything around them.

It only takes a sip of liquid nicotine to potentially cause serious medical effects, including coma, seizures, stopped breathing, or even death. E-cigarettes and liquid nicotine need to be regarded like other dangerous poisons. They should be kept out of sight and reach of children, preferably in a locked location.

The observed 1,500 percent increase in the number of cases is an epidemic by any definition. If this were an infectious disease, this would make headlines across the country. A federal law that became effective in July 2016 requires child-resistant closures for liquid nicotine containers. This is a good first step, but further swift action is needed by the Food and Drug Administration, industry, and others to adequately protect children from the increasing threat of nicotine poisoning associated with e-cigarette use.

This is not primarily a parenting problem. Rather, this is another example of a highly dangerous product being introduced into the places where young children live and play without adequate regard for child safety. It is unacceptable that children are being rushed to emergency departments in coma, with seizures or breathing failure, and dying. Child safety should be put first.

Here are some tips for parents and child caregivers to help children stay safer around liquid nicotine:

- tore e-cigarettes and refill products where children cannot see or reach them—in a locked location is best. Do not store them in a purse, which children can easily access.
- Use and refill alone. Do not use e-cigarettes around children. Because children like to imitate adults, using e-cigarettes and refilling them with children nearby could lead to a dangerous exposure. The images, smells, and colors may be attractive to them.
- If a child has been exposed to liquid nicotine, call the national Poison Help Line (1-800-222- 1222). Save the number in your cell phone and post it near your home phones. Upon calling, you will be connected with an expert who can talk through what to do and whether to seek medical attention.

Learn more about the latest liquid nicotine study from Nationwide Children's Hospital, here:

- The study (Pediatrics, June 2016): http://pediatrics.aap publications.org/content/137/6/e20160041
- Press release: http://www.nationwidechildrens.org/news-room-articles/new-study-finds-child-e-cigarette-exposures-up-1500?contentid=153940
- Multimedia release: https://www.youtube.com/ watch?v=eK09gUtHCxo

Learn more about e-cigarette and liquid nicotine injury prevention here: http://www.nationwidechildrens.org/liquid-nicotine

Getting the Dose Right

Measuring the right dose of a child's medicine is critical; underdosing may result in an ineffective treatment, and overdosing may result in harm to the child. A recent study from NYU School of Medicine—Bellevue Hospital found that nearly all of the parents enrolled in a dosing study made at least one error when measuring their child's liquid medicine.

The 2,110 parents in the study had children aged eight or under and were randomly assigned to one of five study groups based on the units on the medicine bottle (milliliters, teaspoons, or both) and the units on the dosing tool (milliliters, teaspoons, or both). The instructions were written either in English or Spanish depending on the parents' preference.

All parents measured out three amounts of the medicine—2.5, 5.0, and 7.5 mL—three times, once each in three different measuring devices: a dosing cup with a 30 mL capacity, a 10 mL syringe with 0.2 mL markings, and another with 0.5 mL markings. There was no time limit for the parents to measure out the liquid.

The outcome measured was the amount of medicine in the dosing device. Almost all the parents (99.3 percent) made at least one measuring error. Nearly 85 percent made at least one significant error, defined as being off by at least 20 percent. Overdosing was found in 68 percent of the errors. Over 20 percent of the parents made at least one large error (more than twice what was prescribed). The parents' error declined as they went through the nine measurements.

The dosing tool made a real difference. There was no significant difference in the results using the two different syringes. Measurements with the dosing cup tended to be the least accurate, particularly with small doses, by a factor of four.

Liquid medicines are the preferred formulation for children because it's easier to finely adjust the dose and usually easier to convince children to swallow. However, it's harder for parents to measure the medicine. If your child is prescribed a liquid medicine, be sure you know the dose in milliliters and have a dosing syringe that's easy to read and has the unit markings.

Critical Thinking

1. What do adolescents know about the dangers of e-cigarettes?

2. Do adolescents know the difference between e-cigarettes and tobacco-based cigarettes?

3. What have we learned from the history of cigarettes in the United States that we can learn from and apply to our understanding of children and smoking?

Internet References

Are E-cigarettes Leading More Kids to Smoke?
   https://directorsblog.nih.gov/2017/01/31/are-e-cigarettes-leading-more-kids-to-smoke/

E-Cigarettes and Liquid Nicotine
   http://www.aapcc.org/alerts/e-cigarettes/

E-Cigarettes Are Dangerous to Children, Surgeon General Says

https://www.nbcnews.com/health/health-news/e-cigarettes-aren-t-safe-remain-dangerous-children-surgeon-general-n693576

Electronic Cigarettes

http://www.no-smoke.org/getthefacts.php?id=824

LAURA FRIEDENBERG, MA, is a research writer/editor in the Center for Injury Research and Policy of The Research Institute at Nationwide Children's Hospital in Columbus, Ohio. With both a health communications and public health background, she works to translate pediatric injury research into meaningful, accurate messages which motivate the public to make positive behavior changes.

GARY A. SMITH, MD, DrPH, is a Professor of Pediatrics, Emergency Medicine, and Epidemiology at The Ohio State University and is founder and director of the Center for Injury Research and Policy (www.injurycenter.org) of The Research Institute at Nationwide Children's Hospital. He holds the Dimon R. McFerson Endowed Chair in Injury Research. He has been an active researcher and advocate in the field of injury prevention for more than 30 years.

Article   Prepared by: Claire N. Rubman, *Suffolk County Community College, Selden, NY*

Secrets of Our Modern Youth

Brigitte Piniewski

Learning Outcomes

After reading this article, you will be able to:

- Articulate the difference between children's fat cells and adults' fat cells in relation to obesity.

- Explain the concept of a "hormonal functional mix-up."

- Discuss the potential social and emotional impact of obesity during puberty.

As parents, we all know that it is important to prevent our children from becoming overweight. Countless articles warn of health complications that overweight children may face, including becoming overweight adults and increasing their risk of developing serious diseases like diabetes, heart disease, and many cancers. Yet today, the national rate of childhood obesity continues to climb in most states. In fact, in some state, almost one-third of children and teens ages 2–19 are overweight or obese.

In addition to all of the health risks trumpeted in the media, there are two other very important ways that are rarely discussed that overweight harms children. These effects may be devastating, are generally irreversible and they can occur very quickly. The good news is that they are preventable . . . if you know about them.

The first is that overweight children gain weight by gaining more fat cells that they may never be able to lose. Overweight adults who gain or lose weight don't gain or lose fat cells—they simply change the size of the fat cells they already have. This means that it may be much harder for adults who were overweight as children to lose weight.

The second is that fat cells can disrupt sexual maturation during the few short years of puberty. Puberty is an important time for boys and girls. Both males and females have hormones that are a type of floating messenger traveling through their blood streams in search of docking stations called receptors. These receptors are often on the surface of cells and when the hormone docks a specific message or the cell receives instruction. The cell then carries out that instruction.

Both male and females share common hormones that carry the instructions need to mature through puberty. These include testosterone (T), which provides more male-like instructions, as well as estrogen (E2) and estrone (E1), which provide more female-like instructions. Some fat cells produce estrone (E1) suggesting that many fat cells may generate extra amounts of estrone (E1) in both boys and girls with excess weight.

But few of us are aware of a very interesting and surprising truth: though our sex hormones may have pretty specific functions, our receptors are much less narrow-minded and are often willing to bind with other hormones that are not specific to them! In fact, sex hormone receptors share a similar structures and each type gets its name only by the type of hormone that binds BEST to that receptor.

When all things are equal . . . T most often binds to T hormone receptors and likewise E2 hormones often bind to E2 hormone receptors. But when things are not equal—when concentrations of hormones change and one group is more abundant than expected—we may generate a hormonal functional mix up, an involuntary mess that may be irreversible.

Surely hormone concentrations must be well regulated to avoid any unexpected mishaps? Unfortunately, this is not so. Given our modern lifestyles, children and teens may be exposed to shifts in hormonal concentrations; in fact, mismatched hormone/receptor complexes might be the most common scenarios in overweight or obese adolescents.

How could this happen and what does it mean? Are young males experiencing a wave of feminization?

Meet John. He is a 22-year-old who recently had a full physical. Like many adolescents and young adults today, John struggled with excess weight during his childhood. Adolescence was the time when he expected to develop into an adult. But in John's case the transition to adult male did not follow the path he and his parents expected.

At 22, John is about 100 pounds overweight; he has large breasts, an extra-large abdomen, and a small penis and small testes. He is also quite withdrawn. He spends a lot of time alone on the couch at home playing video games. His parents are upset and wish he would try to find a job. John has not been employed yet and is not confident that any one will hire him. He has few friends and has not yet had a steady relationship.

John is not alone. Many students struggle with weight gain, unemployment, and inability to thrive socially. Many young adults like john not only struggle to achieve their full academic and vocational potential but also often suffer from health and social challenges. They have a few friends, early onset type II diabetes, and low self-esteem.

Parents must realize that children may suffer the consequences of being overweight within a few short years of puberty. Helping your child to successfully make this transition into adulthood requires actively avoiding excess weight gain in childhood, well before children reach their early teens.

There are many ways parents can help. The basics outlined in many articles and books center on prudent choices of food and activity. Gone are the days that we can assume our children will eat and exercise sufficiently without deliberately designing their environment to be sure that they will make the right choices. At a minimum, avoid flour products (breads, cold cereals, bagels, muffins, etc.), sharply limit sugar-sweetened beverages such as sodas, fruit juices and power drinks, and encourage children to eat vegetables and whole fruit.

Dr. Larry Wallack, a Portland State University professor of Public Health studies explains, "Our genes are not a blueprint for our future selves, they are instead a package of many possibilities.

Some possibilities are preferred and some are not and in the end we as individuals play a critical but often blind role in expressing our genes."

Said another way, we should accept the responsibility that healthy living has become complicated in our modern would. Yet our scientific industrial complex has not taken the time or the dollars needed to sort out in details what really matters to us as individuals. As a result, we have only basic recommendations for everyone. But we have a choice. We can either continue to wait on standby for science to sort out the things that matter, or we can use readily available technology to deliberately learn together how best to design healthy living for our families.

Today our phones offer apps to help track the food we eat; Fitbit and other wearable devices track movement and sleep. The cost and complexity of using simple sensors is diminishing. A wave of measurement of the basics such as sleep, food, and movement could combine vital information to reveal the actions that really make a difference in our health. Technology can help us to assume greater personal responsibility for our health and will enable our children and future generations to achieve their full human potential.

Critical Thinking

1. Why is puberty such a difficult time for adolescents?
2. Are the emotional and social issues associated with puberty culturally driven or are they universal?
3. Suggest novel ways that parents can help their children to avoid obesity in childhood and adolescence.

Internet References

Childhood obesity: Implications in Pubertal Process
    http://ebook.ecog-obesity.eu/chapter-clinics-complications/childhood-obesity-implications-in-pubertal-process/
Obesity and the Pubertal Transition in Girls and Boys
    https://www.ncbi.nlm.nih.gov/pmc/articles/PMC2931339/
Role of Obesity and Leptin in the Pubertal Process and Pubertal Growth—A Review
    http://www.nature.com/ijo/journal/v27/n8/full/0802328a.html
The Truth behind Early Puberty
    http://www.livescience.com/1824-truth-early-puberty.html

Dr. Brigette Piniewski is a primary care physician with extensive experience in both Canada, and the United States. She is skilled in both patient care as well as medical administration in the role of Chief Medical Officer.

Article   Prepared by: Claire N. Rubman, *Suffolk County Community College, Selden, NY*

Twenty Insider Tips for Working with Adolescents at Camp

KAREN GOELLER

Learning Outcomes

After reading this article, you will be able to:

- Discuss the role of the frontal lobe in the development of more mature thought in adolescence.
- Articulate three suggestions for problem-solving strategies to help the developing adolescent brain in difficult situations.

Camp staff beware and be ready! You may have already been warned about your adolescent campers. Wild mood swings and impulsive behaviors will happen, or if you are lucky, you may simply be ignored. Adolescents do not get a free pass to act this way over and over at camp. Yet, the rest of us do need to take a deep breath and consider that these biological changes are perfectly normal and that we are the ones who must adjust our behavior.

Dr. Jill Bolte Taylor, researcher of the adolescent brain, offers helpful advice with these 20 ready-to-use tips to get you off to a good start this camp season in dealing with your campers' still-developing brains:

Tip One: Learn about Teenage Brain Development

Get a head start on camping with your teens. Watch the YouTube video (16.31 minutes) The Neuroanatomical Transformation of the Teenage Brain: Jill Bolte Taylor at TEDxYouth@Indianapolis. Find out how important brain development is during the teenage years. Taylor will open your eyes to why you need to and how you can help.

Tip Two: Take Charge of Adolescents Right from the Start

Identify campers between the ages of 10 and 19. Quickly learn names and a few logistics. Ask your campers to respond to three quick questions, perhaps about backgrounds, likes/dislikes, and what they hope to gain from camp. Try to remember something special about each camper to help you establish a strong rapport early on. Adolescents want to know you are available and interested in them as individuals.

Tip Three: Stay Focused on Campers' Immaturity

Taylor tells those of us who work with adolescents and teens to "Keep 'em alive 'til 25!" The brain's frontal lobe, responsible for personality makeup, impulse control, and judgment about what is right and wrong, is not completely developed until about age 25. Be alert: Your campers are thinking, speaking, and acting with brains that are not fully mature. This may apply to you, too, as you sort through and make sense of your own behavior.

Tip Four: Create Teachable Moments about the Brain

It is far better to face the known than the unknown! You can find easy-to-use brain games, lesson plans, videos, and project ideas on educational sites like Society for Neuroscience (brainfacts.org). Build in fireside chats and small group discussions around simple brain facts to help adolescents and teens process changes taking place. Letting them talk openly together will lead to a healthier camp community.

Tip Five: Show Your Campers How to Remain Calm

Learning to remain calm starts with you. Explain to your campers that when their anxiety levels are high, they don't feel safe and are less likely to make good choices. Teach them simple strategies like walking away from a problem, taking a deep breath before speaking when angry, and just trying to imagine the situation from another point of view. Work together with your campers to design real-life trigger scenarios and then have fun letting them practice handling these scenarios with simple and positive strategies.

Tip Six: Be the Rock that Adolescents Need

Be that solid, responsible staffer who represents security and consistency during this time of emotional ups and downs. Your positive attitude and smile matter more than you know. Because they are experiencing so many simultaneous physical and neurological changes, adolescents need stability most of all in their lives. Be the responsible person in charge as opposed to being another friend.

Tip Seven: Take Care of Nutrition Essentials

Be the camp staffer who reminds teens that what they are eating is what they are feeding their brain cells. Try to plan simple and healthy snacks as rewards for activities. Cooking healthy snacks together at camp will transfer into improved eating habits throughout later years. Eating healthy snacks yourself, such as fruit and nuts, and drinking plenty of water will help you stay in shape to keep up with them.

Tip Eight: Make Positive Peer Relationships Happen

Peer relationships are everything during adolescence. All teens want to belong at camp, so we must look for ways to include each and every one of them. Making structured introductions at first will be important as well as planning daily activities where campers are paired with different partners. Help campers recognize interests that they have in common. Only by mixing teens together repeatedly will you give them chances to get to know each other well and forge new friendships.

Tip Nine: Insist on a Bedtime Schedule

Keep a structured bedtime schedule for your adolescent campers and for you. Make sure your teenagers get to bed on time so they get plenty of sleep to stay healthy. Taylor emphasizes that sleep is when the brain cleanses itself, so convey that message and don't let your campers shortchange themselves. Even though they won't like it, teenagers need to turn off their technological devices at night to enable their brains to rest.

Tip Ten: Push Campers to Problem Solve Together

Structure time for adolescents to think logically and problem solve together. They can hear peers try out ideas and make group decisions. They can see that doing what is right is not always easy. Join in a group and let your campers watch you thinking aloud and hear you considering pros and cons of options in various situations.

Tip 11: Recognize and Reinforce Positive Emotions

Be on the lookout for ways to help campers know and control their emotions. Look for simple ways during the day where you can recognize and reinforce positive emotions and kind behaviors. You can point out, "I really liked how you smiled and laughed when Emma told her story. You made her feel like such a valuable part of the group." Or you can say, "Thank you for walking with Jose today. He seems tired and your positive energy helped." Teens benefit from concrete examples.

Tip 12: Encourage Teens to Explore New Hobbies, Skills, and Talents

Teenagers are making new connections within their brains. Encourage them to join unfamiliar sports and groups at camp where there is no fear of failure. We want them to try new activities where they will not be ridiculed for not being good. Share how you yourself have tried a new skill and were awkward at first. Taylor stresses that this is the time for them to "plant the seeds and tend the gardens of their minds."

Tip 13: Listen, Listen, and Listen Some More

Be patient and give campers your full attention. Adolescents are moving from dependency to independence, and as Taylor relays, they need a safe haven. Allow them time to work out their own problems if possible. Try to help them better communicate or summarize their issues so they can think more clearly and become more self-sufficient.

Tip 14: Teach the 90-second Rule for Anger Management

Taylor tells us we have 90 seconds to think a thought, feel emotions, and run a physiological response. Teens can recognize how this anger takes over their bodies. Encourage them to wait and observe instead of immediately engaging in actions. Teach them that when they become angry, they can take a deep breath and come back to the present moment.

Tip 15: Seek Help for Self-harmful Behaviors

Be alert for and seek help for campers' dangerous behaviors. They are often influenced by peers to engage in harmful risk-taking behaviors. Taylor shares that teens do not clearly grasp the relationships between their immediate actions and their longer-term consequences. Campers depend on counselors and other staff to learn ways to cope with pressures and make healthier and wiser choices. Tell your supervisor immediately if any camper tells you about self-harmful behavior.

Tip 16: Lead Right Brain, Compassionate Conversations

Develop activities that focus on the brain's right hemisphere, helping adolescents see similarities and the larger picture of how we are all connected. Our right brain focuses on compassion, playfulness, imagination, and caring about the present. As an example, your camp group could read a nature poem by Ralph Waldo Emerson or Emily Dickinson and reflect on how we can all join together to improve our planet. Perhaps, campers can design a nature collage to illustrate their ideas. Right brain lessons at camp will inspire campers to take on more ethical challenges later.

Tip 17: Teach Cooperation, Not Competition

The right brain is all about treating others with respect. Teach campers about respect and good sportsmanship, playing with others instead of against others. Set the tone that games are more for pleasure than for competition. Praise teens who recognize good plays by members of the opposing team. Have them shake hands before and after a game or contest. Your own words and actions matter, so have fun when you play, be a good loser, and be sure not to brag when you win.

Tip 18: Teach Campers How to Leverage Left Brain Skill Sets

We also want campers to understand the verbal and reasoning abilities of the brain's left hemisphere. The left brain is methodical. Adolescents need to know that their left hemisphere is more focused on details, judgment, and boundaries. Teach them to plan camping events using left brain skill sets. Campers can make outlines, thinking through steps to make sure they are logical, realistic, and practical.

Tip 19: Create Your Own Peer Support Group

When you become frustrated or angry at camp, grab two other staff members and form a triad of support. Perhaps they are experiencing similar issues. Be open to the ideas and feedback of others. When you ask their advice about a particular incident, use their perspectives to learn and grow. Reflect together, create new brain-based ideas, and get back in the game. Your campers are depending on you!

Tip 20: Help Campers Recognize Their Power

Taylor encourages us to pay attention to what we are doing with our power. The natural camp setting gives adolescents a chance to put away technological devices and focus attention elsewhere. Emphasize to your campers that they can choose how they respond in emotional situations. They have an awesome responsibility to make the right choices. We want them to leave camp with self-confidence and a positive and more caring attitude about their place in the world.

Final Words for Camp Staff

It is up to you to help your campers understand and appreciate their brain development. Reassure them that it is okay—even better than okay—it is wonderful for them to experience these magnificent changes to their brains. Taylor is quick to point out that the brains our campers bring to camp are not the brains with which they will leave. You are on the front line helping your campers build healthy brains. Be sure to teach them to be mindful of their awesome power to make positive choices at camp and elsewhere in the future.

About Dr. Jill Bolte Taylor

Dr. Jill Bolte Taylor shares a moment-by-moment account of her own severe brain hemorrhage in the New York Times bestseller, My Stroke of Insight: A Brain Scientist's Personal Journey (2008). She explains the intricate steps of losing cognitive abilities during a massive stroke through the lens of a Harvard-trained neuroanatomist who can also recount the anatomy and biology behind the traumatic event. Taylor attributes her recovery to her advantage as a neuroscientist to believe in her brain's ability to retrain its circuitry as well as the love of her mother, who helped her make the connections necessary for her brain to completely heal. She uses her own experiences to inform her research on brain development.

Critical Thinking

1. Are adolescents too old to attend summer camp?
2. Why is there so much change in the adolescent brain during adolescence?
3. Do adolescents relate better to other adolescents or to older councilors in a summer camp situation?

Internet References

9 Great Benefits for Teens Attending Camp
    http://www.michianamom.com/March-2016/9-Great-Benefits-of-Teens-Attending-Camp/
Adolescence and the Agony of Decision-Making
    https://www.psychologytoday.com/blog/surviving-your-childs-adolescence/201303/adolescence-and-the-agony-decision-making
Adolescent Decision-Making: Implications for Prevention Programs
    https://www.nap.edu/read/9468/chapter/2
Risk and Rationality in Adolescent Decision-Making Implications for Theory, Practice, and Public Policy
    http://psi.sagepub.com/content/7/1/1.abstract
Teen Brain: Behavior, Problem Solving, and Decision-Making
    http://www.aacap.org/aacap/families_and_youth/facts_for_families/fff-guide/The-Teen-Brain-Behavior-Problem-Solving-and-Decision-Making-095.aspx

KAREN GOELLER, PhD, lives in Terre Haute, Indiana. She currently serves as deputy superintendent of the Vigo County School Corporation.

Article   Prepared by: Claire N. Rubman, *Suffolk County Community College, Selden, NY*

Substance Abuse Concerns: Heroin and Prescription Drug Use on the Rise among Teens

Learning Outcomes

After reading this article, you will be able to:

- Describe the typical demographic for a first time heroin user.
- Recognize at least six signs of adolescent drug abuse.
- List five suggestions to help adolescents with drug issues.

It seems as though some teenagers have always dabbled in drugs, but with increasing access to dangerous prescription opioids and cheap heroin, the problem is especially acute. For some students, drug experimentation will lead to drug addiction. Village Behavioral Center, a treatment center focusing on teenagers and adolescents, reports that the causes of addiction are unknown, but three factors are linked to whether or not someone will become addicted:

1. **Genetics.** Teens with a parent or sibling who has addictive behaviors are more likely to have an addiction.
2. **Physical factors.** Chronic substance abuse can cause addiction.
3. **Environmental factors.** Teens with parents who abused drugs and/or alcohol are more likely to abuse drugs and/or alcohol later in life. Also, teens who use drugs and/or alcohol at earlier ages are more likely to abuse the substances.

You might have noticed that addiction is receiving more attention in the media and among politicians. Michael Botticelli, the director of the White House Office of National Drug Control, told *The New York Times*:

"Because the demographic of people affected are more white, more middle class, these are parents who are empowered. They know how to call a legislator, they know how to get angry with their insurance company, [and] they know how to advocate."

Startling Facts and Figures

- Drug overdoses cause more deaths every day than car accidents.
- 44 people per day die of opioid (such as OxyContin) medication overdose.
- 1,600 teens begin abusing prescription drugs each day.
- 12–17-year olds abuse prescription pills more than ecstasy, heroin, crack/cocaine, and methamphetamines combined.
- 20 percent of teens who abuse prescription pills did so before they turned 14.

Sources: nytimes.com, 10/30/15; rxsafetymatters.org

Prescription Drug Abuse

After marijuana and alcohol, prescription and over-the-counter drugs are the most commonly abused drugs for Americans aged 14 years and older, reports the National Institute on Drug Abuse (NIDA). In 2012, nearly 20 percent of American 12th graders said they had abused prescription pills at some point in their lives. NIDA says some teens abuse prescription drugs by taking someone else's pills, going over the recommended dosage, and taking pills to get high.

According to the Partnership for Drug-Free Kids, there are two typical routes teenagers take when abusing prescription drugs:

1. Trying them with friends because they are curious—thinking it will feel good or help them concentrate.
2. Receiving them legitimately from a doctor for a health concern and then being unable to stop using them.

The health effects of prescription drug abuse can vary widely based on whether a student is using a depressant, stimulant, or painkiller, writes abovetheinfluence.com. Death by overdose is one common denominator.

Depressants can cause long-term effects including danger-ously low heart rates and respiration, particularly when taken under the influence of alcohol or other drugs. They can also cause depression, exhaustion, and confusion. *Stimulants* can cause irregular heartbeats, seizures, and heart failure, along with vomiting, sweating, and tremors. *Painkiller* overuse can cause nausea, lack of energy, vomiting, and an inability to con-centrate. They are especially dangerous when combined with alcohol and/or other drugs.

Also Known As . . .

Painkillers: Captain Cody, Cody, sizzurp, lean, syrup, schoolboy, doors and fours, loads, oxy, oxycotton, oxy-cet, hillbilly heroin, percs.

Depressants: Downers, downs, barbs, benzos, reds, red birds, phennies, tooies, yellows, yellow jackets, candy, sleeping pills, tranks, xanies.

Stimulants: Uppers, bennies, black beauties, crosses, hearts, truck drivers, JIF, MPH, R-ball, Skippy, the smart drug, vitamin R.

Source: abovelheinfluence.com

Signs, Symptoms, and How to Help

According to rxsafetymatters.org and smartmovessmartchoices.org, physical symptoms vary when a student is abusing pre-scription drugs, based on whether she is using a stimulant (Ritalin), a painkiller (OxyContin), or a depressant (Xanax). Signals that a student might be abusing prescription drugs include:

- Lack of interest in appearance
- Uninterested in extracurricular activities
- Mood swings
- New friend group
- Sleeping excessively, often with an increase in snoring (depressants and painkillers)
- Enlarged (depressants and painkillers) or constricted (stimulants) pupils
- Excessive sweating
- Inability to concentrate (depressants and painkillers)
- Agitation, hostility, and aggression (stimulants)

If you know or suspect that your student could be abus-ing drugs, teachersatrisk.com recommends you take these actions:

- Have a nonjudgmental and nonconfrontational approach to a conversation about drugs.
- Encourage the involvement of parents.
- Help students learn coping skills to get through stressful situations without drugs.
- Connect students with community resources they can utilize without getting into legal trouble.
- Encourage students to seek help from a doctor who can provide a screening.

Heroin

NIDA reports that heroin use has been rising since 2007. Though use among 8th, 10th, and 12th graders is at less than one percent, NIDA emphasizes that heroin use is reported as the biggest drug abuse issue in rural and urban areas. "National Geographic" writes that the rate of teens using heroin soared by 80 percent between 1999 and 2009. Muirwoodteen.com reports that 23 percent of those who try heroin will become addicted.

Trends to Keep an Eye On . . .

E-cigarettes: "E-cigs" deliver nicotine through a vapor that contains flavoring and propylene glycol. Adolescents who use them report 30 percent more respiratory problems, like coughing and phlegm, than nonusers.

Hand sanitizer: Teens can add salt to gel hand sanitizer to extract its ethyl alcohol, which has a proof of 120. Just a few shots can land a teenager in the hospital.

Marijuana edibles: There's no standard "serving" for the amount of THC in marijuana edibles, which look like normal candy. Teenagers might eat a whole candy bar, not realizing they've ingested an extremely dangerous amount of marijuana.

Synthetic marijuana/cannabinoids: These manmade chemicals, cannabinoids, are sprayed on plants and then smoked or inhaled. Though marketed as "safe marijuana," they are unpredictable and might cause similar effects to marijuana such as hallucinations, violent behavior, and suicidal thoughts.

Sources: drugfree.org; NYTimes.com; rueters.com; drugabuse.gov

The *New York Times* collected statistics about the heroin epidemic that has garnering attention from concerned citizens, politicians, and the media:

- There has been a 39 percent increase in heroin related deaths from 2012 to 2013.
- 90 percent of first-time users are white.
- Increasing numbers of first-time users are middle or upper class.
- 75 percent of heroin users used prescription painkillers before using heroin, with 40 percent of those individuals abusing opioid painkillers.

NIDA has found that some teenagers start taking heroin because it is much cheaper than prescription pills. Serious health problems involved with heroin include:

- Infectious diseases like HIV and hepatitis.
- Collapsed veins and infection of the heart lining and valves.
- Death by overdose.
- Liver and kidney disease.

Signals That a Student May Be on Heroin

Muir Wood Adolescent and Family Services, a California-based treatment program for boys' ages 12–17, and Village Behavior Health list signs a teen could be addicted to heroin:

- Acting slow and sedated, then intensely hyperactive
- Extreme sleepiness, with cold and clammy skin, runny nose, and pinprick pupils
- Uninterested in extracurricular activities and academics
- Inattention to cleanliness
- Nausea
- Unexplained changes in friends, hangouts, and hobbies
- Weight loss
- Unable to pay attention or problem solve

Critical Thinking

1. Why are drugs so appealing to some adolescents?
2. What advice would you give to parents of adolescents who want to prevent their children from using drugs?
3. What can we, as a society, do to prevent prescription drug abuse in our adolescent population?

Internet References

Abuse of Prescription ADHD Drugs Rising on College Campuses
http://healthcare.utah.edu/healthlibrary/related/doc.php?type=1&id=23617

Heroin|NIDA for Teens
https://teens.drugabuse.gov/drug-facts/heroin

How Teens Abuse Medicine
https://www.dea.gov/pr/multimedia-library/publications/prescription_for_disaster_english.pdf

Prescription Drug Abuse—Adolescents and Young Adults
https://www.drugabuse.gov/publications/research-reports/prescription-drugs/trends-in-prescription-drug-abuse/adolescents-young-adults

Article   Prepared by: Claire N. Rubman, *Suffolk County Community College, Selden, NY*

High Anxiety: Colleges Are Seeing an Increase in the Number of Students with Diagnosable Mental Illness, Anxiety, and Depression

Sandra Long Weaver

Learning Outcomes

After reading this article, you will be able to:

- Discuss three of the symptoms of anxiety or depression.

- Give two reasons why anxiety and depression are on the rise among college students.

- Articulate some of the stressors that contribute to mental health issues on college campuses.

Students seeking psychological help on their campuses are increasingly reporting anxiety over just about everything related to college life. "The students lack coping skills and emotional skills," said Mari Ross-Alexander, interim director of the counseling center at Tennessee State University in Nashville. "If the smallest thing goes wrong, they go from zero to one hundred that they want to die."

Those things could be a bad grade, breaking up in a relationship or just having a bad day.

"Nearly one in six college students has been diagnosed with or treated for anxiety within the last 12 months," according to a recent national survey by the American College Health Association.

Anxiety symptoms include panicky feelings, faster heart rates or insomnia. Students sometimes complain of feeling sweaty and just feel overwhelmed, according to the survey.

A 2013–2014 study by the Association for University and College Counseling Center Directors (AUCCCD) found that 47.4 percent of students had some type of anxiety, followed by 39.7 percent with some depression. Ross-Alexander said a higher number of Tennessee State students than usual participated in a depression-screening day on the campus last fall.

"In high school, the students were helped a lot to make sure they were successful," Ross-Alexander said. "They had hovercraft parents. They don't know what to do with their independence. They were used to getting good grades and when they get a bad grade, they want to kill themselves."

Some symptoms for depression are feelings of sadness, loss of appetite, change in weight, slowed thinking or speech, loss of interest in activities or social gatherings, guilt or anger over past failures, anger or frustration for no distinct reason.

The 400 directors who completed the AUCCCD Survey in 2012 reported that the number of students with severe psychological problems on their campus has increased in the past year. About 9–12 percent of students at small colleges, and 6–7 percent at larger colleges and universities seek help, the report said. New research also shows high-achieving African-American students enrolled in the fields of science, technology, engineering and mathematics (STEM) often face mental stress as well. Dr. Ebony McGee, assistant professor of diversity and urban schooling at Vanderbilt's Peabody College of Education and Human Development, found African-American students had "unexpected emotion and trauma." The study she coauthored with

David Stovall of the University of Illinois was recently published in the educational journal "Educational Theory."

"Racism is a real thing on the college campus," McGee said. "When students look to counseling, they are often told their racialized experiences are in their head—that the college or university is color blind." The student "is told they are overly racially sensitive," she said, and often the campus has no black counselors for the students to see.

McGee, who has interviewed more than 200 students since 2009, said she's "seen too much black pain." The students are told they need to suck up the pain and just deal with it. The answer can't be, "Just be more gritty." These are students who are the best and brightest.

"It is troubling how much we are asking black students to endure. They need a way to talk about their suffering," she said.

The mental stress is not just faced by black students at majority white campuses, she said. The problem also exists on historically black college and university campuses (HBCUs).

"Black students work hard to please the encouraging, caring black faculty," McGee said. "The black faculty tells the student you know you have to work twice as hard because you are at an HBCU. And the students work very hard trying to meet the expectations of the caring black professors."

In addition, black students at HBCUs in STEM fields often have a disproportionate number of foreign-born professors who have their own stereotypes of black students, McGee said. Asian students often work to unhealthy mental levels as well, she added. "They are working twice as hard to prove the stereotype of the model student right, that they are naturally intelligent," the researcher said. "Black students are working twice as hard to prove the stereotype that they are intellectually inferior about them wrong."

The students of East Indian descent she has talked with say they face another layer of racism—that they sometimes are accused of building bombs or being a terrorist. "And that's not what they are thinking about at all," McGee said.

Victor Schwartz, MD, medical director of The Jed Foundation in New York, agrees the rates of anxiety compared with depression have gone up.

"It's not clear that we can make the claim that students are sicker," he said. "But more want to talk about it (what's bothering them)."

Schwartz said more students are worried about the economy, the debt they are taking on to pay school costs and their job prospects down the road. "More people are seeking help and asking for help sooner," he said.

Not all students who may need it seek help, and those that do might have to wait because the ratio of mental health staff to students is high on most campuses. The AUCCCD 2012 Survey said the ratio of paid mental health staff to students was one for every 664 students at small colleges, 1,864 for midsize colleges/universities, and 2,731 for large universities.

Research conducted by the National Alliance on Mental Illness on mental health on college campuses shows that one in four students have a diagnosable illness.

That research also shows:

* 40 percent do not seek help
* 80 percent feel overwhelmed by responsibilities
* 50 percent are anxious because they struggled in school

However, Schwartz noted that mental health services in the communities students come from are worse than they were 20 years ago. Because of managed care, students sometimes have less access before they get to their college campus. "Now they are using the campus counseling centers because they have better access," he said.

The Jed Foundation was founded in 2000 by a family who lost a son to suicide. It works to promote the emotional health among college students, providing support to more than 1,500 colleges and universities through online programs and written guides and other materials for the schools to use.

Outreach efforts are very important to help students who may have mental health issues, according to Dr. Karen Hofmann, director of Counseling and Psychological Services at the University of Central Florida.

"There is still a great stigma. Students don't want to be labeled as crazy or feel ashamed because they are seeking help," she said.

Sources of Stress

In the last five years, Hofmann said anxiety has taken over as the No. 1 problem students have.

"For this generation, the world is different," she said. "We have national news 24/7. The world is more challenging. They are more aware of life events happening. It's more costly, more competitive . . . Parents are more involved. And the bar is higher for academic achievement. We can see why they are more anxious."

UCF has a number of programs to "get people in the door" to counseling in a less stressful environment and provide education. Hofmann said they use an animal-assisted therapy program, as well as smaller group programs that target racial, ethnic, LGBT, athletic or educational demographics such as the STEM students. Hofmann said there are staff liaisons for different groups like the STEM students.

"Students need somebody they can see. . . . They can call a staff member and ask, 'What should I do?' if they are struggling," she said.

"We've been very proactive reaching out to ethnic students," she added. Eighty African American students registered in the fall for a special program that connected each student with a mentor and offered sessions on being successful in college.

"We know there is a great need to break the stigma so you are not seen as a failure or weak if you get support or help," Hofmann said. "Students have to believe you understand where they are coming from. You have to be culturally aware of the students' needs as well."

Critical Thinking

1. Thinking about the American college experience, what could be changed to reduce anxiety or depression among students?

2. As a college student yourself, what causes you the most anxiety or contributes to a depressing environment for you?

3. Are mental health issues overdiagnosed among the adolescent population?

Internet References

Anxiety the Most Common Mental Health Diagnosis in College Students
https://www.bu.edu/today/2016/college-students-anxiety-and-depression/

Mental Health Disorders—The Office of Adolescent Health
http://www.hhs.gov/ash/oah/adolescent-health-topics/mental-health/mental-health-disorders.html

Mental Health on College Campuses: A Look at the Numbers
http://college.usatoday.com/2016/01/30/mental-health-by-the-numbers/

Normal Teenage Behavior versus Early Warning Signs of Mental Illness
http://www.asmfmh.org/resources/publications/normal-teenage-behaviour-vs-early-warning-signs-of-mental-illness/

SANDRA LONG WEAVER is a freelance editor and writer who is the managing partner of Tea and Conversations, a communications consulting firm.

Article   Prepared by: Claire N. Rubman, *Suffolk County Community College, Selden, NY*

High-Tech Bullies

Suicides have made administrators aware that acts of aggression in the wireless, viral world of the Internet demand action to protect targeted students.

INGRID STURGIS

Learning Outcomes

After reading this article, you will be able to:

- Identify the most vulnerable members of our society who are most prone to bullying.

- Describe what colleges and universities are doing to combat cyberbullying.

Cases of cyberbullying have made headlines over the past decade, raising awareness about the number of young people who have committed suicide or otherwise been harmed as a result of being on the receiving end of constant Internet harassment or shaming.

Bullying that started in email and chat rooms in the early days of the Internet has evolved into other forms—mostly social networking sites and instant messaging, as well as video and pictures, Justin W. Patchin, PhD, co-director of the Cyberbullying Research Center at the University of Wisconsin-Eau Claire, agrees.

"It's constantly changing," he said. "The bullies are pretty creative. Now there is a level of permanence that is not evident in traditional bullying. Early adopters are most likely to use new technology. It's amazing how creative some can be to cause harm."

Patchin, author of *Words Wound: Delete Cyberbullying and Make Kindness Go Viral* (Free Spirit Publishing, December 2013), has been studying cyberbullying among secondary students for more than a decade, starting in 2001. He has surveyed nearly 15,000 students across the United States.

Most cases seem to involve middle school or high school students, whom experts say, are in the primary age group for such behavior.

However, as social media continues its pervasive intrusion into everyday lives, cyberbullying is trickling up to college campuses and even into the workplace. Researchers, law-enforcement lawyers, college officials, and students say there are more reported incidents of acts of cyberbullying cropping up on campus and a rise in incidents of teenage suicide has coincided with the rise in incidents of cyberbullying. In fact, the suicide of Rutgers University freshman Tyler Clementi in 2010, who was the target of a campaign of intimidation by his roommate, put universities on notice that what might have once been treated as a college prank could lead to suicide for vulnerable students. Clementi jumped off the George Washington Bridge after learning that his roommate spied on him during a romantic encounter with a man using a webcam. Clementi also learned that his roommate conspired to "out" him by alerting Twitter followers to a second viewing.

Attacking the Vulnerable

Cyberbullies often target gays, women or people of color. Students who are different in some way (race, ethnicity, sexual orientation, religion, or appearance) or high-profile students (athletes, student government officers) are often the most vulnerable.

Jiyoon Yoon, associate professor and director of the elementary education program at University of Texas at Arlington, said via email that while nearly anyone can be a victim, most victims are targeted because of perceived differences from a group and weaknesses.

"Students who do not fit in may become the prime targets of cyberbullying," she said. "In many contexts, students of minority status and/or lower economic privilege may be more susceptible to the abuse."

Yoon said victims of such bullying are more likely to report feelings of depression than other groups of students, which interfere with their scholastic achievement, social skills, and sense of well-being. She has conducted research with Dr. Julie Smith on cyberbullying among college students and says it is increasing. According to survey responses conducted by Yoon and Smith within a Midwestern university system, 10.1 percent of the students said they experienced cyberbullying by another student; 2.9 percent of the students had been cyberbullied by instructors, and 27.5 percent of the students witnessed cyberbullying behavior by a student toward another student.

This is consistent with other studies on cyberbullying. In one study conducted at Indiana State University, 22 percent of college students reported being cyberbullied, and 9 percent reported cyberbullying someone.

"People thought cyberbullying happened mostly among teenagers who are familiar with and willingly use electronic technology," Yoon said. "However, as portability and accessibility of technology for distance learning increases daily in higher education, incidents of cyberbullying are rising on college campuses."

Dawn Harner, a training coordinator and counselor at Salisbury University, said a potent mix of 24/7, always-on communication lends itself to abuses. She cited the pervasive use of connected mobile devices, multiple social media profiles from Facebook to Twitter to Instagram, growth in text messaging and decline in phone conversations, the illusion of anonymity and the international reach of the Internet, coupled with students' immaturity and newly found freedom.

"It is much more common for students to be connected to social media," Harner said. "Now, as opposed to seven years ago, phones connect to Internet as well."

Researchers are just starting to examine the rise in university-level bullying. Today, universities are obligated to face the problem before another student is hurt. First, they must define cyberbullying.

"A lot of times as academics, we debate definitions," said Patchin. "What's the difference between hazing, bullying and harassing? All could be the same behaviors. We don't focus on it until something happens. We have to focus on behaviors that repeatedly cause harm to another person." Although definitions vary, cyberbullying can be defined as acts of aggression and subterfuge against someone that gain power through digital technology.

The problems can range from the use of gossip sites like JuicyCampus, College Anonymous Confessions Board or College Wall of Shame to "revenge porn sites," in which former lovers upload photos of ex-girl friends and to stalking by emails and text messages. Some of the most popular vehicles for cyberbullying, said Yoon, are Facebook texting, email, Twitter, and YouTube. Other technologies or applications and online gaming technologies, such as AOL Instant Messenger, MSN Messenger MySpace and League of Legends, as well as online forums, message boards, blogs, are also used. Researchers have identified several types of aggression, which include online stalking, flaming, fights, and arguments; posting embarrassing or incriminating photos of a victim; outing, revealing secrets; exclusion and masquerading as someone else.

Aggressors may send mean text messages or emails, spread rumors by email or social networking sites, and they may post videos, put up embarrassing websites, or create fake profiles of a victim. The use of technology means that victims can be exposed to an audience of millions and may be unable to escape scrutiny.

Students also face dangers from impersonation, fraud and trickery online. In one infamous incident, Manti Te'o, the Notre Dame star linebacker and a finalist for the Heisman Trophy, became a victim of "catfishing." He met someone online who pretended to become his "girlfriend" even though they had never met. The ruse was uncovered by a sports website after she was reported to have died. Similarly, MTV's reality TV show called "Catfish" focuses on deceptions in online dating and is popular among college students.

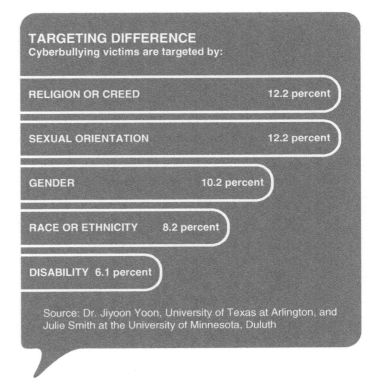

TARGETING DIFFERENCE
Cyberbullying victims are targeted by:

RELIGION OR CREED	12.2 percent
SEXUAL ORIENTATION	12.2 percent
GENDER	10.2 percent
RACE OR ETHNICITY	8.2 percent
DISABILITY	6.1 percent

Source: Dr. Jiyoon Yoon, University of Texas at Arlington, and Julie Smith at the University of Minnesota, Duluth

Handling the Cyberbully

Colleges and universities are developing courses, starting anti-bully campaigns and offering mentoring relationships and other tools to deal with the emerging social issue of cyberbullying. Rutgers University opened the Tyler Clementi Center to help students adjust to college life. Other colleges and universities are developing anti-bullying policies and taking other actions to combat problems of cyberbullying and "online incivility."

In many states, schools are required to address cyberbullying in their anti-bullying policy. Some state laws also cover off-campus behavior that creates a hostile school environment. Some universities also address direct punishment of the cyberbullying and provide special reporting tools when cyberbullying is exhibited.

University instructors/faculty are also required to report cyberbullying incidents. University IT staffs record and track incidences and courses on college campuses contain "netiquette" rules in syllabi. As most colleges and universities realize the seriousness of cyberbullying on campus, said Dr. Jiyoon Yoon, associate professor and director of the elementary education program at University of Texas at Arlington, they start to incorporate anti-cyberbullying policies into the student handbook or student code of conduct and employment standards for faculty and staff. These policies are clear about what constitutes cyberbullying and what the penalties may be.

Dawn Harner, a training coordinator and counselor at Salisbury University, said the university has a program training first-year students as leaders and asking them to refer students to a counseling center if they are experiencing anxiety or depression as related to bullying.

Whitney Gibson, head of the Internet crises group for Vorys, Sater, Seymour, and Pease LLP, s said victims should tell someone at school or get help by talking to police or school officials or an expert to get screen shots of the offending posts, chats, messages, videos, or emails.

Yoon recommends that victims:

- Take immediate action but do not respond or forward cyberbullying messages.
- Keep evidence of cyberbullying.
- Learn how to use privacy settings to block the bully.
- Report cyberbullying to the social media site, law enforcement officials, the school and online service providers.
- Review the terms and conditions of service at social media sites and Internet service providers.

—Ingrid Sturgis

One of the main characteristics of the cyberbullying is that bullies believe they can act anonymously, said Yoon. "They can harass their victims without the victims ever knowing who or why they are being cyberbullied," she said. "The various forms of current professional technology on campus allow the victims to be continually victimized without identifying the perpetrators." Experts can determine the identities of the abusers, however. The pervasiveness of social media, said Elaine Heath, PhD, dean for Student Services at Howard University, and the fact that the reasoning capabilities in adolescents do not fully mature until age 25, makes students emotionally ill equipped to handle the consequences of being a bully or being bullied.

"They are not mature enough to pick up social cues to determine this is inappropriate behavior," Heath said. "They are shocked when you tell them. Young people don't understand the boundaries and the appropriateness of how to use it."

Heath said bullying often reveals a degree of anger and deep-seated emotions. "It will start within the person and then triggers an outward manifestation," she said. "Anger or emotional problems will be acted out. They will continue the conversation with social media. It's a lack of impulse control."

When Heath asks students why they do it, she said many have given no thought to their actions. "Bottom line, people don't think about it," she said. "They are angry and want to get their story and their say out. These children live in reality TV."

"It's about power and control to instill fear," she said. "People don't fear the consequences. There is a lack of empathy, lack of control, and immaturity around relationships. A lot people don't know how to have healthy relationships."

Patchin of the Cyberbullying Research Center said parents and teachers who may not use social media sometimes underestimate the seriousness of the issue. He said some adults ask cyberbullied students questions like, "Why can't you turn it off?"

"For high school and college students, it's a big part of their social lives," he said. "If you don't know anything about it, it's not a big problem."

Cyberbullying can have implications beyond the campus and maybe even have long-lasting legal ramifications for students. Whitney Gibson, a partner at Vorys, Sater, Seymour, and Pease LLP and head of the firm's Internet crises group, works with schools to help them educate students about the unintended consequences of Internet use.

"What I see is a lot of students using technology," he said. "A lot of students don't think what they are doing is a big deal . . . They don't understand how quickly that goes viral, and they can never get it down. There is a rise of serious damage being done to people on the Internet. People are dying. Kids are getting arrested for felony."

Gibson said students often don't realize that their online behavior, including posting pictures while drinking or using marijuana, as well as acts of bullying, can affect their scholarships or job prospects as more recruiters check social media sites. In addition, Gibson said, college students think they can conceal their identities with fake names.

"They don't realize that it is very hard to remain anonymous on the Internet," he said. "They end up getting in big trouble."

Critical Thinking

1. How much supervision and monitoring is appropriate at the college level?

2. Where do we draw the line between teasing and cyberbullying?

3. How does technology like instagram, vine, and flikr contribute to cyberbullying?

Internet References

buzzfeed.com 9 Teenage Suicides In The Last Year Were Linked to Cyber-Bullying on Social Network Ask.fm
http://www.buzzfeed.com/ryanhatesthis/a-ninth-teenager-since-last-september-has-committed-suicide

cyberpsychology.eu Cyberbullying in Adolescent Victims: Perception and Coping
http://www.cyberpsychology.eu/view.php?cisloclanku=2011121901

Huffingtonpost.com 8 Scary Social Networking Sites Every Parent Should Know
http://www.huffingtonpost.com/michael-gregg/8-scary-social-network-sites-every-parents-should-know_b_4178055.html

thementalelf.net Bullying and Cyberbullying Increase the Risk of Suicidal Ideation and Suicide Attempts in Adolescents
http://www.thementalelf.net/populations-and-settings/child-and-adolescent/bullying-and-cyberbullying-increase-the-risk-of-suicidal-ideation-and-suicide-attempts-in-adolescents

tylerclementi.org The Tyler Clementi Foundation
http://www.tylerclementi.org/

INGRID STURGIS is an author, journalist, and assistant professor specializing in new media in the Department of Media, Journalism and Film at Howard University.

Sturgis, Ingrid. "High-Tech Bullies." *Diverse: Issues in Higher Education, Convergence Supplement.* (February, 27, 2014): 19–23. Used with permission.

Article   Prepared by: Claire N. Rubman, *Suffolk County Community College, Selden, NY*

Pathways to Adulthood

Dare to dream big about what senior year could be.

JEREMY KNOLL

Learning Outcomes

After reading this article, you will be able to:

- Describe three ideal assignments for a 12th-grade English class.

- Explain why an English class is the ideal platform for exploration and growth in 12th grade.

- Describe one potential benefit of the "common application" essay for college entrance applications.

I remember building pathways around my house as a kid. I used everything I could get my hands on, from trash cans to hula hoops to hockey pucks. Sometimes alone, sometimes with friends, I would dedicate whole afternoons to building the most random routes I could conceive. The pathways did not lead anywhere. They were simply a means of passing the time.

At many high schools, senior year is the academic equivalent of one of my childhood pathways. Under the guise of curricula, we set up a few hoops for students to jump through, but nothing resembling a cohesive experience that leads in a definitive direction. We allow students to simply pass time. In doing so, we lose the opportunity to prepare them to become the best citizens they can be.

Senior Year: Past and Present

Six years ago, Walter Kirn wrote a piece for *The New York Times Magazine* titled "Class Dismissed." He bemoans a senior year that is "less a climatic academic experience than an occasion for oafish goofing off, chronic truancy, random bullying, [and] sloppy dancing." He goes on to say that "seniors rule" not because they have done anything significant, but rather because

"it's tradition, and seniors crave tradition. They crave it because they know, deep down, they're lost, and tradition helps them hide this fear."

His accusation—that senior year was simply a holding pattern that encouraged sloth and academic atrophy—made me take a good look at my 12th-grade English students. They are lost, I thought. I was lost when I was a senior. I did not know what I stood for or believed in. I did not know how I felt about the social issues facing my community, country, or world. My K-12 education did precious little to teach me about self-reflection or agency.

What Senior Year Could Be

By allowing senior year to remain a blow-off year, we are missing an opportunity to help students navigate the transformation from high school student to full-fledged members of society—and missing an opportunity to create a more just world.

For many students, leaving high school offers the unique opportunity to redefine themselves. Even if they aren't moving to a new community, they will most likely be surrounded by a different cohort of people who don't have preconceived expectations about who they are. They have the chance to review the details of their first 18 years and decide what to keep and what to toss. If we want to prepare thoughtful citizens, we must support this process.

Do our seniors have an opportunity to practice self-reflection and self-assessment? Do you ask them to think about how their race, gender, or family income opened or closed doors? Do they have opportunities to ponder whether fairness and ethics are more important than profit margins? Do they understand the difference between inequality and inequity? As guides, teachers need to keep pointing to and questioning life beyond the classroom walls.

Seniors want to talk about tough issues. They want to have their beliefs challenged and debate with their peers. They just need fuel to ignite the glowing embers burning in their chests.

Ask Students about Themselves

Not enough students from inner-city schools are given internships at prestigious law firms and investment banks. Not enough students driving BMWs to school are aware that some kids attend elementary schools with crumbling ceiling tiles. Regardless of whether we, as educators, can succeed at making the huge systemic changes necessary to level these inequities, we can do a lot with just the written and spoken word.

English classes, especially during senior year, have the ability to transcend boundaries dictated by curricula. College admission essays are a good place to start the process of self-discovery that should be the foundation of senior year.

One of the questions for the 2016 Common Application asked students to reflect on aspects of their "background, identity, interest, or talent" that set them apart. Having students write about themselves, coupled with peer editing, can open their eyes. Suddenly, they see themselves as agents within society, or they see peers in a totally different light. From that moment, a teacher can lead the conversation to how little we know about the people we interact with each day, the judgments we make without facts, and how we can work to better understand the people around us.

Another application prompt asks students to write about "a time when [they] challenged a belief or idea." This offers a great starting point for potentially life-altering conversations. Students can gain strength from hearing others' stories of standing up for or against an idea they felt was wrong. Those who may never have done such a thing are forced to ask themselves, "Why?"

Ask Difficult Questions

What is education? What is purpose? Fairness? Poverty? These are questions I was asked when I was a senior in high school in a series of "personal definition papers." I use the questions now with my students.

While, academically, these writing exercises focus on writing concisely, using examples to illustrate central claims and explaining complex ideas, that's not what matters most. What matters most is students' abilities to decide where they stand. Asking about education, fairness, and poverty requires students to confront the inequities at the foundation of our public school system. The paper might prompt them, for example, to ask how

a student from a school that is poorly funded or inadequately staffed is expected to compete with a student from a school funded by a reliable budget and staffed by professionals with master's degrees.

For students from low-income schools, this question may highlight realities they are aware of but don't know how to address. For the more affluent, it may be the first time they've considered this type of inequity.

Writing about fairness forces students to look back at years of hallway interactions, news headlines, and family dinner conversations and to develop their opinions independently. By analyzing the injustices around them, many realize they want to challenge the status quo rather than tolerate it, ignore it, or actively support it.

Ask Students to Share Their Voices

For my students, senior year now ends with 10-min commencement speeches delivered formally in front of the class and other people the students invite. The task is simple: Share what they have learned from their education so far. Students must mine the depths of their experience for moments when they have learned something about strength, integrity, or grace.

These speeches force students to move past their objections that, at their age, they don't have anything to teach anyone. They challenge the cozy stereotypes we all use as tools to navigate and simplify the world we live in. Students talk about the struggle of quitting baseball despite a father's angry objection, about battling eating disorders and drug addictions, about losing parents. They talk about bullying and coming out and devotion to God. They talk about all different aspects of their 18 years, and in the process shock themselves and their classmates.

It all comes from self-reflection and open conversation. It all leads to students better prepared to contribute to a world with less hatred and greater understanding.

Offer Challenges, Not Hoops

I am all for pushing students to excel academically, but let's make sure that effort is focused on challenges rather than arbitrary obstacles, on character development rather than box-checking. The tasks of senior year need to be more than the disconnected pathways I laid out in my yard years ago. This, of all years, needs cohesion; there needs to be a point.

What better thematic thread to weave over the course of students' culminating high school year than an exploration of self?

Critical Thinking

1. What were your hopes and fears during your senior year of high school?
2. Describe your "ideal" senior year for high schoolers.
3. What is the function and purpose of a high school education?

Internet References

4 Universal Truths about Senior Year of High School
https://www.collegexpress.com/articles-and-advice/student-life/blog/4-universal-truths-about-senior-year-high-school/

5 Things High School Seniors Should Be Doing Now
https://www.usnews.com/education/blogs/the-college-solution/2011/07/26/5-things-high-school-seniors-should-be-doing-now

How to Conquer the Admissions Essay
https://www.nytimes.com/2017/08/02/education/edlife/college-application-essay-admissions.html

How to Prepare for College during Your Senior Year of High School
https://www.mycollegeoptions.org/Core/SiteContent/Students/Advice/College-Resource-Center/Getting-in---Applying-to-College/College-Admissions-Guides/Senior-Year.aspx

What Is the Purpose of the American High School?
http://edge.ascd.org/blogpost/what-is-the-purpose-of-the-american-high-school

JEREMY KNOLL has taught English for nearly two decades since graduating from Middlebury College in VT.

Article   Prepared by: Claire N. Rubman, *Suffolk County Community College, Selden, NY*

Pediatricians' Primer on Sexting

Understanding what adolescents experience online with sexting and digital technology can help pediatricians counsel teenagers about the dangers of this practice.

PAT F. BASS III

Learning Outcomes

After reading this article, you will be able to:

- Describe three reasons why adolescents sext.

- Discuss other behaviors associated with adolescents who sext.

- Explain the relationship between sexting and substance abuse, sexual activity and underage drinking.

Sexting is the act of sending or receiving sexually explicit or sexually suggestive photos, messages, or videos digitally by text, e-mail, or instant messaging from a smartphone or computer device. It is more common among teenagers than one might think. Some adolescents do not realize or appreciate the long-term, serious implications sexting may have. Others understand the consequences, but a sense of invulnerability, impulsivity, or sexual desire are stronger motivators.

Some of the consequences of sexting can be severe. The following examples received a great deal of media attention, but unfortunately such instances are not that uncommon:

- **In 2008,** 2 months after going on a Cincinnati television station to discuss the consequences of sexting gone bad following a relationship breakup so that others might not go through her pain, 18-year-old Jessica Logan committed suicide.

- **In 2012,** Amanda Todd was blackmailed by an online predator into showing herself via her webcam. When she refused to continue, the online predator would find her classmates and send them a topless picture Amanda had sent. To deal with her anxiety, Amanda began using drugs, alcohol, and sex. Peers ostracized her. Ultimately, she also committed suicide.

- **In 2015,** a Colorado district attorney considered felony criminal charges against high school and middle school students that resulted from hundreds of nude pictures being swapped among students.

Sexting among adolescents has increased along with access to smartphones. Some teenagers may fail to appreciate the long-term consequences of their actions, although others have sexted with nothing bad happening to them. Pediatricians need to be aware of trends surrounding sexting and develop awareness and counseling skills to help patients and their families as needed.

Sexting Is Common

Sexting is common among adults, with 8 of 10 respondents to an online poll admitting to sexting (defined as sending or receiving sexually suggestive or explicit content via text) in the prior year. Among adults, 75 percent sexted as part of a committed relationship whereas more than 40 percent did so as part of a more casual relationship.

Among adolescents, it is difficult to determine exactly how many are sexting. In a 2009 Pew Research Center report on teenagers and sexting, 4 percent of cell-owning teenagers sent sexually suggestive nude images of themselves via text. More recent reports estimate prevalence of sexting as between 15 percent and 28 percent of adolescents, with the numbers much greater after they enter college.

Why Teenagers Sext

There are several reasons why adolescents may engage in sexting. Perhaps for some, it may be a joke or a way to get attention. Teenagers also may see celebrities they admire having lewd pictures and videos exposed, only to have their fame and popularity increase rather than suffer humiliation and ruined reputations that teenagers may experience. For others, sexting is a form of flirtation—seen as cool or a way to become more popular. Finally, peer pressure to sext and the perception that "everyone is doing it" may lead teenagers to report this behavior as normal.

Current literature finds three general themes for why teenagers sext:

- To initiate sexual activity with a boyfriend or a girlfriend;
- As an experimental phase prior to beginning sexual relationships;
- As a way to enhance current sexual relationships.

In the context of a relationship, the sext is sent as a tool to initiate, keep, or gain attention. Approximately ⅔ of young women often describe the activity as a "sexy" present for a boyfriend, whereas more than half of young men describe sexting as an attempt to "be fun and flirtatious."

Pressure or coercion also is a common motivation for teenaged sexting. Girls are significantly more likely to report being pressured, coerced, blackmailed, or threatened into sexting.

In one report, half of sexts among girls are coerced, which is twice the rate among boys. Teenagers seem to be thinking about their relationships when they sext. The most common reasons they report sexting include that a date or boyfriend/girlfriend wants the picture (66 percent) and to attract someone's interest (65 percent). Increasing their popularity (22 percent) and proving that they completely trust a boyfriend or a girlfriend (17 percent) are less common reasons for sexting. Some experts argue that boys tend to sext from peer pressure of male friends but girls tend to receive pressure from males.

In relation to pressured sexts, nearly 70 percent of requests come from a date, nearly 20 percent from a friend, and less than 10 percent result from blackmail or a threat.

Some studies have demonstrated certain personality traits may be associated with an increased risk of sexting. Adolescents scoring high on assessments of sensation seeking and experiential thinking were more likely to participate in sexting, whereas adolescents scoring higher in rational thinking were less likely to sext. Similarly, adolescents displaying higher degrees of impulsivity were also more likely to sext.

Advice for Pediatricians

Pediatricians are in a unique position to help parents not only understand what their children are experiencing online and with digital technology but also suggest strategies for preventing and dealing with online or offline incidents. Pediatricians can:

- Develop their own knowledge base related to digital technology and topics such as sexting.
- Take careful sexual histories and explicitly ask about use of cell phones, texting, sending of sexual messages, and use of social media sites such as Snapchat, Facebook, and Twitter.
- Advise parents to talk with their children about the whole range of online and digital issues that their children face.
- Advise parents to become more educated and participate in the technologies their kids are using.
- Develop a policy of review of privacy settings and review online footprints of their adolescent. The emphasis and tenor should be one of good citizenship rather than punitive for indiscretions unless an incident truly merits such. (See "Living life online: Talking to parents about social media," *Contemporary Pediatrics*, May 2016.)
- Help parents develop strategies to supervise online and cell phone activity via active participation and communication rather than solely relying on some sort of remote monitoring program.

Resources for Pediatricians and Parents

- *ThatsNotCool.com*
  https://thatsnotcool.com
  Site provides teen and parent with tools to talk about and deal with consequences of sexting.
- *Sexting in America: When Privates Go Public*
  http://on.mtv.com/29IU50M
  The MTV 4-part special looks at sexting and its unintended emotional and legal consequences. Encouraging parents and teenagers to watch together or using it as part of a talk to parents or adolescents can not only educate but also generate discussion about the topic.
- *Amanda Todd's Story: Struggling, Bullying, Suicide, Self-Harm*
  bit.ly/amanda-todd-story
  Powerful video that can be used as a topic with teenagers or recommended to parents to watch with their child.

Sexting Links to Other Behaviors

Sexting is associated with a number of other behaviors such as sexual activity and substance use.

Among 1,285 students in Los Angeles middle schools participating in the 2012 Youth Risk Behavior Survey, more than $2/3$ (68 percent) owned their own cell phone. Of these students, approximately 20 percent of those with a text-capable cell phone reported receiving a sext and 5 percent reported sending one. Sending or receiving sexts significantly increased the odds of sexual activity among middle school students (odds ratio [OR], 3.2; 95% confidence interval [CI], 1.3–8.1; and OR, 7.0; 95% CI, 4.0–12.1, respectively). Sending more than 100 texts per day also was associated with both sexting and sexual activity.

In other studies, sexting is associated with an increased number of sexual partners for both sexual intercourse as well as oral sex. One study found that among young adults, sexting was related to unprotected sex, sex after drinking, and sex after drug use. The relationship of high-risk sexual behaviors associated with sexting, however, does not appear to be consistent across studies. Overall, the literature strongly supports that sexting is associated with sexual behavior compared with those who have not sexted, including a study that found sexting predicted sexual behavior.

Similarly, sexting appears to be associated with substance use. In a study of 763 young adults, sexting was associated with a significantly increased use of recreational drugs such as alcohol (58.1 percent vs. 42.2 percent), marijuana (39.5 percent vs. 24.8 percent), ecstasy (6.8 percent vs. 3.3 percent), and cocaine (4.7 percent vs. 2.1 percent) compared with those who did not sext. Further, another study of adolescents including 937 ethnically diverse boys and girls found that sexting was associated with both substance use and impulsivity, but was not a marker of mental health.

Although not often discussed regularly in the research related to sexting, the spread of images without consent and the social exclusion, shame, or insult that are suffered when a teenager no longer has control of the images is a form of cyberbullying. The literature is replete with the negative consequences of this form of abuse.

Legal Implications

Although many states have passed laws that significantly lessen penalties for sexting, other states prosecute the sending of a nude picture of a minor under child pornography laws. As a result, a couple of 17-year-olds can legally consent to have sex with each other, but sharing a nude photograph can be prosecuted as child pornography even if the picture is voluntarily shared between two people. Any sort of sext between two minors is basically a crime. Prosecution is rare, but sexting by minors has led to both criminal and civil cases and subsequent legislative action in many states.

A 2012 article in *Pediatrics* identified 3,477 cases of "youth-produced sexual images," with approximately 2,291 different law enforcement agencies seeing at least one case during 2008 and 2009. The study depicts a large heterogeneity of cases that are potentially difficult to prosecute under a single simple law.

In this sample, 67 percent were considered aggravated and 33 percent experimental. Aggravated incidents are considered criminal or abusive over and above the creation, possession, or sending of images. The aggravated group was further classified as having adult involvement in cases in which adults solicited or were the recipient of a solicited image versus youth only. Youth-only aggravated incidents involved some sort of intent to harm such as maliciousness, sexual abuse, extortion, or reckless distribution without the knowledge or against the will of the person in the image.

An incident was considered experimental when adults were not involved, recklessness was not demonstrated, and there did not appear an intent to harm. Experimental was further subdivided into romantic incidents between boyfriend/girlfriend; attention-seeking incidents in the process of attempting to generate a romantic interest or other general attention seeking; and another category that was not readily classifiable.

Of all cases, 36 percent involved adults. Although this included sexual abuse and exploitation cases, 10 percent of this number were 18- or 19-year-old high school students who likely should have been classified as part of the adolescent peer group, and 5 percent of adult-involved cases were minors soliciting sex from adults.

Of "youth-only" aggravated cases, 31 percent demonstrated malicious, nonconsensual, or criminal behaviors. Most cases in this category (57 percent) resulted from lack of consent in sending images. However, 19 percent involved criminal behavior such as blackmail or abuse in addition to the creation, possession, or sending of images.

Of cases that came to the attention of law enforcement, 33 percent were considered "experimental" without aggravating factors (32 percent romantic; 57 percent attention seeking; 11 percent other).

Arrests occurred in 62 percent of cases where adults were involved, 36 percent of youth-only aggravated cases, and 18 percent of experimental cases. In the youth-only aggravated cases, 5 percent of those arrested were subject to sex offender registration. This study demonstrates the behaviors from sexting display a spectrum, from criminal activity, to malicious behavior among adolescents, to what can be considered experimental relationship development, and sexual attention-seeking behaviors among adolescents with no malicious intent.

Advice for Parents

Pediatricians can make the following recommendations to parents:

- Openly discuss sexting with children before an incident occurs, explaining that they must let the parent know without fear of reprisal if an incident does occur.
- Role play with a child what he/she will do if pressured to send an inappropriate photo. Remind the child that the potential social humiliation is much worse than standing up to peer pressure.
- Empower their children that they are responsible for whether they allow pictures of themselves to be taken or sent and that they should immediately delete or show to an adult any picture that they receive.
- Use an incident of sexting (or a talk about sexting) as an opportunity to talk with children and adolescents about sex (comprehensive safe sex education). Remind parents to discuss with their child that the images cannot be retrieved once sent.

This report clearly refutes that sexting is a harmless activity to be thought of as a normal part of adolescence. Sexting can be seen as a risky behavior even if it does not become a police matter.

Two-thirds of cases identified in this study met federal definitions of child pornography, but comparatively few cases were prosecuted as such. Some cases result in having to register as a sex offender when an individual is not much older than the person whose picture he/she has or transmits. Importantly, 2/3 of all images were confined to a device and not available over the Internet where further exploitation could occur. The heterogeneity of enforcement indicates that law enforcement has not developed a clear consensus on how to handle these cases. It is possible that the 18 percent of experimental cases prosecuted might have been better handled informally with the family and clinician rather than through the legal system.

Since 2009, many state legislatures have passed laws specific to sexting. States have created statutes that specify sexting as a misdemeanor, escalate penalties with multiple offenses, create educational diversion programs, or institute civil fines as punishment.

Florida, for example, now has an escalating penalty based on the number of offenses. For a first offense, the Florida law allows for issuance of a citation and a combination of penalties including: 8 hr of community service, a $60 civil penalty, and participation in a cyber safety program. Failure to comply can result in loss of one's driver's license. A second offense is prosecutable as a misdemeanor and a third as a felony. Laws such as these have taken sexting away from child pornography prosecutions and given district attorneys leeway.

The pediatrician needs to develop awareness and skills that help identify and bridge the gap between adolescents and adults. Identifying adolescent experimentation versus dangerous behaviors can be difficult for the pediatrician. Failure to understand the dangerous implications of sexting and its place in adolescent sexual behavior can be detrimental for patients, families, and pediatricians.

Critical Thinking

1. Give three suggestions that parents could implement to reduce the likelihood of their child sexting.
2. Discuss the relationship between self-esteem and sexting.

Internet References

House Passes Bill That Could Have Teens Facing 15 Years for Trying to Sext

https://www.forbes.com/sites/janetwburns/2017/06/02/house-passes-bill-that-could-jail-teens-15-years-for-sexting/#75c6a94f4cf6

How Popular is Sexting among Teens?

https://www.psychologytoday.com/blog/attraction-evolved/201703/how-popular-is-sexting-among-teens

Parent of Teen Involved in Sexting

http://www.focusonthefamily.com/family-q-and-a/parenting/parent-of-teen-involved-in-sexting

Sexting and Teenagers

http://raisingchildren.net.au/articles/sexting.html

Why Kids Sext

https://www.theatlantic.com/magazine/archive/2014/11/why-kids-sext/380798/

Dr. Pat F. Bass is a chief medical information officer and an associate professor of Medicine and of Pediatrics, Louisiana State University Health Sciences Center—Shreve port. The author has nothing to disclose in regard to affiliations with or financial interests in any organizations that may have an interest in any part of this article.

Unit 6

UNIT

Prepared by: Claire N. Rubman, *Suffolk County Community College, Selden, NY*

Development during Emerging and Early Adulthood

As our adolescents begin to take on adult responsibilities such as jobs, family responsibilities, and a position in society, so they enter the world of "emerging adulthood." This is a shift away from adolescence and a step toward adulthood. This period is fraught with contradictions such as trying to raise a child while addicted to drugs, gang membership and its justification, self-harm and a cry for help, trying to stay in high school while raising an infant, safe school sports that allow for competition and the toxic environment of the 21st century that our adolescents are trying to successfully navigate.

Some adolescents become pregnant but would like to complete their high school education. Rabiah and Russo (2016) explore the challenges faced by student parents including whether or not they should be separated from the remaining student population.

Not all students manage to stay on school and out of trouble. Some turn to drugs to soothe themselves or escape from their problems. One young mother describes her descent into desperation as she focused her attention on drugs instead of her child. Read about Betsy's battle to locate and consume over 200 pills per week. Read about addiction to oxycodone, fentanyl, and other opioids and the havoc they can wreak. Zimmerman's article, "To Hell and Back" (2016) is a firsthand account of a shy high schooler's descent into addiction, homelessness, and despair. Learn how Tracy turned her life around and about her advocacy work for others.

Many adolescents feel isolated and alone. For some, the allure of gang membership and inclusion may lead to a life of crime. Gangs are discussed by Jang (2016) in her article

"Beneath the Ink: A Deeper Look at Gang Violence in El Salvador." Jang traces the history of the MS 13 gang from El Salvador. She describes how gang members are seduced by this life of crime. Read about government efforts to intervene and prevent impressionable adolescents from falling prey to this lifestyle.

Some adolescents try to overcome the pain of their isolation, depression, or anxiety by engaging in self-harm. Learn about the primary and secondary risk factors associated with self-harm. Read about examples and triggers. Discover intervention techniques and awareness programs that are designed for emerging adults. Rae (2016) discusses these issues in her article titled "Introducing the Topic of Self-Harm in Schools."

As adolescents journey toward adulthood, they sometimes encounter the harsh realities of life such as the inequity of wealth, unemployment, low wages, and the decrease in social mobility in our society. Two articles address some of these issues in two very different ways. Clark (2016) discusses the inequity of the minimal prison sentence that Brock Turner received for raping a college student while she was passed out. The incident gained national attention and focused on the rapist's Ivy League education, his ample financial resources and social standing. Read about Turner's father's reaction to his son's behavior.

The final article discusses the social, emotional, and psychological toll that the 21st century is taking on our emerging adult population. Read Eberstadt's account of the devastating job market, demoralizing salaries, and the dismal outlook for social mobility. How do we empower our adolescents to develop resilience and find a positive outlook on life . . . .

Article   Prepared by: Claire N. Rubman, *Suffolk County Community College, Selden, NY*

Meeting the Needs of Student Parents

RABIAH GUL AND CHARLES J. RUSSO

Learning Outcomes

After reading this article, you will be able to:

- Discuss how pregnancy and teen parenting impacts educational goals and high school completion.

- Explain the implications of Title IX of the Education Amendment of 1972.

- Discuss the policy changes advocated by Gul and Russo.

In 2014, almost 249,000 children were born to adolescent females ages 15–19, according to the National Center for Health Statistics. One in six births were to adolescent females who already had one or more babies.

In addition to the struggles teenage parents and their children face, in 2010, teen childbearing also costs taxpayers between \$9.4 and \$28 billion a year for such expenditures as public assistance payments, lost tax revenue, and public health care, foster care, and schooling, according to the Department of Health and Human Services (United States Department of Health and Human Services 2016).

In light of the budgeting and social costs of teenage pregnancies and parenting, this is an issue about which educational leaders should be aware.

Consequences of Teenage Pregnancies

The teen birth rate has declined almost continuously over the past 20 years (United States Department of Health and Human Services 2016). In 1991, for example, the rate of teen births was 61.8 for every 1,000 adolescent females, compared with 24.2 births in 2014. HHS attributes the decline in births to the fact that more teens are waiting longer before engaging in sexual relations and those who do engage are using contraceptives more frequently. Still, the teen birth rate in the United States is higher than that of many developed countries, including Canada and the United Kingdom (United States Department of Health and Human Services 2016).

Giving birth is the primary reason teen mothers do not graduate from high school. In fact, once teen mothers give birth, their levels of schooling decline dramatically. Based on data from 2010, the Centers for Disease Control (CDC 2015), reports that only about 50% of teen mothers graduate secondary school before age 22 while approximately 90% of their peers who had not given birth during high school earn their diplomas. Teen mothers also are more likely to have more health problems and face unemployment as young adults (CDC 2015).

Teenage Pregnancy and the Law

The United States Supreme Court ruled that education is "not among the rights afforded explicit protection under our Federal Constitution. Nor do we find any basis for saying it is implicitly so protected" (*San Antonio v. Rodriguez* 1973, p. 35). Yet, recognizing education as perhaps the most important function of state and local governments *(Brown v. Board of Education* 1954), state constitutions safeguard the educational rights of all students, including those who are pregnant and parenting.

The rights of pregnant and parenting teens receive significant protection under Title IX of the Education Amendments of 1972. According to this law, no one in the United States can be excluded from participation in or be denied the benefits of any education program or activity that receives federal funding on the basis of sex. As reflected in an accompanying regulation, Title IX protects females from discrimination based on pregnancy and childbirth.

The regulation highlights four provisions applicable to public school systems that receive federal financial aid:

1. Boards of education cannot discriminate against any student, or exclude any student from its education program or activity, including any class or

extracurricular activity, on the basis of the student's "pregnancy, childbirth, false pregnancy, termination of pregnancy or recovery therefrom, unless the student requests voluntarily to participate in a separate portion of the program or activity . . ." (34 C.F.R. § 106.40(b)(1)).

2. If a board provides a portion of its education program or activity separately for pregnant students who volunteer for the program, the program must be comparable to what's offered to non-pregnant students (34 C.F.R. § 106.40(b)(3)).

3. Districts that receive federal funding must "treat pregnancy, childbirth, false pregnancy, termination of pregnancy and recovery therefrom in the same manner and under the same policies as any other temporary disability with respect to any medical or hospital benefit, service, plan or policy which such recipient administers, operates, offers, or participates in with respect to students admitted to the recipient's educational program or activity" (34 C.F.R. § 106.40(b)(4)).

4. If a school board that does not maintain a leave policy for its students, or if a student does not otherwise qualify for leave under such a policy, the district must treat "pregnancy, childbirth, false pregnancy, termination of pregnancy, and recovery therefrom" as a justification for a leave of absence for the period of time deemed medically necessary by the student's physician. At the conclusion of that time, the student must be reinstated to the status she held when the leave began (34 C.F.R. § 106.40(b)(5)).

A closer reading of the regulation reveals three key protections for students who are pregnant and parenting (Fershee 2009). First, the regulation guarantees access to education by forbidding officials from expelling students who are pregnant and parenting. Second, the regulation requires officials to grant students covered by these provisions the right to choose whether and where they wish to attend school. Third, the regulation requires boards to ensure that if they offer alternative schools to teens who are pregnant and parenting, the programs must be comparable to those offered in mainstream schools.

Associated Litigation

To date, little reported litigation addresses the rights of pregnant and parenting teens. Even so, students prevailed in two cases when they sought to become members of the National Honor Society (NHS).

In a case from Arizona, the Ninth Circuit affirmed an injunction in favor of a pregnant, unmarried student in Arizona who was not living with the child's father, thereby ordering her acceptance into the NHS. The court found that educators acted in bad faith in calling for her exclusion (*Cazares v. Barber* 1992).

In like manner, a federal trial court in Kentucky granted a preliminary injunction to unmarried high school students who were excluded from the NHS after becoming pregnant and giving birth (*Chipman v. Grant County School District* 1998). The court ruled that the students showed the strong likelihood of success on the merits of their claims and that they would have suffered irreparable injury if it did not grant their request that they be admitted to the NHS.

Policy Suggestions

When seeking to meet the needs of students who are pregnant and parenting, the following policy suggestions are offered as food for thought for SBOs and other education leaders.

1. Education leaders should create broad-based policy writing and revision teams to address issues related to teen pregnancies. Teams should include a board member, a central office official such as the SBO, a parent, a community representative, a building level administrator, a teacher, a school health-care worker, a school counselor, public health and medical care professionals, and perhaps a student or two at the high school—ideally a young woman who has given birth and returned to school along with another who is pregnant and attending school. These young women should be able to help other members appreciate the importance of a pregnancy policy.

2. When they devise or revise policies, teams should contact their state education and health departments along with other school boards in their area to learn about effective approaches to addressing the needs of pregnant and parenting students.

3. When it becomes obvious that students are pregnant or when they reveal their conditions, building-level educators should meet with each young woman, her parent(s), the school counselor, the school nurse, and perhaps her partner and his parents to devise support systems to help the expectant mothers remain in school.

   If pregnant teens decide to leave school before graduation, officials should conduct follow-up activities to determine why. Educators should analyze the data they collect to see how pregnancy and parenthood affect the district's dropout rate, and how those issues can be addressed or resolved.

4. Counselors and/or other personnel such as the school nurse should contact pregnant and parenting students who have dropped out of school and encourage them to return.

5. School counselors should confer with pregnant and parenting students individually to devise graduation plans tailored to their individual needs. Plans may include academic credit-recovery, online programming, and home instruction for students who have fallen behind.

6. Boards should create support groups to help pregnant and parenting students stay in school. As part of program activities, districts should consider using peer counseling in which pregnant and parenting students share their experiences regarding how they have been able remain in school and work toward their diplomas.

7. When students who have given birth return to school, educators should make supports available such as designating a private room where they can breastfeed their babies, pump milk, or address other needs related to breastfeeding during the school day. Also, a school nurse or other health-care professional should be available to answer questions for new mothers.

8. Teachers should encourage students who are pregnant and parenting to seek the assistance of school counselors who can provide support to help them remain in school. In addition, teachers should be flexible with regard to assignments and other academic matters.

9. Officials should provide professional development sessions for all school personnel to help them to understand the needs of and work with pregnant and parenting students.

10. Educators should provide instruction in appropriate settings such as health classes or school assemblies to remind students about the need to be supportive of their peers who are pregnant and parenting.

11. Boards should provide information sessions for parents of students who are pregnant and parenting, reminding them of available services to assist them and their daughters through the potentially challenging transitions they are experiencing.

12. Officials should include board policies identifying the services provided to pregnant and parenting teens in faculty and student handbooks, in materials provided to parents, and on district websites.

Conclusion

Meeting the needs of students who are pregnant and parenting is both sensitive and challenging for educators and school communities. Suggestions provided here should, we hope, guide district officials as they devise policies and programs to support students who are pregnant and parenting.

References

Brown v. Board of Education, 347 U.S. 483 (1954).
Cazares v. Barber, 959 F.2d 753 (9th Cir. 1992).
Chipman v. Grant County School District, 30 F. Supp.2d 975 (E.D. Ky. 1998).
Center for Disease Control. 2015, May 19. *About Teen Pregnancy: Teen Pregnancies in the United States.* www.cdc.gov/teenpregnancy/about/index.htm
San Antonio v. Rodriguez, 411 U.S. I (1973).
Code of Federal Regulations, 34 C.F.R. § 106.40.
Fershee, K. 2009. Hollow promises for pregnant students: How the regulations governing Title IX fail to prevent pregnancy discrimination in school. 43 Indiana L. Rev. 79, 92–95.
Title IX of the Education Amendments of 1972, 20 U.S.C. § 1681(a).
United States Department of Health and Human Services. 2016, Feb. 23. *Trends in Teen Pregnancy and Childbearing.* Available at www.hhs.gov/ash/oah/adolescent-health-topics/reproductive-health/teen-pregnancy/trends.html#

Critical Thinking

1. What are the short- and long-term consequences of teen parents not pursuing their educational goals?
2. Discuss the advantages and disadvantages of teens becoming parents.
3. Will the "morning after" pill benefit or hurt teens?

Internet References

Postcard: Teen Pregnancy Affects Graduation Rates
http://www.ncsl.org/research/health/teen-pregnancy-affects-graduation-rates-postcard.aspx
Reproductive Health—Teen Pregnancy
https://www.cdc.gov/teenpregnancy/index.htm
The Dropout Crisis and Teen Pregnancy
http://www.progressivepolicy.org/blog/the-drop-out-crisis-and-teen-pregnancy/
The National Campaign to Prevent Teen and Unplanned Pregnancy
https://thenationalcampaign.org/

RABIAH GUL, JD, is a 2016 graduate of the University of Dayton (Ohio) School of Law, hopes to become a human rights attorney.

CHARLES J. RUSSO, JD, EdD, is a Joseph Panzer Chair of Education in the School of Education and Health Sciences (SEHS), director of SEHS's PhD Program in Educational Leadership, and adjunct professor in the School of Law at the University of Dayton, Ohio.

Article   Prepared by: Claire N. Rubman, *Suffolk County Community College, Selden, NY*

Stanford Sexual-Assault Case Reveals the Chasm that Privilege Creates

Naeemah Clark

Learning Outcomes

After reading this article, you will be able to:

- Explain the concept of "white privilege" as a social phenomenon.
- Discuss the conversation that Brock Turner should have with other white males.

My social media feeds recently were full of friends' and colleagues' dismay and frustration with the controversial—some would say ludicrous—statement that Dan Turner had made on behalf of his son Brock, a former Stanford University student who had just been sentenced to six months in jail after being found guilty of sexually assaulting a woman he met at a fraternity party. But, in between the excuses he made for his son and the tone-deaf language he used to describe the assault—"20 minutes of action"—he has a great idea. It's an idea that could shape the lives of hundreds of people, even though it's a lesson he and his son will probably never fully understand.

Turner's father, perhaps trying to counter the viral social-media outcry after the victim's statement, wrote a letter to the judge about his son's despondency over the accusation and his subsequent conviction and impending imprisonment. In his father's mind, Brock isn't a sexual predator; he's simply a college-age male who became an overly amorous jerk after a night of drinking. Dan Turner suggests that Brock shouldn't go to jail but receive probation, so he can visit college campuses speaking about the dangers of "alcohol consumption and sexual promiscuity."

And this is where I agree with him: His son, convicted of sexual assault, should go on a mandatory tour of colleges, talking about his crime and its consequences.

However, that mandatory tour must be done at his expense—and after he has served his six months in jail. Another caveat: The audiences must be made up solely of white males.

This purposeful segregation is much needed on campuses around the country. It will probably never happen, yet it could be the most important moment in the college experiences of white men.

More often than not, when I hear of students facing university discipline for substance, verbal, or physical abuse, the perpetrators are white males. What is going on with these guys?

Of course, most white males on campus are not irresponsible drinkers, vandals, or abusers; most are bright and informed. Still, they are products of a system that shields them from facing the devastating harm they can cause.

White privilege, a societal phenomenon in which the majority benefits simply by being in the majority, means that the white men on campus have been born with systemic advantages that give them access to opportunities that I, as an African American woman, cannot fathom.

It is this privilege that has created a chasm, or deficit, for the white guys. It is assumed that these young men have every advantage and, therefore, are not in need of tending and nurturing. That's simply not true.

It's not a coincidence that at a time when colleges are getting better at diversity and inclusion, news stories reveal white guys on college campuses acting up while struggling to find themselves. For them, philanthropy and brotherhood get lost in a culture of drinking and sexism celebrated in fraternities and dorms.

I teach at a predominantly white institution that is also predominantly female. Like many other such institutions, we make efforts to bring diversity to our expansive lawns. As a result, we have seen an increase in minority students, students who are openly gay, and students who are transgender.

We not only recruit these students, but we also offer them programs, reading rooms, and mentoring services designed to make them feel at home on our campus. And I'm so proud of our work. But I have to ask: Would all of the programs we offer to empower women, students of color, and LGBT students be as necessary if there were programs that taught cisgender white male students to be more empathetic members of our campus community?

To not talk about how white males contribute to a culture of micro- and macroaggressions puts the onus on the abused to remedy the problem. Also, to ignore the relationship of these guys to the problem does a disservice to them, as they desperately need a good push into responsible adulthood. In fact, to give white males ownership of these issues is to acknowledge the tremendous responsibilities their postgraduation privilege will give them.

So, in this rare case, I have some privilege as a black woman on a predominantly white campus. I can shout that the white guys need help, and no one assumes I'm being racist.

The consternation that would be caused by the creation of a white-male support group that required mandatory membership upon matriculation would surely be counterproductive. Instead, alternative efforts should be considered. For example, all-male residence halls should take the lead on school-spirit efforts like responsible tailgates and planning the campus's late-night activities.

Additionally, colleges should hone the mentoring skills of young white male employees. These faculty and staff members can talk with the students in ways that will encourage them to listen.

And Brock Turner may just be the ideal voice to talk about how a privileged life can be destroyed by 20 minutes of irresponsible, selfish, and hurtful actions. It's a conversation that needs to be had, white guy to white guy.

Critical Thinking

1. What are college campuses doing to safeguard women from social predators and sexual assault?
2. What are college campuses doing to uphold the law and prevent underage drinking?
3. What can be done to level the playing field in terms of privilege, the judicial system, ethnicity, and social class?

Internet References

Brock Turner's Stanford Rape Case: Everything You Need to Know
    http://www.usmagazine.com/celebrity-news/news/brock-turners-stanford-rape-case-everything-you-need-to-know-w209237

Brock Turner to Leave Jail after Serving 3 Months for Sexual Assault
    http://www.cnn.com/2016/09/01/us/brock-turner-release/

Light Sentence for Brock Turner in Stanford Rape Case Draws Outrage
    http://www.nytimes.com/2016/06/07/us/outrage-in-stanford-rape-case-over-dueling-statements-of-victim-and-attackers-father.html?_r=0

Stanford Rape Case: Read the Impact Statement of Brock Turner's Victim
    http://www.independent.co.uk/news/people/stanford-rape-case-read-the-impact-statement-of-brock-turners-victim-a7222371.html

Stanford Rapist Brock Turner Faces Extra Probation Requirements
    http://www.nbcnews.com/news/us-news/stanford-rapist-brock-turner-faces-extra-probation-requirements-n609071

Naeemah Clark is an associate professor in the School of Communications and director of the Communications Fellows Program at Elon University.

Article   Prepared by: Claire N. Rubman, *Suffolk County Community College, Selden, NY*

To Hell and Back

Tracey Helton Mitchell is fighting to beat heroin, over and over again.

JULIE IRWIN ZIMMERMAN

Learning Outcomes

After reading this article, you will be able to:

- Discuss how Tracy became addicted to heroin?
- Describe Tracy's recovery from addiction.
- Talk about how Tracy's success has helped others to overcome their addiction.

Staring into the glassy-eyed mug shots of heroin users—people who have prostituted their own daughters or shot up in their children's hospital rooms—one question usually comes to mind: *What the hell were they thinking?*

Tracey Helton Mitchell knows, and she's using that knowledge to help anyone she can from meeting that same fate. In her memoir, *The Big Fix: Hope After Heroin,* published by Seal Press this spring, the West Chester native explains in harrowing detail what it's like to fall into heroin addiction, and what it took to get her out. Mitchell was an Ursuline High School student in the late 1980s—shy, studious, depressed, and lacking self-confidence—when a dentist prescribed opioid painkillers following surgery to remove her wisdom teeth.

Mitchell spent the next few years trying to recapture the euphoria opioids granted her. Scrounging for excess pills eventually gave way to trying heroin as a student at the University of Cincinnati; a move across the country to San Francisco, homelessness, and addiction soon followed. She documents her descent with unblinking honesty: trading sex for money so she could afford more heroin; shooting the drug into her feet because she had no working veins left on her body; the arrests and abscesses she endured as friends were dying all around her from overdoses and AIDS.

Convinced she'd be dead soon too, Mitchell agreed to be profiled in the 1999 documentary *Black Tar Heroin: The Dark End of the Street* that explored an earlier strain of the epidemic. She still runs into people who recognize her from the film, in which she was shown injecting heroin into her legs, arguing with a boyfriend, trying in vain to kick the habit, and talking on a pay phone to her mother in West Chester. Before the film's release, cornered by cops for yet another arrest, Mitchell decided it was time to end her addiction.

The damage wrought by heroin is well-trodden territory, but Mitchell's account illuminates the seemingly endless and insurmountable obstacles on the path to recovery. She's initially rejected when she tries to return to school. Her teeth are a mess. She gains weight as soon as she stops using. She has to train herself not to store money in a sweaty bra or refer to all women as "bitches." The depression and shyness her drug habit papered over are again conspicuous, as is the legacy of what she characterizes as an alcoholic father and an enabling mother. But with heroin out of her life, she's forced to find other ways to cope.

Mitchell slowly climbs out of her addiction, landing a job, then going back to school, then settling into a career in mental health counseling in the San Francisco Bay Area with her husband and three children. She even becomes a PTA mom, albeit one who carries the overdose-reversing drug Naloxone in her purse at all times.

In fact, Mitchell has become a Naloxone fairy godmother of sorts, distributing it as much as possible. The drug's price soared in recent years, from less than $5 a dose to as much as $100, making it harder for those without insurance to get their hands on it. Once, having lunch while visiting here in town, she jumped up from her meal and crossed the street to give it to someone who looked to be in need. People e-mail, call, and text, asking her for it almost daily, and she counts nearly 200 lives saved because she sent Naloxone to them or their loved ones. Her advocacy has become a defining pillar of the journey from addict to activist, though she's battling more than the debilitating power of dependence. "It's not just opioid overdoses," says Mitchell. "It's Hepatitis C, and there are cities where HIV rates are going back up."

She knows how hard the habit is to kick. But that's why Mitchell offers her success story any chance she gets, as testimony that an addiction is not automatically terminal.

"When parents of addicts contact me, the first thing I say is, *Take a deep breath.* There's a deficit of hope when it comes to heroin," she says. "We need to keep people alive until they're ready to get better. A person can't get clean if they're dead."

Critical Thinking

1. What are the alternative pain medications to opioids for teenagers and college students after surgery or wisdom tooth extraction?

2. Make two suggestions that could reduce addiction rates among teenagers.

Internet References

Emerging Trends and Innovations in the Identification and Management of Drug Use among Adolescents and Young Adults
https://www.ncbi.nlm.nih.gov/pmc/articles/PMC4119795/

Drug Addiction among Adolescents
https://www.ncbi.nlm.nih.gov/pubmed/6561047

Heroin
https://teens.drugabuse.gov/drug-facts/heroin

Heroin Addiction's Stranglehold on Adolescents
http://www.timesunion.com/local/article/Heroin-addiction-s-stranglehold-on-adolescents-5981314.php

Heroin Use on the Rise among Teens and Adolescents
http://www.sun-sentinel.com/features/south-florida-parenting/stages/preteen-teen/sfp-heroin-is-on-the-rise-amongst-teens-2014-story.html

Article   Prepared by: Claire N. Rubman, *Suffolk County Community College, Selden, NY*

Introducing the Topic of Self-harm in Schools: Developing an Educational and Preventative Support Intervention

Tina Rae

Learning Outcomes

After reading this article, you will be able to:

- Define self-harm.
- Explain the primary and secondary factors associated with self-harm and suicide.
- Discuss the most common form of self-harm and why people engage in it.

Promoting the mental health of young people and the prevention of self-harm which emanates from psychological pain is undoubtedly the most challenging task faced by professionals working with young people today. Data from the Department of Health (Meltzer 2000) regarding the mental health of 12,529 children and adolescents indicated that 10 percent of children aged 5–15 years had a mental disorder and these children were also more likely to be boys living in a lower-income family with one parent. Of these children, ½ had been referred to a professional from the educational services and almost ¼ had access to specialist health-care services, while ⅓ had contact with Social Services.

According to the DfES (2004), young people are unable to learn and remain included in the school context if they do not feel safe or if health or social problems create barriers to learning. Education is seen as the most effective route for young people out of both poverty and disaffection.

Many families today are exposed to high level of daily stress and the incidence of childhood depression is increasing.

An estimated 10 per cent of children in any school experience serious depression, such as going through extended periods of despair and even engaging in suicidal thoughts. Young people do not enjoy carefree childhoods but instead have to cope with the devastating effects of divorce, exposure to drugs, and bullying among other significant stressors. Young people are most vulnerable to negative emotions and at risk of developing depression at the age of 11, when they move from primary to secondary education (Reivich and Shatte 2002).

Professionals appear to be in agreement that any kind of intervention which purports to protect and improve the mental health of young people would need to:

- be implemented at an early stage/age
- be targeted primarily at boys
- include and actively involve parents, carers, education, health, and the judicial system
- be concerned with both skills and knowledge, for example, self-esteem, self-confidence, emotional literacy and relationship building
- be focused on health, decision-making, and risk-taking behaviors.

Shifting the Emphasis

Consequently, in understanding health and therefore mental, emotional, and social health, there needs to be a shift from the more usual focus of illness to also embracing the notion of positive well-being. Mental health should clearly be linked to, or described as, an increase in the general degree of happiness, vitality, sense of worth and achievement, alongside their concern/empathy for others. Within a school context this would suggest that the curriculum would need to actively prevent unhappiness—bullying, violence, and conflict—while also encourage learners and those supporting them in schools to achieve their goals; to feel love; to feel joyful; to be energetic, and to care about others (Weare 2000).

Consequently, when schools attempt to engage in mental health promotion, they would need to ensure the following:

- The development of a healthy schools policy which includes mental, social, and emotional health, for example, policies which actively prevent bullying violence and conflict.
- The development of personal skills, including emotional literacy skills, among staff and students alike. These will consequently enable all stakeholders to deal effectively with bullying and conflict and will also ensure that there is an ethos of motivation, energy, and a real sense of happiness within the school community.
- The creation of supportive environments, for example, where all individuals actively and openly care for each other.
- The strengthening of community action, for example, appropriate and significant contributions from a range of agencies, including Education, Health, Social Services, and agencies within the wider community context.
- The encouragement of the whole school approach to mental health promotion which may involve the reorientation of some services (adapted from the Ottawa Charter, 1986).

Understanding Suicide and Self-harm

Of all the areas of mental health promotion, suicide and self-harm are probably the most challenging for both the professionals and the target groups involved. If suicide rates are to be reduced and the damage that stems from self-harm is to be ameliorated, then it is essential that these issues are addressed in a coherent manner with both those supporting these vulnerable teenagers and the students themselves.

Suicide rates among young men in the United Kingdom rose significantly during the 1980s and early 1990s. This has led to a significant amount of public attention being drawn to this topic and rightly so, given the fact that the rates of suicide in England and Wales for young men between the ages of 15 and 24 years rose by approximately 60 percent within the 10 year period from 1981 to 1991. This led to the Government setting a goal in 1991 (Health of the Nation Strategy Document) to reduce the rate of youth suicide by 15 percent by the end of the century. The rate has been reduced by approximately 16 per 100,000 in 1990 to 12 per 100,000 in 2000.

In order to further support the Government's health strategy in this area, a specific 'National Suicide Prevention Strategy for England' was issued in 2002. This strategy has six identified objectives, including reducing risk in key high-risk groups, for example, men, and promoting mental health well-being in the wider population, alongside reducing the availability and lethal nature of suicide methods. It seems still the case that young men are far more likely to commit suicide than young women. In England and Wales in the year 2000, the rate for young men was 12 per 100,000, while it was only 4 per 100,000 for young women, that is, three times as many young men as young women commit suicide every year. The UK's rate is close to that of other comparable European countries but less than the rates in North America, Australia, New Zealand, and Ireland. It is also concerning that the rate for young men in Scotland in the year 2000 was 36 per 100,000, that is, three times the rate in England and Wales. Regional variations of this type are of great concern, having implications for service provision and public policy.

Risk Factors

The risk factors associated with suicide can be divided between primary and secondary factors. Clearly no one young person will experience all of these factors but are likely to experience a significant combination. Such a combination will then lead to an increased risk of suicide.

Primary risk factors include the following:

- Alcohol and drug abuse
- A sense of real hopelessness concerning the future
- Serious depression
- A previous attempt at suicide
- Some form of psychiatric disorder

Secondary risk factors include:

- A severe dent to self-esteem which may lead to a sense of guilt or shame
- A recent loss or bereavement
- A family history of suicide
- Experiencing a significant other (e.g., a friend or significant adult) committing suicide.

Added to these factors, there are also groups of young people who are at much higher risk than would be expected within the mainstream group, including young people in custody, looked-after children, gay/lesbian or bisexual children and those who inhabit more isolated rural communities.

Self-harm
Definition

There has been a significant level of debate as to how to define self-harm. John Coleman (2004) suggests that we, "take the view that it is most helpful to consider self-harm as a continuum, ranging from behavior which has a strong suicidal intent (e.g., some kinds of overdose) to behavior which is intended to help the person stay alive (e.g., cutting)" (p. 6). Coleman adds that the problem with the term "deliberate self-harm" is that it has an implication of willfulness about it, which may be unhelpful to young people if they believe they have little control over their behavior. Similarly, the problem with the term "attempted suicide" is that some young people take an overdose with little suicidal intent (p. 7). Self-harm therefore appears to be the best term to use in order to describe this continuum of behaviors while also maintaining a focus on the degree of suicidal intent.

Evidence

There is consistent and converging evidence (Whitlock et al. 2008) that the most commonly chosen form of self-harm is cutting the body with a knife or razor, typically on the arm or leg or stomach. Other common forms include scratching or scraping the skin until blood is drawn, burning the skin, or inserting objects (such as pins) under the skin. Less frequently reported forms include hitting or biting oneself, pulling out hair, or picking at wounds.

Data

Data concerning hospital admissions (Hawton et al. 2003) suggest an increasing trend over these behaviors over the last two decades; while anecdotal reports from clinicians, other health professionals, and teachers also indicate a marked rise in these behaviors over the recent past. Rates of self-harm are far more difficult to identify than those for suicide. The reasons for this are clear and obvious. In a study carried out by Hawton and Rodham (2006) for the Samaritans, 10.6 percent of a 4,500 sample of secondary school pupils were found to have been involved in some form of self-harming behavior. However, within this particular group many more had been involved in cutting (7.4 percent) than in self-poison (3.2 percent). The gender ratio here was approximately 3:1, that is, more females than males were involved in this kind of behavior.

Assessment

When working with young people, the professionals involved have to be able to assess the degree of suicidal intent in such behaviors. The criteria most usefully utilized are as follows:

- The length of time that the attempt at suicide was actually being planned. If the planning period is extensive, then the risk will be greater.

- The level and severity and intensity of depression that the young person is experiencing.
- The sense of hopelessness the young person is experiencing.
- If the young person was alone at the time of the self-harm incident, that is, if the young person knows that they are not entirely alone, then this would indicate a lower degree of risk.

Why Self-harm?
Self-poisoning

There are many reasons for self-harming and there are many meanings to each of the acts perpetrated by the individuals concerned. It may well be the case that when a young person attempts to self-poison, there is a serious attempt to die. However, this attempt could also simply be a wish to escape from a terrible situation or a perceived terrible situation. It may be the only way out that the young person considers to be possible at this point in time. He/she may also feel that they have no control over the situation and feel a total lack of self-efficacy while also experiencing a sense of life being simply too much to bear or cope with. Ultimately, many professionals would consider self-poisoning as a means of communication and according to Coleman (2004) "Concentrating on the meaning of the communication may help to prevent a repetition of the act" (p. 8). Coleman also makes the significant point that, "It is frequently the case that troubled relationships, either with the parent or a close friend, lie at the heart of an episode of self-poisoning. For this reason it is especially important that, following such an episode, the young person has the opportunity to talk with a caring adult, and to give expression to some of the painful emotions caused by her/his relationship difficulties" (Coleman 2004, p. 8).

Mutilation

In the same way that self-poisoning can be motivated by painful relationships and experiences, cutting and other forms of mutilation are also similarly motivated. However, it is important to point out that self-harm is at the opposite end of the continuum in terms of suicidal intent. Cutting, itself, is frequently a way or means of being able to stay alive as opposed to achieving death. Generally, forms of self-mutilation are an attempt to gain release from severe emotional tension or distress. This form of self-abuse may also be a means of the young person redirecting the anger that they feel, that is, they may hate their abuser but be unable to express that hatred toward that individual and this form of mutilation provides them with an outlet for these feelings.

Range of Behaviors

Overall, self-harm refers to a range of behaviors along a continuum ranging from low to high suicidal intent. In general, young people who tend to mutilate or cut themselves are likely to have a lower suicidal intent, while those who take an overdose may have a higher suicidal intent. What is important is that the young person accesses appropriate assessment procedures within the context of a mental health organization. Part of this assessment would include identifying risk factors which are similar to those identified with suicide. However, risk factors for self-harm also include physical, sexual, or emotional abuse, low self-esteem and anxiety and difficulties in relationships.

The Development of a School-based Awareness Raising Intervention

Keith Hawton (2015) has most recently identified the essential necessity to develop and deliver school-based interventions which educate and inform all young people about the causes and triggers to self-harm and suicide.

A key question to ask is: Whom do young people talk to first when they disclose their self-harming behaviors? We know that it is most likely that they will talk to their friends at school and not to parents in the home context or to teachers in school. Young people need to feel skilled up and confident in terms of talking about these issues, what to say to a friend who discloses to them, how to manage when they see images on line which are triggering, how to cope with pressure to engage in self-harm behaviors from peers and how to build effective thinking and resilience in order to manage the emotions and triggers to anxiety which may result in these behaviors.

It is this perspective that led to the development of this preventative program for young people (Rae and Walshe 2016). It was developed for high school students and aimed to raise awareness as to these risk factors for both suicide and self-harm behaviors among young people and those who care for them. Consequently, within the resource, attention is paid to identifying and further analyzing such factors alongside also attempting to increase the mental health of the young people concerned or targeted by the program. As stated previously, the authors were not simply concerned here with prevention of illness but also with the promotion of young people's vitality, validity, sense of self-worth, and general degree of happiness. A key aim was to really ensure that young people have the opportunity within the school context to feel and be free from bullying, violence, and conflict and to be able to engage in the learning process in an energetic, motivated, and caring manner.

Trialing the Resource—An On-going Initiative

To date, the resource has been trialed in three high schools and students and staff perceptions of the impact have been measured via scaling questionnaires and focus groups. The process is on-going and it is expected that data will be analyzed via thematic analysis (Braun and Clarke 2006) and the themes identified will support on-going development of the program while also providing evidence of its efficacy in terms of changing perceptions and building resilience and coping skills in the students themselves.

At the outset, it was vital to enlist the support of the staff team and to ensure that the necessity for including the program as part of their PSHE/Well-being curriculum. Overcoming the stigma and discussing concerns regarding any "contagion effect" was an essential at the outset. An awareness raising and information session was delivered by the facilitators in order to ensure that staff in schools felt comfortable with both the approach and the content of the program. They were also assured that delivery would be undertaken in partnership with the schools educational and child psychologist and that adequate debriefing for both staff and students would be made available to both staff and individual students as and when needed. The program was delivered on the understanding that school-based staff would work together to formulate and agree a whole school policy regarding the management of self-harm in the school. Guidance was provided as to how to both inform and involve parents/carers.

Using the Resource

With these aims in mind the resource was consequently divided into two parts, aiming to ensure that knowledge and skills were developed at three different levels: the whole school level, the group level, and at the individual level.

Part 1—Working at the Whole School Level

- The first part of this resource is a training session designed to educate and raise awareness among professionals working with young people. A PowerPoint presentation is accompanied by a facilitator's script with detailed notes relating to each of the slides. The idea here is to provide much of the information provided in the introduction to the program as published, alongside activities which provide the opportunity to gain a further insight into the nature of self-harm and suicide among young people.

- The appendices then highlight the ways in which school-based staff can develop a policy and raise awareness among the whole school as to best practice in this area. Key aspects of the policy are addressed and a sample policy is also provided within the appendices.
- The appendices also provide information leaflets for parents, staff, and pupils as to the nature of self-harm among young people alongside resources and sources of support. The idea here is to dispel any myths and to ensure that accurate, up-to-date facts are provided so that many of the fears around these issues can, to a certain extent, be changed.

Part 2—Working at the Group Level

This section is designed as an eight-session program which can be delivered to groups of young people in a school or youth education context. The eight sessions are designed to cover the main issues surrounding self-harm and suicide in young people and to provide a safe framework in which students can develop preventative strategies and techniques alongside recognizing the importance of peer support and appropriate access to therapeutic agencies.

The program is divided into the sessions as follows:

Session 1   What is self-harm?—Myths and realities and tackling the stigma

Session 2   Understanding stress and anxiety

Session 3   Triggers and traumas—the impact of social media and the Internet

Session 4   Stopping the cycle of self-harm—key tools and strategies

Session 5   Supporting friends who self-harm—key issues and sources of support

Session 6   Key tools from Cognitive Behavior Therapy to practice and use

Session 7   Using tools from positive psychology to create a more positive mind-set

Session 8   Breaking the cycle and moving forward

An Important Point

It is very important to remember that young people participating in the group activities and staff involved in the training aspects of this program may find themselves experiencing and dealing with some very strong feelings and emotions. Self-harm and suicide clearly involve very sensitive issues. Many of the people involved in this work may have been affected by self-harming behaviors or suicidal tendencies or behaviors within their own families. Some people may be engaged in or have engaged in these behaviors themselves. Consequently, it is recommended that prior to delivering the introductory INSET or work on policy and raising awareness or work at a group level in particular, that the facilitators ensure adequate time is spent in enabling group members to feel relaxed and get to know each other and that appropriate risk assessments are undertaken to ensure the emotional and physical safety of all involved.

Session 1 of the group work in which the students formulate ground rules should also perhaps be undertaken prior to delivering the training with any group of professionals. Trust needs to be established among participants regardless of which part of the program they are working on. It is also important for the facilitator to feel skilled, knowledgeable, and secure in delivering these materials and dealing with many of the strong emotions that may erupt during the course of delivery. Being trained or having access to training in this area can result in some emotional and unpredictable responses. It is consequently recommended that facilitators are trained in group work and group dynamics and also that a minimum of two facilitators deliver the training and group work. It is also vital that facilitators have access to supervision and appropriate levels of support themselves if they are to be truly effective in both delivering the key aspects of this program and maintaining their own well-being.

Conclusion

It is hoped that the resource developed and trialed within the high schools will be disseminated further in a range of educational contexts. The drive to promote well-being and prevent the escalation of mental health difficulties and associated self-harming behaviors remains of vital importance to those of us who work with children and young people in the educational context and beyond. Interventions at a school level are essential in order to dispel myths, develop awareness and resilience skills and also to prevent the escalation of anxiety which leads to such behaviors in the first instance. A review of findings by Nock (2010) indicates that most individuals known to engage in self-harm report having access to psychological support or medication. However, there appear to be few (if any) current interventions (clinic- or community-based) that have a solid evidence base, although various forms of established treatment (behavioral therapy, cognitive therapy, and psychodynamic therapy) have been modified to target self-harm. We therefore hope that with additional trials we can identify the evidence base for our intervention for working with young people at a preventative level.

Also, having focused upon students at high school level and becoming aware of the fact that younger children are now engaging in these behaviors, the next step for the authors is to identify how to support and intervene at primary level. We know that self-harm has been witnessed in primary school aged children as young as six years (Palmer and Martin, 2014; Nock and Prinstein, 2004; Barrocas et al. 2012). It is therefore essential for us to consider how to create preventative approaches and interventions which are both effective and age appropriate. This is clearly a much-needed work in progress.

References

Barrocas, A. L., Hankin, B. L., Young, J. F. and Abela, J. R. Z. 2012. Rates of nonsuicidal self-injury in youth: Age, sex, and behavioral methods in a community sample. *Pediatrics,* 130(1), 39–45.

Braun, V. and Clarke, V. 2006. Using thematic analysis in psychology. *Qualitative Research in Psychology.* 3 (2), 77–101.

Coleman, J. 2004. *Teenage Suicide and Self-harm—A Training Pack for Professionals.* Brighton. Trust for the Study of Adolescence.

DFEs. 2004. *Removing Barriers to Achievement The Government's strategy for SEN* (DfES 0117/2004).

DOH. 2002. National Suicide Prevention Strategy for England Consultation document Department of Health.

Hawton, K. 2015. *The All-Party Parliamentary Group (APPG) on Suicide and self-harm prevention.* Inquiry into local suicide plans in England.

Hawton, K. and Rodham, E. 2006. *By their own hand—deliberate self-harm and suicidal ideas in adolescence.* London: Jessica Kingsley Publishers.

Hawton K., Hall S. and Simkin, S. 2003. Deliberate self-harm in adolescents: a study of characteristics and trends in Oxford. *Journal of Child Psychology and Psychiatry* 44: 1191–1198.

Meltzer, H. 2000. *Mental Health of Children and Adolescents in Great Britain.* ISBN: 0-11-621373-6.

Nock, M. J. and Prinstein, M. J. 2004. A functional approach to the assessment of non-suicidal self-injury. *Journal of Consulting and Clinical Psychology,* 72(5), 885–890.

Nock M. 2010. Self-Injury *Annual Review of Clinical Psychology* 6: 339–363.

Palmer, B. and Martin, G. 2014. *An investigation into the factors associated with self-harm in a sample of seven to 14 year old inpatients.* Manuscript Submitted to Child Abuse and Neglect.

Rae, T. and Walshe, J. 2016. *Understanding and Preventing self-harm in schools key strategies for identifying and supporting vulnerable young people.* Buckingham: Hinton House Publishers.

Reivich, K. and Shatte, A. 2002. *The Resilience Factor: 7 Keys to Finding Your Inner Strength and Overcoming Life's Hurdles.* Broadway.

Weare, K. 2000. *Promoting Mental, Emotional and Social Health. A Whole School Approach.* London: Routledge.

Whitlock J., Muchlenkamp J. and Eckenrode J. 2008. Variation in nonsuicidal self-injury *Journal of Clinical Child and Adolescent Psychology* 37:725–735.

Critical Thinking

1. What changes could we make in the lives of adolescents to promote better self-esteem and reduce depression rates?

2. Give two suggestions to help to combat drug use among teens.

Internet References

6 Things Your Child Needs from You to Reduce Cutting (Self-harm) Behaviors
https://www.newhavenrtc.com/effective-therapies-for-adolescent-cutting/

Non-suicidal Self-injury in Adolescents
https://www.ncbi.nlm.nih.gov/pmc/articles/PMC2695720/

Self-injury in Adolescents
http://www.aacap.org/AACAP/Families_and_Youth/Facts_for_Families/FFF-Guide/Self-Injury-In-Adolescents-073.aspx

Teens and Self-cutting (Self-harm): Information for Parents
http://aces.nmsu.edu/pubs/_i/I104/

The Adolescent Self Injury Foundation
http://www.adolescentselfinjuryfoundation.com/

Dr. Tina Rae is a professional and academic tutor, Doctorate in Educational and Child Psychology, University of East London.

Article   Prepared by: Claire N. Rubman, *Suffolk County Community College, Selden, NY*

The Real Science Behind Concussions

New imaging techniques are much better equipped to see inside the living brain.

Michelle Taylor

Learning Outcomes

After reading this article, you will be able to:

- Articulate what Dr. Omalu's findings revealed.
- Explain the role of "tau" protein in traumatic brain injury.
- Discuss what "Diffusion Tensor Imaging" and "fMRI" technology has added to our understanding of traumatic brain injury.

On Christmas Day, Sony Pictures released *Concussion*, a biographical sports medical drama film based on research by Dr. Bennet Omalu identifying chronic traumatic encephalopathy (CTE) in retired NFL players. While the movie may be classified as entertainment, the story is real, and the scientific research behind it is very real.

CTE is a type of traumatic brain injury associated with repeated blows to the head. The progressive degenerative disease can be spurred on by symptomatic concussions as well as sub-concussive hits to the head that do not cause immediate symptoms. Thanks to Omalu's work, CTE has most commonly been found in the brains of professional athletes participating in football, but is also associated with other contact sports, such as ice hockey, wrestling and boxing, and cheerleading. The disease is characterized by degradation of brain tissue and the accumulation of tau protein, causing symptoms such as memory loss, aggression, confusion, and deep depression that generally appear years after initial brain trauma.

Omalu first encountered CTE in 2002 during the autopsy of former Pittsburg Steelers center Mike Webster when he was a forensic pathologist with the Allegheny County, Penn. coroner's office. With the help of former Steelers team doctor Julian Bailes, Omalu published a paper on his findings, which was initially dismissed by the NFL. *Concussion* follows the "David vs. Goliath" story of Omalu trying to reveal the truth with the NFL being less than cooperative. Eventually, Omalu is vindicated and amid growing scrutiny from retired players and Congress, the NFL is forced to take the concussion issue more seriously.

Although the circumstances have changed mightily since 2002, the same problem exists today for CTE research—it can only be diagnosed posthumously. However, thanks to continued research by Omalu and fellow researchers at UCLA, as well as significant research out of Boston University, we are getting closer and closer to the goal line of more accurate diagnosis.

UCLA's Positron Emission Tomography (PET) Imaging Technique

CTE is characterized by the accumulation of the protein tau in regions of the brain that control mood, cognition, and motor function. Tau is also one of the abnormal protein deposits found in the brains of people with Alzheimer's, sometimes making it difficult to image the difference between CTE and Alzheimer's.

In 2013, Gary Small, Director of the Geriatric Psychiatry Memory and Aging Research Center at UCLA, conducted a study that became the first to identify the abnormal tau proteins associated with CTE in five retired NFL players who were still living.

The study—which included Omalu and Bailes as authors—relied on a chemical marker Small and collaborator Jorge Barrio previously created for assessing neurological changes associated with Alzheimer's disease. The marker, FDDNP, binds to deposits of amyloid beta plaques and tau tangles, which are the hallmarks of Alzheimer's.

After the players received intravenous injections of FDDNP, the researchers used PET imaging to perform brain scans on the living players. Compared to healthy men, the NFL players had elevated levels of FDDNP in the amygdala and subcortical regions of the brain. According to the study, the FDDNP binding patterns in the players' scans were consistent with tau deposit patterns that have been observed at autopsy in CTE cases.

"Early detection of tau proteins may help us understand what is happening sooner in the brains of these injured athletes," Small told *Laboratory Equipment*.

Small and his colleagues further elaborated on this work in an April 2015 paper published in PNAS. The new, larger study included 14 retired NFL players (including the five previously used), in addition to 12 men and 12 women with Alzheimer's disease and 19 men and 9 women with healthy brains as controls.

The researchers identified four distinctive patterns of brain FDDNP PET signal in the 14 retired NFL players, each of whom has suffered at least one concussion. The four stages of deposits could signify early to advanced levels of CTE.

According to the paper, the observed deposit patterns are defined as follows:

(i) Pattern T1 is predominantly subcortical in brainstem (midbrain) with localized involvement of the limbic medial temporal lobe (MTL) structures (limited to amygdala).

(ii) Pattern T2 shows FDDNP PET signal in all subcortical areas analyzed in this study, in all limbic MTL areas [amygdala and MTL; hippocampus, entorhinal cortex, and parahippocampal gyrus], and in parts of the frontal cortex, including anterior cingulate gyrus.

(iii) Pattern T3 shows further increases in signal intensity and pattern complexity: all affected areas in the T2 pattern plus additional cortical areas [posterior cingulate gyrus, lateral temporal lobe, and parietal lobe]; this pattern is not associated with severe ventricular enlargement and prominent cortical atrophy commonly observed in aged retired boxers with dementia pugilistica.

(iv) Pattern T4 shows high FDDNP PET signal throughout the cortical, subcortical, and limbic MTL structures, as well as in the white matter areas; this pattern was associated with significant brain atrophy (MRI or CT); possible comorbidity of CTE with other neurodegenerative diseases may be suspected, such as Alzheimer's or end-stage CTE progressing to and simulating Alzheimer's disease.

Verifying—and extending—the results of the 2013 study, the PET scans revealed the former athletes had higher levels of FDDNP in the amygdala and subcortical regions of the brain, which are areas that control learning, memory, behavior, emotions, and other mental and physical functions. These are also the types of symptoms experienced by some of the former players in the study, as well as former players diagnosed with CTE postmortem. In contrast, those subjects with Alzheimer's disease had higher levels of FDDNP in areas of the cerebral cortex that control memory, thinking, attention, and other cognitive abilities.

"The distribution pattern of the abnormal brain proteins, primarily tau, observed in these PET scans presents a 'fingerprint' characteristic of CTE," said Barrio.

"One of the advantages of FDDNP is it shows both amyloid and tau proteins, which are important in many forms of neurodegeneration," explained Small. "It's not the specific protein that is useful at this point, but it's the pattern of deposition that seems to be informative."

The present work, according to researchers, suggests the use of neuropathology deposition as a brain tissue target for PET molecular imaging probes. But, since tau deposits are not specific to CTE, probes can only provide significant *in vivo* information when combined with the regional sensitivity of PET. The resulting information must then also be in agreement with CTE autopsy results and known mood/cognitive symptoms.

"We want to understand how these imaging tools [like FDDNP PET] predict future cognitive decline," said Small. "For years we've worked with Alzheimer's to try to use these tools to identify problems early so we can test interventions to help people. The article is exciting [since] it shows there are patterns that appear to differentiate these two subject groups."

Multimodal, Multicenter Technique

Barrio and Small note in their paper that FDDNP PET scan is just one approach to *in vivo* CTE detection—with alternative techniques such as blood-based biomarkers, functional MRI, and diffusion tensor imaging being explored by other researchers.

In fact, on December 22, 2015, researchers from Boston University, the Cleveland Clinic, Banner Alzheimer's Institute and Brigham and Women's Hospital were awarded a seven-year $16 million grant from the National Institutes of Health/National Institute of Neurological Disorders and Stroke (NIH/NINDS). The multicenter grant will be used to create methods for detecting and diagnosing CTE during life, including examining risk factors for CTE through the use of multiple advanced imaging modalities.

The study is headed by Robert Stern, Clinical Core director of the Boston University Alzheimer's Disease and CTE Center.

Other PI's include Cleveland Clinic's Jeffrey Cummings; Eric Reiman from the Banner Alzheimer's Institute; and Brigham and Women's Hospital's (BWH) imaging expert Martha Shenton.

"Years ago, people stopped using imaging to detect mild-TBI because, for the most part, it was not informative," said Shenton, Director of the Psychiatry Neuroimaging Laboratory at BWH and professor of psychiatry and radiology at Harvard Medical School. "What this translates to, and what this means, is that the right technology was not developed yet, nor were [the researchers] using the right tools. But we are now."

Among the "right" tools Shenton will be using throughout the duration of the grant is a technique known as diffusion tensor imaging (DTI). General diffusion imaging is a type of MRI developed in the early 1990s for use in humans that is based on the random motion of water molecules. According to a 2012 paper by Shenton, this motion in the brain is affected by the speed of water displacement depending on the tissue properties and type, such as gray or white matter.

What makes DTI especially suited for *in vivo* CTE brain imaging is its ability to provide information about white matter that is not possible using other imaging techniques? DTI differs from CT and conventional MRI in that it is sensitive to microstructural changes. Thus, subtle changes using DTI can reveal microstructural axonal injuries, which is the most common injury in concussions.

DTI data can be used to perform tractography—a 3-D modeling technique used to visually represent neural tracts—within white matter. Tractography is a useful tool for measuring deficits in white matter. Its estimation of fiber orientation and strength is increasingly accurate, making DTI the most sensitive way to view elements of the brain indicative of possible CTE.

The researchers involved in the grant will image retired NFL players, former college football players, and a control group of individuals without any history of contact sport or brain injury.

"We're going to be looking at structural imaging for volume or area changes," Shenton told *Laboratory Equipment*. "We will be focusing on neural inflammation since we're going to be examining college athletes as well to see if we can pick up early signs of problems. And we're also going to be using PET with florbetapir to measure the buildup of amyloid beta plaques in the brain, as well as T-807, a tau ligand, to measure the buildup of tau proteins in the brain."

The latter is important as tau pathology seems to have a different signature in the brain in postmortem findings where CTE is diagnosed than is observed in, for example, Alzheimer's disease.

The additional use of magnetic resonance spectroscopy will allow the researchers to see any metabolic changes affecting the brain. They intend to use a method to look at many different biochemical peaks in the MRS spectrum, not just the typical five or six peaks researchers use most of the time.

"If you combine a lot of these imaging techniques in the same patients, you're looking at multiple images with different information from each of the imaging modalities," explained Shenton. "It will make a big difference in terms of getting a full picture for us to characterize what is really going on in the brain. You'll have the neural chemistry, the structure and what is going on in terms of changes in the ligands. We think this kind of multimodal approach is going to be very important to understanding what is going on in the brain so that we can try to pinpoint what some of the consequences of repetitive head impacts are, including CTE. Eventually, we may be able to intercede early to try to prevent the cascade of changes that occur before they become neurodegenerative. Once you are able to diagnose it, you may be able to predict better prognosis. Is there anything you can do that is neuroprotective that will help? You can't even try treatment until you are able to detect and diagnose. That is the first step."

In addition to state-of-the-art imaging methods, participants in the study will undergo extensive clinical examinations, experimental blood tests, genetic testing, and head impact exposure tests to refine and validate specific criteria for the diagnosis of CTE.

Not everyone who plays football ends up with a neurodegenerative disease like CTE. That's why it's important to use methods that identify a wider range—not just symptomatic, but asymptomatic as well, said Shenton. This will give researchers a better idea of what the contributing factors of the disease are, what predicts who will get it and who won't, and what makes some brains more prone to CTE than others.

The project involves a group of approximately 50 investigators representing 17 research institutions, with all patient examinations taking place at four centers across the country. This allows the study to combine the efforts of the best researchers with differing/complimentary expertise across the best sites. And—perhaps more importantly—more sites means more subjects.

"This is true in a number of studies," said Shenton. "You are always trying to acquire more and more data. Everything is moving toward multisite because it allows you to do that. The more you sample anything, the more representative your findings are."

Critical Thinking

1. Which parts of the brain are adversely affected by CTE and how does that affect behavior.

2. How do present day findings change and how we play sports such as football, boxing, cheer leading, and so on in high school?

3. Suggest three changes that could be made to professional sports as a result of the research on CTE.

Internet References

Advanced stages of CTE found in Aaron Hernandez's brain
http://www.espn.com/nfl/story/_/id/20777856/lawyer-says-aaron-hernandez-had-advanced-stages-cte

"Concussion" Doctor: Letting Kids Play Football is "Definition of Child Abuse"
https://www.si.com/nfl/2017/08/08/bennet-omalu-cte-football

What is CTE?
https://concussionfoundation.org/CTE-resources/what-is-CTE

Will a New Way to Diagnose CTE Change Football?
https://www.theatlantic.com/health/archive/2017/09/football-brain-injury-chronic-traumatic-encephalopathy/540459/

Article

Prepared by: Claire N. Rubman, *Suffolk County Community College, Selden, NY*

Our Miserable 21st Century

From work to income to health to social mobility, the year 2000 marked the beginning of what has become a distressing era for the United States.

NICHOLAS EBERSTADT

Learning Outcomes

After reading this article, you will be able to:

- Explain the term "America's Second Gilded Age."

- Describe the conditions that have led to a "dreadful collapse of work."

- Describe the work trajectory rates for women since World War 2.

On the morning of November 8, 2016, America's elite—its talking and deciding classes—woke up to a country they did not know. To most privileged and well-educated Americans, especially those living in its bicoastal bastions, the election of Donald Trump had been a thing almost impossible even to imagine. What sort of country would go and elect someone like Trump as president? Certainly not one they were familiar with, or understood anything about.

Whatever else it may or may not have accomplished, the 2016 election was a sort of shock therapy for Americans living within what Charles Murray famously termed "the bubble" (the protective barrier of prosperity and self-selected associations that increasingly shield our best and brightest from contact with the rest of their society). The very fact of Trump's election served as a truth broadcast about a reality that could no longer be denied: *Things out there in America are a whole lot different from what you thought.*

Yes, things are very different indeed these days in the "real America" outside the bubble. In fact, things have been going badly wrong in America since the beginning of the 21st century.

It turns out that the year 2000 marks a grim historical milestone of sorts for our nation. For whatever reasons, the Great American Escalator, which had lifted successive generations of Americans to ever higher standards of living and levels of social well-being, broke down around then—and broke down very badly.

The warning lights have been flashing, and the klaxons sounding, for more than a decade and a half. But our pundits and prognosticators and professors and policy makers, ensconced as they generally are deep within the bubble, were for the most part too distant from the distress of the general population to see or hear it. (So much for the vaunted "information era" and "big-data revolution.") Now that those signals are no longer possible to ignore, it is high time for experts and intellectuals to reacquaint themselves with the country in which they live and to begin the task of describing what has befallen the country in which we have lived since the dawn of the new century.

II

Consider the condition of the American economy. In some circles people still widely believe, as one recent *New York Times* business-section article cluelessly insisted before the inauguration, that "Mr. Trump will inherit an economy that is fundamentally solid." But this is patent nonsense. By now it should be painfully obvious that the U.S. economy has been in the grip of deep dysfunction since the dawn of the new century. And in retrospect, it should also be apparent that America's strange new economic maladies were almost perfectly designed to set the stage for a populist storm.

Ever since 2000, basic indicators have offered oddly inconsistent readings on America's economic performance and prospects. It is curious and highly uncharacteristic to find such measures so very far out of alignment with one another. We are witnessing an ominous and growing divergence between three trends that should ordinarily move in tandem: wealth, output,

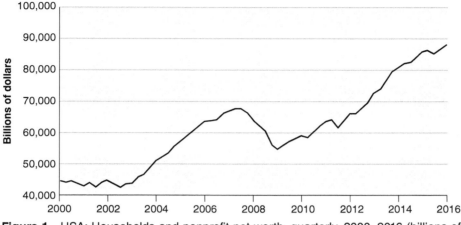

Figure 1   USA: Households and nonprofit net worth, quarterly, 2000–2016 (billions of current US dollars).

and employment. Depending upon which of these three indicators you choose, America looks to be heading up, down, or more or less nowhere.

From the standpoint of wealth creation, the 21st century is off to a roaring start. By this yardstick, it looks as if Americans have never had it so good and as if the future is full of promise. Between early 2000 and late 2016, the estimated net worth of American households and nonprofit institutions more than doubled, from $44 trillion to $90 trillion (see Figure 1).

Although that wealth is not evenly distributed, it is still a fantastic sum of money—an average of over a million dollars for every notional family of four. This upsurge of wealth took place despite the crash of 2008—indeed, private wealth holdings are over $20 trillion higher now than they were at their precrash apogee. The value of American real-estate assets is near or at all-time highs, and America's businesses appear to be thriving. Even before the "Trump rally" of late 2016 and early 2017, U.S. equities markets were hitting new highs—and since stock prices are strongly shaped by expectations of future profits, investors evidently are counting on the continuation of the current happy days for U.S. asset holders for some time to come.

A rather less cheering picture, though, emerges if we look instead at real trends for the macroeconomy. Here, performance since the start of the century might charitably be described as mediocre, and prospects today are no better than guarded.

The recovery from the crash of 2008—which unleashed the worst recession since the Great Depression—has been singularly slow and weak. According to the Bureau of Economic Analysis (BEA), it took nearly four years for America's gross domestic product (GDP) to reattain its late 2007 level. As of late 2016, total value added to the U.S. economy was just 12 percent higher than in 2007 (see Figure 2). The situation is even

more sobering if we consider per capita growth. It took America six and a half years—until mid-2014—to get back to its late 2007 per capita production levels. And in late 2016, per capita output was just 4 percent higher than in late 2007—nine years earlier. By this reckoning, the American economy looks to have suffered something close to a lost decade.

But there was clearly trouble brewing in America's macroeconomy well before the 2008 crash, too. Between late 2000 and late 2007, per capita GDP growth averaged less than 1.5 percent per annum. That compares with the nation's long-term postwar 1948–2000 per capita growth rate of almost 2.3 percent, which in turn can be compared to the "snapback" tempo of 1.1 percent per annum since per capita GDP bottomed out in 2009. Between 2000 and 2016, per capita growth in America has averaged less than 1 percent a year. To state it plainly: *With postwar, pre-21st-century rates for the years 2000–2016, per capita GDP in America would be more than 20 percent higher than it is today.*

The reasons for America's newly fitful and halting macroeconomic performance are still a puzzlement to economists and a subject of considerable contention and debate.* Economists are generally in consensus, however, in one area: They have begun redefining the growth potential of the U.S. economy downward. The U.S. Congressional Budget Office, for example, suggests that the "potential growth" rate for the U.S. economy at full employment of factors of production has now dropped below 1.7 percent a year, implying a sustainable long-term annual per capita economic growth rate for America today of well under 1 percent.

Then there is the employment situation. If 21st-century America's GDP trends have been disappointing, labor-force trends have been utterly dismal. Work rates have fallen off a cliff since the year 2000 and are at their lowest levels in decades. We

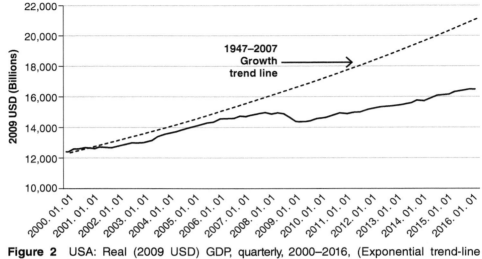

Figure 2 USA: Real (2009 USD) GDP, quarterly, 2000–2016, (Exponential trend-line 1947–2007).

can see this by looking at the estimates by the Bureau of Labor Statistics (BLS) for the civilian employment rate, the jobs-to-population ratio for adult civilian men and women (see Figure 3). Between early 2000 and late 2016, America's overall work rate for Americans age 20 and older underwent a drastic decline. It plunged by almost 5 percentage points (from 64.6 to 59.7). Unless you are a labor economist, you may not appreciate just how severe a falloff in employment such numbers attest to. Postwar America never experienced anything comparable.

From peak to trough, the collapse in work rates for U.S. adults between 2008 and 2010 was roughly twice the amplitude of what had previously been the country's worst postwar recession, back in the early 1980s. In that previous steep recession, it took America five years to re-attain the adult work rates recorded at the start of 1980. This time, the U.S. job market has as yet, in early 2017, scarcely begun to claw its way back up to the work rates of 2007—much less back to the work rates from early 2000.

As may be seen in Figure 3, U.S. adult work rates never recovered entirely from the recession of 2001—much less the crash of '08. And the work rates being measured here include people who are engaged in *any* paid employment—any job, at any wage, for any number of hours of work at all.

On Wall Street and in some parts of Washington these days, one hears that America has gotten back to "near full employment." For Americans outside the bubble, such talk must seem nonsensical. It is true that the oft-cited "civilian unemployment rate" looked pretty good by the end of the Obama era—in December 2016, it was down to 4.7 percent, about the same as it had been back in 1965, at a time of genuine full employment.

The problem here is that the unemployment rate only tracks joblessness for those still in the labor force; it takes no account of workforce dropouts. Alas, the exodus out of the workforce has been the big labor-market story for America's new century. (At this writing, for every unemployed American man between 25 and 55 years of age, there are another three who are neither working nor looking for work.) Thus the "unemployment rate" increasingly looks like an antique index devised for some earlier and increasingly distant war: the economic equivalent of a musket inventory or a cavalry count.

By the criterion of adult work rates, by contrast, employment conditions in America remain remarkably bleak. From late 2009 through early 2014, the country's work rates more or less flatlined. So far as can be told, this is the only "recovery" in U.S. economic history in which that basic labor-market indicator almost completely failed to respond.

Since 2014, there has finally been a measure of improvement in the work rate—but it would be unwise to exaggerate the dimensions of that turnaround. As of late 2016, the adult work rate in America was still at its lowest level in more than 30 years. To put things another way: *If our nation's work rate today were back up to its start-of-the-century highs, well over 10 million more Americans would currently have paying jobs.*

There is no way to sugarcoat these awful numbers. They are not a statistical artifact that can be explained away by population aging, or by increased educational enrollment for adult students, or by any other genuine change in contemporary American society. The plain fact is that 21st-century America has witnessed a dreadful collapse of work.

Figure 3 Employment to population ratio for 20+ population: United States, 2000–17 (Seasonally adjusted).

---

*Some economists suggest the reason has to do with the unusual nature of the Great Recession: that downturns born of major financial crises intrinsically require longer adjustment and correction periods than the more familiar, ordinary business-cycle downturn. Others have proposed theories to explain why the U.S. economy may instead have downshifted to a more tepid tempo in the Bush–Obama era. One such theory holds that the pace of productivity is dropping because the scale of recent technological innovation is unrepeatable. There is also a "secular stagnation" hypothesis, surmising we have entered into an age of very low "natural real interest rates" consonant with significantly reduced demand for investment. What is incontestable is that the 10-year moving average for per capita economic growth is lower for America today than at any time since the Korean War—and that the slowdown in growth commenced in the decade before the 2008 crash. (It is also possible that the anemic status of the U.S. macroeconomy is being exaggerated by measurement issues—productivity improvements from information technology, for example, have been oddly elusive in our officially reported national output—but few today would suggest that such concealed gains would totally transform our view of the real economy's true performance.)

For an apples-to-apples look at America's 21st-century jobs problem, we can focus on the 25–54 population—known to labor economists for self-evident reasons as the "prime working age" group. For this key labor-force cohort, work rates in late 2016 were down almost 4 percentage points from their year-2000 highs. That is a jobs gap approaching 5 million for this group alone.

It is not only that work rates for prime-age males have fallen since the year 2000—they have, but the collapse of work for American men is a tale that goes back at least half a century. (I wrote a short book last year about this sad saga.*) What is perhaps more startling is the unexpected and largely unnoticed falloff in work rates for prime-age women. In the United States and all other Western societies, postwar labor markets underwent an epochal transformation. After World War II, work rates for prime women surged, and continued to rise—until the year 2000. Since then, they too have declined. Current work rates for prime-age women are back to where they were a generation ago, in the late 1980s. The 21st-century U.S. economy has been brutal for male and female laborers alike—and the wreckage in the labor market has been sufficiently powerful to cancel, and even reverse, one of our society's most distinctive postwar trends: the rise of paid work for women outside the household.

In our era of no more than indifferent economic growth, 21st-century America has somehow managed to produce markedly more wealth for its wealthholders even as it provided markedly less work for its workers. And trends for paid hours of work look even worse than the work rates themselves. Between 2000 and 2015, according to the BEA, total paid hours of work in America increased by just 4 percent (as against a 35 percent increase for 1985–2000, the 15-year period immediately preceding this one). Over the 2000–2015 period, however, the adult civilian population rose by almost 18 percent—meaning that paid hours of work per adult civilian have plummeted by a shocking 12 percent thus far in our new American century.

This is the terrible contradiction of economic life in what we might call America's Second Gilded Age (2000–). It is a paradox that may help us understand a number of overarching

---

*Nicholas Eberstadt, *Men Without Work: America's Invisible Crisis* (Templeton Press, 2016).

features of our new century. These include the consistent findings that public trust in almost all U.S. institutions has sharply declined since 2000, even as growing majorities hold that America is "heading in the wrong direction." It provides an immediate answer to why overwhelming majorities of respondents in public-opinion surveys continue to tell pollsters, year after year, that our ever-richer America is still stuck in the middle of a recession. The mounting economic woes of the "little people" may not have been generally recognized by those inside the bubble, or even by many bubble inhabitants who claimed to be economic specialists—but they proved to be potent fuel for the populist fire that raged through American politics in 2016.

III

So general economic conditions for many ordinary Americans—not least of these, Americans who did not fit within the academy's designated victim classes—have been rather more insecure than those within the comfort of the bubble understood. But the anxiety, dissatisfaction, anger, and despair that range within our borders today are not wholly a reaction to the way our economy is misfiring. On the nonmaterial front, it is likewise clear that many things in our society are going wrong and yet seem beyond our powers to correct.

Some of these gnawing problems are by no means new: A number of them (such as family breakdown) can be traced back at least to the 1960s, while others are arguably as old as modernity itself (anomie and isolation in big anonymous communities, secularization and the decline of faith). But a number have roared down upon us by surprise since the turn of the century—and others have redoubled with fearsome new intensity since roughly the year 2000.

American health conditions seem to have taken a seriously wrong turn in the new century. It is not just that overall health progress has been shockingly slow, despite the trillions we devote to medical services each year. (Which "Cold War babies" among us would have predicted we'd live to see the day when life expectancy in East Germany was higher than in the United States, as is the case today?)

Alas, the problem is not just slowdowns in health progress—there also appears to have been positive retrogression for broad and heretofore seemingly untroubled segments of the national population. A short but electrifying 2015 paper by Anne Case and Nobel Economics Laureate Angus Deaton talked about a mortality trend that had gone almost unnoticed until then: rising death rates for middle-aged U.S. Whites. By Case and Deaton's reckoning, death rates rose somewhat slightly over the 1999–2013 period for all non-Hispanic White men and women 45–54 years of age—but they rose sharply for those with high school degrees or less, and for this less-educated grouping most

of the rise in death rates was accounted for by suicides, chronic liver cirrhosis, and poisonings (including drug overdoses).

Though some researchers, for highly technical reasons, suggested that the mortality spike might not have been quite as sharp as Case and Deaton reckoned, there is little doubt that the spike itself has taken place. Health has been deteriorating for a significant swath of white America in our new century, thanks in large part to drug and alcohol abuse. All this sounds a little too close for comfort to the story of modern Russia, with its devastating vodka- and drug-binging health setbacks. Yes: It *can* happen here, and it has. Welcome to our new America.

In December 2016, the Centers for Disease Control and Prevention (CDC) reported that for the first time in decades, life expectancy at birth in the United States had dropped very slightly (to 78.8 years in 2015, from 78.9 years in 2014). Though the decline was small, it was statistically meaningful—rising death rates were characteristic of males and females alike; of Blacks and Whites and Latinos together. (Only Black women avoided mortality increases—their death levels were stagnant.) A jump in "unintentional injuries" accounted for much of the overall uptick.

It would be unwarranted to place too much portent in a single year's mortality changes; slight annual drops in U.S. life expectancy have occasionally been registered in the past, too, followed by continued improvements. But given other developments we are witnessing in our new America, we must wonder whether the 2015 decline in life expectancy is just a blip, or the start of a new trend. We will find out soon enough. It cannot be encouraging, though, that the Human Mortality Database, an international consortium of demographers who vet national data to improve comparability between countries, has suggested that health progress in America essentially ceased in 2012—that the United States gained on average only about a single day of life expectancy at birth between 2012 and 2014, before the 2015 turndown.

The opioid epidemic of pain pills and heroin that has been ravaging and shortening lives from coast to coast is a new plague for our new century. The terrifying novelty of this particular drug epidemic, of course, is that it has gone (so to speak) "mainstream" this time, effecting breakout from disadvantaged minority communities to Main Street White America. By 2013, according to a 2015 report by the Drug Enforcement Administration, more Americans died from drug overdoses (largely but not wholly opioid abuse) than from either traffic fatalities or guns. The dimensions of the opioid epidemic in the real America are still not fully appreciated within the bubble, where drug use tends to be more carefully limited and recreational. In *Dreamland*, his harrowing and magisterial account of modern America's opioid explosion, the journalist Sam Quinones notes in passing that "in one threemonth period" just a few years ago, according to the Ohio Department of Health, "fully 11 percent of all Ohioans were prescribed opiates." And of course many Americans self-medicate with licit or illicit painkillers without doctors' orders.

In the fall of 2016, Alan Krueger, former chairman of the President's Council of Economic Advisers, released a study that further refined the picture of the real existing opioid epidemic in America: According to his work, nearly half of all prime working-age male labor-force dropouts—an army now totaling roughly 7 million men—currently take pain medication on a daily basis.

We already knew from other sources (such as BLS "time use" surveys) that the overwhelming majority of the prime-age men in this un-working army generally don't "do civil society" (charitable work, religious activities, and volunteering), or for that matter much in the way of childcare or help for others in the home either, despite the abundance of time on their hands. Their routine, instead, typically centers on watching—watching TV, DVDs, Internet, hand-held devices, and so on—and indeed watching for an average of 2,000 hr a year, as if it were a full-time job. But Krueger's study adds a poignant and immensely sad detail to this portrait of daily life in 21st-century America: In our mind's eye we can now picture many millions of un-working men in the prime of life, out of work and not looking for jobs, sitting in front of screens—stoned.

But how did so many millions of un-working men, whose incomes are limited, manage en masse to afford a constant supply of pain medication? Oxycontin is not cheap. As *Dreamland* carefully explains, one main mechanism today has been the welfare state: more specifically, Medicaid, Uncle Sam's means-tested health-benefits program. Here is how it works (we are with Quinones in Portsmouth, Ohio):

> [The Medicaid card] pays for medicine—whatever pills a doctor deems that the insured patient needs. Among those who receive Medicaid cards are people on state welfare or on a federal disability program known as SSI . . .If you could get a prescription from a willing doctor—and Portsmouth had plenty of them—Medicaid health-insurance cards paid for that prescription every month. For a three-dollar Medicaid co-pay, therefore, addicts got pills priced at thousands of dollars, with the difference paid for by U.S. and state taxpayers. A user could turn around and sell those pills, obtained for that three-dollar co-pay, for as much as ten thousand dollars on the street.

In 21st-century America, "dependence on government" has thus come to take on an entirely new meaning.

You may now wish to ask: What share of prime-working-age men these days are enrolled in Medicaid? According to the Census Bureau's SIPP survey (Survey of Income and Program Participation), as of 2013, over ⅕ (21 percent) of *all* civilian men between 25 and 55 years of age were Medicaid beneficiaries. For prime-age people not in the labor force, the share was over half (53 percent). And for un-working Anglos (non-Hispanic White men not in the labor force) of prime working age the share enrolled in Medicaid was 48 percent.

By the way: Of the entire un-working prime-age male Anglo population in 2013, nearly ⅗ (57 percent) were reportedly collecting disability benefit from one or more government disability program in 2013. Disability checks and means-tested benefit cannot support a lavish lifestyle. But they can offer a permanent alternative to paid employment, and for growing numbers of American men, they do. The rise of these programs has coincided with the death of work for larger and larger numbers of American men not yet of retirement age. We cannot say that these programs *caused* the death of work for millions upon millions of younger men: What is incontrovertible, however, is that they have *finance* it—just as Medicaid inadvertently helped finance America's immense and increasing appetite for opioids in our new century.

It is intriguing to note that America's nationwide opioid epidemic has *not* been accompanied by a nationwide crime wave (excepting of course the apparent explosion of illicit heroin use). Just the opposite: As best can be told, national victimization rates for violent crimes and property crimes have both reportedly dropped by about ⅔ over the past two decades.* The drop in crime over the past generation has done great things for the general quality of life in much of America. There is one complication from this drama, however, that inhabitants of the bubble may not be aware of, even though it is all too well known to a great many residents of the real America. This is the extraordinary expansion of what some have termed America's "criminal class"—the population sentenced to prison or convicted of felony offenses—in recent decades. This trend did not begin in our century, but it has taken on breathtaking enormity since the year 2000.

Most well-informed readers know that the United States currently has a higher share of its populace in jail or prison than almost any other country on earth, that Barack Obama and others talk of our criminal-justice process as "mass incarceration," and know that well over 2 million men were in prison or jail in recent years.** But only a tiny fraction of all living Americans ever convicted of a felony is actually incarcerated

*This is not to ignore the gruesome exceptions—places like Chicago and Baltimore—or to neglect the risk that crime may make a more general comeback: It is simply to acknowledge one of the bright trends for America in the new century.

**In 2013, roughly 2.3 million men were behind bars according to the Bureau of Justice Statistics.

at this very moment. Quite the contrary: Maybe 90 percent of all sentenced felons today are out of confinement and living more or less among us. The reason: the basic arithmetic of sentencing and incarceration in America today. Correctional release and sentenced community supervision (probation and parole) guarantee a steady annual "flow " of convicted felons back into society to augment the very considerable "stock" of felons and ex-felons already there. And this "stock" is by now truly enormous.

One forthcoming demographic study by Sarah Shannon and five other researchers estimates that the cohort of current and former felons in America very nearly reached 20 million by the year 2010. If its estimates are roughly accurate, and if America's felon population has continued to grow at more or less the same tempo traced out for the years leading up to 2010, we would expect it to surpass 23 million persons by the end of 2016 at the latest. Very rough calculations might therefore suggest that at this writing, America's population of non-institutionalized adults with a felony conviction somewhere in their past has almost certainly broken the 20 million mark by the end of 2016. A little more rough arithmetic suggests that about 17 million men in our general population have a felony conviction somewhere in their CV. That works out to one of every eight adult males in America today.

We have to use rough estimates here, rather than precise official numbers, because the government does not collect any data at all on the size or socioeconomic circumstances of this population of 20 million, and never has. Amazing as this may sound and scandalous though it may be, America has, at least to date, effectively banished this huge group—a group roughly twice the total size of our illegal-immigrant population and an adult population larger than that in any state but California—to a near-total and seemingly unending statistical invisibility. Our ex-cons are, so to speak, statistical outcasts who live in a darkness our polity does not care enough to illuminate—beyond the scope or interest of public policy, unless and until they next run afoul of the law.

Thus, we cannot describe with any precision or certainty what has become of those who make up our "criminal class" after their (latest) sentencing or release. In the most stylized terms, however, we might guess that their odds in the real America are not all that favorable. And when we consider some of the other trends we have already mentioned—employment, health, addiction, and welfare dependence—we can see the emergence of a malign new nationwide undertow, pulling downward against social mobility.

Social mobility has always been the jewel in the crown of the American mythos and ethos. The idea (not without a measure of truth to back it up) was that people in America are free to achieve according to their merit and their grit—unlike in other places, where they are trapped by barriers of class or the misfortune of misrule. Nearly two decades into our new century, there are unmistakable signs that America's fabled social mobility is in trouble—perhaps even in serious trouble.

Consider the following facts. First, according to the Census Bureau, geographical mobility in America has been on the decline for three decades, and in 2016, the annual movement of households from one location to the next was reportedly at an all-time (postwar) low. Second, as a study by three Federal Reserve economists and a Notre Dame colleague demonstrated last year, "labor market fluidity"—the churning between jobs that among other things allows people to get ahead—has been on the decline in the American labor market for decades, with no sign as yet of a turnaround. Finally, and not least important, a December 2016 report by the "Equal Opportunity Project," a team led by the formidable Stanford economist Raj Chetty, calculated that the odds of a 30-year-old's earning more than his parents at the same age was now just 51 percent: down from 86 percent 40 years ago. Other researchers who have examined the same data argue that the odds may not be quite as low as the Chetty team concludes, but agree that the chances of surpassing one's parents' real income have been on the down-swing and are probably lower now than ever before in postwar America.

Thus, the bittersweet reality of life for real Americans in the early 21st century: Even though the American economy still remains the world's unrivaled engine of wealth generation, those outside the bubble may have less of a shot at the American Dream than has been the case for decades, maybe generations—possibly even since the Great Depression.

IV

The funny thing is, people inside the bubble are forever talking about "economic inequality," that wonderful seminar construct, and forever virtue-signaling about how personally opposed they are to it. By contrast, "economic insecurity" is akin to a phrase from an unknown language. But if we were somehow to find a "Google Translate" function for communicating from real America into the bubble, an important message might be conveyed.

The abstraction of "inequality" doesn't matter a lot to ordinary Americans. The reality of economic insecurity does. The Great American Escalator is broken—and it badly needs to be fixed.

With the election of 2016, Americans within the bubble finally learned that the 21st century has gotten off to a very bad start in America. Welcome to the reality. We have a lot of work to do together to turn this around.

Critical Thinking

1. How can adults maintain a good psychological outlook in light of such a gloomy report of our society?

2. How can we reduce the opioid epidemic?

3. How can we create a better outlook for our nation?

Internet References

A Bad Economy Means More Reasons to Watch Our Mental Health at Work

https://beta.theglobeandmail.com/report-on-business/rob-commentary/a-bad-economy-means-more-reasons-to-watch-our-mental-health-at-work/article26373227/?ref=http://www.theglobeandmail.com

Distress, Status Wars and Immoral Behaviour: The Psychological Impacts of Inequality

https://theconversation.com/distress-status-wars-and-immoral-behaviour-the-psychological-impacts-of-inequality-75183

How Do Psychological Factors Affect the Economy?

http://bigthink.com/videos/re-how-do-psychological-factors-affect-the-economy

The Effect of Economic, Physical, and Psychological Abuse on Mental Health: A Population-based Study of Women in the Philippines

https://www.hindawi.com/journals/ijfm/2014/852317/

What the Economic Downturn Means for Children, Youth, and Families

http://www.apa.org/pi/families/resources/economy.aspx

NICHOLAS EBERSTADT holds the Henry Wendt Chair in Political Economy at the American Enterprise Institute and is author of Men Without Work: America's Invisible Crisis (Templeton Press, 2016), upon which this essay draws and extends. He has been writing for Commentary since 1980.

Unit 7

UNIT

Prepared by: Claire N. Rubman, *Suffolk County Community College, Selden, NY*

Development during Middle to Late Adulthood

The focus shifts in this final unit as we shine the spotlight on ourselves as we age. This collection of articles focuses primarily on retirement, declines in our brain as we age and elder abuse. Do we plan properly for our retirement? Can we plan for the inevitable declines in our cognitive capacity and physical well-being? What can we do to delay that inevitable decline in our brains and how can we enjoy living our life to the fullest extent even as we age? Finally, how can we identify and prevent the abuse of the elderly in our society?

As our aging population focuses on retirement, they have to contend with a lack of, or change in, routine. Retirement today has increased in time as a result of an increase in life expectancy for both men and women. The impact of more education, more years in the workforce, and more retirement years is discussed in Clark's article titled "Pick Your Path to Retirement."

During the normal course of development our brain will age along with our body. Barry Volk discusses the particulars of what we can expect as we age. Our brain will shrink, we lose dopamine and our dendrites lose their connectivity. We also face a deterioration in our myelin sheath that insulates our neural pathways. Volk (2015) suggests several ways to combat these losses including the consumption of polyphenols (eat pomegranates!) and resveratrol (eat red grapes!) in his article titled "Combat Age-Related Brain Atrophy." Similarly, Rivington (2016)

touts the benefits of magnesium in the adult diet. Read about this development by MIT scientists as they discuss neural plasticity, memory, and learning as we age. The discussion continues as Klein and Price (2016) suggest that the dinner that we eat could potentially save us from Alzheimer's disease. Read about the benefits of a Mediterranean diet versus a high carbohydrate diet in "Could Cooking a Different Dinner Save You From Alzheimer's?"

As our brains deteriorate and our health declines, changes in the brain can lead some elderly people to believe that they have been mistreated. Sadly, this is often true. The tragic subject of elder abuse is discussed in "The Shock of Elder Abuse in Assisted Living." Lois Bowers is appalled to discover elder abuse in assisted living facilities. She suggests ways to combat physical, psychological, and sexual abuse including neglect, medication errors, and inappropriate behaviors. Learn about warning sign that elder abuse is occurring. She offers a myriad of suggestions to combat this abuse.

This Unit ends with a depressing and scathing condemnation of our society's treatment of the elderly. Bacon (2016) describes the lives of our elderly as "undignified" characterizes them as "vulnerable and precarious." He even suggests that their human rights are being violated. Perhaps we can collectively find a better way to honor the seniors in our lives.

Article   Prepared by: Claire N. Rubman, *Suffolk County Community College, Selden, NY*

PICK Your PATH to Retirement

Once, retirement meant hitting the golf course or sitting by the pool. The new retirement? Whatever you want it to be.

JANE BENNETT CLARK

Learning Outcomes

After reading this article, you will be able to:

- Explain what is meant by the term "the new retirement."

- Articulate 6 tips that may lead to a more enjoyable retirement.

Look up *retire* in the dictionary and here's what you'll find: "To retreat from action or danger. To withdraw for privacy, to recede. To conclude a career."

Retreat, recede, conclude are not words in Priscilla Jackman's vocabulary. In 2008, she retired from a 33-year teaching career in the Steel Valley school district, outside Pittsburgh, and immediately returned to the same district as a consultant on literacy programs. Four years later, she "retired" from that gig and took a five- to seven-hour-a-week job mentoring student teachers at a nearby university. Now 61, Jackman enjoys mentoring, but she says, "I don't see myself doing it until I'm 70." She definitely sees herself doing "something else"—maybe tutoring elementary school kids as a volunteer.

The beauty of Jackman's setup is that with a shorter work schedule, she has plenty of time to take guitar and violin lessons, act as social director for her extended family, sing in a volunteer hospital program and explore back roads with her husband, Tom, who is also retired. "We set the GPS and see where it takes us," she says. "We love finding great little towns and great diners." Rather than define her postcareer life as a slow fade into the sunset, she says, "I'm in awe of what it's possible to do as a retiree."

In fact, demographic changes have turned the standard definition of retirement upside down. Life expectancy has increased steadily over the decades. Now, a man who reaches 65 can expect to live another 18 years; a 65-year-old woman can expect to live 20 years. Plus, people work longer than in past decades, thanks to better health and a higher level of education, which generally leads to more gratifying, less-strenuous work.

With more time and opportunities, many retirees are phasing in and out of work, taking part-time, seasonal or consulting jobs or acting as entrepreneurs. Some post-66-ers work because they need the money, but the majority are taking advantage of the resources they have (including Social Security, savings and maybe a pension) to seek work that is more enjoyable and less stressful than their career was, says Nicole Maestas, a senior economist at the Rand Corp. who has studied older workers. For many, "retirement connotes a broader set of options," she says. "It's a new phase of life."

Explore the Possibilities

Having more time to work and play may sound delightful, but figuring out how to do it over 20 or 30 years is no last-minute exercise. Experiment by pursuing hobbies, volunteering at places where you might want to work, and thinking carefully about whether you want to downsize or move to another city altogether, says Larry Rosenthal, a certified financial planner in Manassas, Va. "People retire to a place and then think, *The grandkids are back where we were,* and they want to move back. Or they discover that Florida gets really hot in the summer."

One way to get a sense of what you want to do a few years hence is through a "practice retirement." That idea, proposed by investment firm T. Rowe Price, has you continue to work at your career job but back off on saving for retirement—say, by contributing only enough to your 401(k) to get the company match. Then you can use the money you've freed up (plus vacation time) to try out your ideas, such as traveling cross-country or turning your hobby into a side business.

Cutting back on contributions to savings in your early sixties may sound like heresy, but the key is staying on the job and waiting to take Social Security until full retirement age (66 until 2021) or later. For each year you delay taking Social Security after 66 until age 70, you get an 8% bump in benefits. And while you're still pulling in a paycheck, you can let your retirement savings grow, even if you're not contributing to your accounts. "It's a way to stay in the workforce and have a little fun while doing it," says Judith Ward, a senior financial planner at T. Rowe Price.

Plan to Work Longer

In most professions, employers can no longer require you to retire at a certain age, but keeping yourself relevant in your current career or attractive to your next employer is on you, says Catherine Collinson, president of the Transamerica Center for Retirement Studies. That includes keeping your skills up-to-date, maintaining and expanding your network, staying on top of the job market, and taking classes or going to school for another degree.

Peter Sefton of Alexandria, Va., accepted the challenge and took it to a whole new level. After working for the U.S. Census Bureau for 24 years, he enrolled in a master's degree program at the University of Virginia, leaving his wife, Linda, to hold down the fort in Alexandria for the next two years. "My retirement party was on Friday. I packed up my desk, and on Monday morning, I was in Charlottesville with the 25-year-olds," says Sefton, who was then 59. A federal pension provided financial underpinning. In addition, he was awarded a fellowship to help pay for his degree in architectural history, an extension of his longtime interest in historic preservation. Now 63, he works about 25 hours a week as a consultant on building preservation (and is happily back in Alexandria with his wife).

Look into phasing out

Not interested in reinventing yourself? Consider staying at the job you have but changing from full-time to part-time work or to a less demanding role. Some employers offer formal phased-retirement programs that let you cut your hours or work only part of the year, or trade managerial responsibilities for a mentoring role. The federal government recently launched a program in which eligible employees can work half-time, training less-experienced employees.

If your employer has no formal program, scope out the feasibility of making your own arrangement. Start by checking with the human resources department. "Have a clear vision of what you want and be very specific," says Collinson. Some companies only want full-time employees, she says; proposing anything else is a nonstarter. "There's homework to be done before you even have a conversation with your boss," she says.

While you're talking to HR, find out how changing from full-time to part-time status would affect your eligibility for employee benefits. Only half of the employers who offer 401(k) allow part-time employees to participate in the plan, according to a recent survey by the Transamerica Center. And a report by the Employee Benefit Research Institute shows that fewer than half of large employers (those with 200 or more employees) and one-third of smaller employers offer health coverage to part-time workers.

If you continue to work past 65, you'll have to coordinate your health coverage with Medicare. At 65, you qualify for Medicare Part A, which covers hospital services and is free. At that point, you can also enroll in Medicare Part B (for doctor visits) and buy Medicare supplemental coverage and Part D (for prescription drugs), or enroll in a Medicare Advantage plan, which combines the two and offers other benefits.

If your company has 20 or more employees, employer-based coverage pays first, and you can stay on it if you work enough hours to be eligible. In that case, just sign up for Part A; when you do retire, you can sign up for Part B and the other coverage without penalty or having to wait for open enrollment. If your company has fewer than 20 employees, Medicare becomes your primary insurance, even if your employer offers its own coverage—so if you don't sign up for Medicare, you may not be covered at all. Be sure to talk to your employer about what your options are.

Line Up Your Finances

Whether you figure on working well past retirement age or kicking back on day one, anticipate how you'll handle ongoing expenses plus potential curveballs, such as a downturn in the stock market or a health problem that could force you to retire early. Mark Thorndyke, a Merrill Lynch wealth management adviser in Chicago, works with clients who are three to five years out to put together a financial plan and plug in what-if scenarios. "That helps clients get a good idea of what's achievable and what kind of planning they need to do now."

Start with a budget for necessary expenses, including food, housing and health care, as well as nice-to-haves, such as travel and trips to see the grandkids. Match the need-to-haves with guaranteed income, such as Social Security, pensions and maybe an annuity, and plan to tap your retirement portfolio to pay for the wants.

Many retirement planners recommend that you withdraw no more than 4% of total assets the first year and the same amount, adjusted for inflation, every year after that. But working longer lets you leave more of your savings intact and makes it easier to defer Social Security (and collect a bigger benefit). And because your earning power offsets risk, you can afford to take more risk in how you invest, says Matt Sadowsky, director of retirement at TD Ameritrade. "Instead of a traditional balanced portfolio in retirement—say, 50% stocks and 50% bonds—you might allocate 60% or more of your portfolio to stocks."

Not everyone delays taking Social Security. In fact, most people take it before 66. Be aware that your benefit is reduced based on the number of months you take it before full retirement age. Start taking it as soon as you turn 62 and it gets dinged by 25%. If you keep working after claiming Social Security but before you reach full retirement age, you'll also be subject to an earnings test, in which $1 is deducted from your benefit for every $2 you earn above the annual limit—$15,720 in 2015. (In the year you reach full retirement age, $1 is deducted in benefits for every $3 you earn above a higher limit, which is $41,880 in 2015.)

Another option: Claim Social Security at 66 but keep working and use your benefit checks to, say, travel or pay for college for the grandkids. "All of a sudden you get a couple of thousand dollars a month coming in—there's a lot you can do with that," says Rosenthal.

Don't forget about taxes

Up to 85% of your Social Security benefits may be subject to tax. That becomes almost a certainty if you're pulling in a paycheck while collecting benefits. Working can also put you in a higher tax bracket or keep you there, meaning you'll owe more on distributions from your pretax retirement accounts. From a tax perspective, you might be better off if you delay claiming Social Security until 70 and hold off on tapping pretax accounts until you turn 70½, when you are required to take minimum distributions.

Or keep your options open by funneling money into a Roth IRA. As long as you're older than 59½ and have had the account for at least five years, distributions, including earnings, are tax-free (you can withdraw contributions tax-free at any time). If most of your money is in a tax-deferred account, consider paying the necessary tax bill to convert a chunk of that money each year into a Roth. If you convert $10,000 a year from age 60 to 70, at 70 you will have $100,000 plus earnings sitting in a tax-free account. By about that time, says Rosenthal, "you're on Social Security and taking required minimum distributions, and you can take tax-free dollars to minimize the taxes."

Retire, Rinse, Repeat

Almost 20 years ago, Gregory Contro, now 52, had a frenetic, lucrative career as the head of a futures brokerage group on the Chicago Mercantile Exchange. By age 37, he was ready to move on. An avid tennis player, he retired from his first career and became a tennis coach for young, highlevel players in the Chicago area, a job he had already been doing on the side. "I had achieved a lot of my goals on the exchange and was going to try this new challenge."

Most people don't have the resources to retire at 52, much less 37. In making the transition, Contro had the luxury of knowing he could afford to hang up his career altogether. "I was able to save and got familiar with the concept of wealth management early. When I left the Merc, I knew I could pretty much do what I wanted if I didn't mess it up." He managed his assets conservatively, working with financial adviser Gayle Ronan, who has since retired. "She made me understand what I needed to live on comfortably, taking into account shocks that investments go through and shocks in your personal life that you have to account for," he says. "You have to build in some safety nets"—including, in his case, umbrella insurance because he works with kids in a physically demanding setting.

Contro could still retire if he chose to. "I work because I like to work," he says. But, like others his age, he has started preparing for a next act. Inspired by his relationship with companies including Fila sportswear and Wilson Racquet Sports, Contro is working toward a master's degree at Northwestern University in sports marketing, a career he hopes will last him until he fully retires. "Going back to school has been incredibly exhilarating for me mentally," says Contro, who is by far the oldest in his class.

Contro's experience reflects the growing awareness that productivity doesn't stop when a career ends. "You think, I want to make enough money to get out of the game, and then you realize, I'm just too young to retire—there are a lot of challenges out there," says Contro. "You become thirsty for something different."

So when does he actually plan to retire? He's not sure. "The one thing I do know is, I don't want to sit still."

Critical Thinking

1. Why has the concept of retirement changed in the twenty-first century?

2. What advice should be given to adolescents and young adults to allow them to plan for the optimal retirement experience?

Internet References

A Timeline of the Evolution of Retirement in the United States
   http://scholarship.law.georgetown.edu/cgi/viewcontent.cgi?article=1049 &context=legal&sei-redir=1&referer=http%3A%2F%2Fwww.bing.com%2 Fsearch%3Fq%3Dthe%2520history%2520of%2520retirement%26qs%3Dn%26

form%3DQBRE%26pq%3Dthe%2520history%2520of%2520retirement%26
sc%3D8-25%26sp%3D-1%26sk%3D%26cvid%3D583F98DAC8E4425BB481
4B4178DB15F9#search=%22history%20retirement%22

Retirement Planning Advice for Teens to 50+
http://hereandnow.wbur.org/2014/04/03/jaffe-rethinking-retirement

Retirement in the 21st Century
https://www.jrf.org.uk/report/retirement-21st-century

Retirement Planning in the 21st Century
https://www.piu.org/communicators/retirement-planning-in-the-21st-century

Article   Prepared by: Claire N. Rubman, *Suffolk County Community College, Selden, NY*

Combat Age-Related Brain Atrophy

BARRY VOLK

Learning Outcomes

After reading this article, you will be able to:

- Describe how to avoid brain shrinkage.

- Discuss the role that the amino acid homocusteine plays in brain shrinkage.

- Explain the "therapeutic window of opportunity."

Even if you seem perfectly healthy, you may be losing as much as 0.4% of your *brain mass* every year.[1,2] The rate of brain shrinkage increases with age and is a major factor in early cognitive decline and premature death.[2–7]

Studies show that older adults with significant brain shrinkage are much more likely to have cognitive and movement disorders than similarly aged people with normal brain size. They are also at an increased risk of vascular death and ischemic stroke.[4, 8–10]

In addition, atrophy of specific brain regions has been associated with a variety of cognitive, behavioral, and mental health problems. Shrinkage of the temporal lobes, for example, is associated with a 181% increase in the risk of major depression.[7]

Perhaps most alarmingly, brain shrinkage sharply increases risk of early death:

- Younger individuals with overall brain shrinkage have as much as a 70% increase in the chance of dying,[5]

- In a study of people aged 85, temporal lobe atrophy is associated with a 60% increase in the risk of dying,[2]

- Severe atrophy of the frontal lobe (behind the forehead) increases the risk of death by 30%.[2]

Brains also shrink from the inside out, resulting in enlargement of the fluid-filled *ventricles,* or hollow spaces on the interior of the brain; such shrinkage has its own modest effect on early death.[2]

Even though brain shrinkage is progressive, a growing number of neuroscientists believe that brain shrinkage can be *slowed* or even *reversed.*[11–13] In this article, we will share with you how lifestyle changes and proper supplementation can help prevent this devastating cause of cognitive decline and premature death.

Brain Shrinkage Is Not Inevitable

Like so many of the symptoms of aging, brain shrinkage was long thought to be simply an inevitable consequence of growing older. However, we are learning that brain atrophy is by no means inevitable. A host of conditions—from cardiovascular disease and diabetes to sleep and anxiety disorders to lifestyle choices—have been associated with brain shrinkage. Since many of these are reversible or at least preventable, it's important to understand their impact on brain shrinkage, cognition, and life span.

The Connection Between Cardiovascular Disease and Brain Shrinkage

Although we don't often hear about this, there is a strong connection between cardiovascular disease and brain shrinkage.

Perhaps the most obvious connection is the one between blood vessel disease (atherosclerosis) and brain volume. Atherosclerosis occurs when plaque builds up inside your arteries and restricts blood flow throughout the body. Although we typically think of the negative effect atherosclerosis has on the heart, its effect on your brain can be equally devastating.

When blood flow to the brain is restricted, your brain receives less oxygen and fewer nutrients, causing it to shrink. Studies show that people with lower levels of blood flow to the brain have smaller total brain volumes and total thickness of the cortex (the active surface layer of the brain)—resulting in poorer performance on tests of cognitive function.[14]

In addition, disease of the coronary arteries (the arteries that feed the heart muscle) is also associated with decreased brain volume. When compared to healthy controls, patients with coronary artery disease had significantly smaller gray matter volume in several regions of their brains.[15] This is especially significant since gray matter is where all thinking, feeling, sensory, and motor function originates.

The relationship between cardiovascular disease and brain volume operates in both directions: People with smaller brain volumes have been found to have a 58% increase in the risk of death from all causes, a 69% increase in risk of vascular death, and a 96% increase in the risk of stroke, compared with those having normal brain volumes.[10]

Several other risk factors commonly associated with cardiovascular disease may also predict brain shrinkage. For example, people carrying the **ApoE4 gene variant** have significantly smaller overall brain size—with a specific decrease in brain areas that process memory and emotion.[16]

High levels of the amino acid **homocysteine**, another risk factor typically associated with heart disease, have now also been connected to brain shrinkage (independent of its impact on cardiovascular disease).

Specifically, studies have shown that people with high levels of homocysteine have smaller volumes of gray matter in the brain—and as a result, have worse scores on many tests of cognitive function.[17]

This was especially evident in a study of a group of people who had recently suffered strokes. The researchers found that those with the highest homocysteine levels had a tremendous **8.8-fold** increase in risk of brain shrinkage (compared with those having the lowest).[18] Other studies have demonstrated that the higher the level of plasma homocysteine, the greater the rate of brain atrophy and the risk for Parkinson's and Alzheimer's diseases.[19–22]

A deficiency of B vitamins has also been tied to brain shrinkage. This makes sense, since inadequate amounts of vitamins B6, B12, and folic acid can lead to elevated homocysteine levels. This occurs because these vitamins play a role in converting homocysteine into an important protein building block and when there's a shortage of B vitamins, that conversion process isn't as efficient, and homocysteine levels increase.[13,23]

Close associations have been found between low levels of folate, for example, and severe gray matter atrophy and atrophy of the hippocampus, a main memory-processing center in the brain.[24,25] Similarly, people with lower vitamin B12 levels have been shown to have progressive brain atrophy, with rates of brain volume loss 517% greater than those with higher levels.[13,26]

Remarkably, it has been found that brain shrinkage due to high homocysteine levels must reach a critical level before cognitive decline sets in.[21] This is another example of the "therapeutic window of opportunity" during which brain shrinkage may be prevented by adequate supplementation, as we'll see later.[27]

Protect Against Brain Shrinkage

- Your brain is shrinking as you age, costing you memories and mental sharpness.
- Worse, brain shrinkage has been directly associated with premature death.
- Causes of brain shrinkage are closely related to symptoms of aging, including cardiovascular disease, obesity, diabetes, and even poor sleep habits and distress.
- You may be able to prevent brain shrinkage by adopting healthy lifestyle habits and using supplements that target your own aging body's vulnerabilities.
- Supplements that reduce your cardiovascular risk, lower your blood sugar, or improve your sleep, for example, may do double duty in slowing or stopping brain shrinkage and improving your chances for a long, mentally fit life.

The Connection Between Diabetes and Brain Shrinkage

Diabetes is notorious for causing problems with the **peripheral nervous system**,[28] leading to conditions such as painful diabetic neuropathy and blindness-inducing diabetic retinopathy. New findings suggest that high blood sugar levels—and the *advanced glycation end products* (AGEs) that they produce—cause damage to the **central nervous system** as well, specifically neurodegeneration and brain atrophy.[29–31]

Studies have shown that, when compared to non-diabetic people of similar age, diabetics have an average of **4%** smaller hippocampal volume, a nearly 3% reduction in whole brain volume, and double the risk of mild cognitive impairment.[32,33]

In addition to causing brain shrinkage, studies now suggest that diabetes induces toxic, misfolded proteins quite similar to those found in neurodegenerative diseases such as Alzheimer's, pointing to yet another way that diabetes can damage brain cells.[34] Indeed, diabetes and Alzheimer's disease share many properties, including defective insulin release and signaling, impaired glucose uptake from the blood, increased oxidative stress, stimulation of brain cell death by apoptosis,[35,36] blood vessel abnormalities, and problems with energy production in mitochondria.[37,38]

Obesity and Your Brain

Like diabetes, obesity is a known cause of brain atrophy.[39] Even in people with normal cognition, higher body mass index (BMI, a measure of obesity) is associated with lower brain volume in obese and overweight people.[40]

Obesity and diabetes share many similar mechanisms, including insulin resistance and oxidative stress, both of which are known to contribute to brain atrophy.[38,41] In addition, fat deposits produce huge amounts of inflammatory signaling molecules (cytokines) that may contribute to brain cell death and brain volume loss.[39]

Additional links between obesity and brain shrinkage may be even more fundamental. About **46%** of Western Europeans and their descendants carry a gene variant called *FTO,* which is associated with fat mass and obesity. People who carry this gene weigh on average about **2.64 pounds** more and have an extra half-inch of waist circumference compared to those who lack the gene variant.[42] Recent findings show that carriers of the FTO gene variant have approximately 8% smaller frontal lobe volumes, and **12%** smaller occipital (back of the brain) volumes than people who don't carry this gene variant. These changes were *not* associated with differences in cholesterol levels or blood pressure, suggesting an independent relationship.[42]

Sleep Disruptions

Sleep disruptions and anxiety also contribute to loss of brain volume. Relatively healthy older adults with short sleep duration have significantly smaller brains than those with longer sleep duration. In addition, for every hour of reduced sleep duration, they experience a **0.59%** yearly increase in the size of the blood-filled ventricles, and a **0.67%** decrease in cognitive performance.[43] Similarly, increases in brain shrinkage are associated with decreased quality of sleep as well.[44]

Poor sleep and anxiety, of course, are related, and one study has shown that middle-aged women who have had longstanding psychological distress (based on a standard questionnaire) are at a **51%** increased risk of moderate-to-severe atrophy of the temporal lobes.[6]

Smoking and Drinking

Smoking has been recognized as a cause of brain shrinkage since at least 1987.[45,46] More recent studies have confirmed and extended this association, with evidence that any lifetime history of smoking (even if you currently do not smoke) is associated with faster brain shrinkage in multiple brain regions, compared with people who never smoked.[47]

Chronic alcohol consumption has also been associated with brain shrinkage, but in a dose-dependent way. While light-to-moderate drinkers have *larger* total brain volume than nondrinkers,[48] heavy drinkers are **80%** more likely than nondrinkers to sustain frontal lobe shrinkage, compared with nondrinkers,[49] and **32%** more likely to have enlargement of the ventricles, indicating shrinkage from within.[50] (A heavy drinker is defined as someone who consumes more than about **15 ounces** of pure alcohol per week. A standard drink is equal to **14.0 grams,** or **0.6 ounces,** of pure alcohol.)

Natural Supplements That Protect Brain Volume

Even though the array of factors that can cause brain shrinkage can be daunting, there is good news. Since brain shrinkage results from the same basic processes that cause other symptoms of aging, it's likely that brain shrinkage is preventable— *especially when caught early enough.*

That's why we want to provide you with information on key nutrients that have been shown to powerfully protect the brain. Here are four of the most potent brain-protecting nutrients.

B Vitamins

B vitamins are essential for supporting normal metabolic function, especially in the regulation of homocysteine[51] (and elevated homocysteine, as we have seen, leads to significant brain shrinkage and dementia, especially when B-vitamins are deficient).[18,27,52,53]

Elderly people are now generally advised to maintain optimal B-vitamin status—and for good reason.[13,54] Studies show that people with higher folate levels have slower rates of brain atrophy and a lower rate of conversion from mild cognitive impairment to actual dementia, and those who take folate or B12 have lower grades of brain white matter abnormalities.[53,55]

While each of these B vitamins provides its own unique benefits, several recent studies show why it's beneficial to supplement with a combination of folate, vitamin B6, and vitamin B12. This was clearly seen in a double-blind, placebo-controlled clinical trial in adults over age 70 who had mild cognitive impairment.[56]

For the study, one group of subjects took folate (**800 mcg/day**), vitamin B12 (**500 mcg/day**), and vitamin B6 (**20 mg/day**), while the other group took placebo.[56] After two years, supplemented patients' brains shrank at an annual rate that was **30%** slower than those taking the placebo. Supplemented patients whose homocysteine levels were abnormally high at baseline had a **53%** slower brain shrinkage rate than unsupplemented patients, showing that supplementing with B vitamins is especially important in people who have high homocysteine levels.

A follow-up study showed that brain areas most susceptible to atrophy in the early development of Alzheimer's disease are especially well-protected by the same B-vitamin regimen, with supplemented patients experiencing as much as a **7-fold** reduction in shrinkage of those regions.[57] Another study, using the same doses of B vitamins, found that supplemented patients had 30% lower mean plasma homocysteine levels, and slower rates of cognitive decline on multiple standard tests.[58]

Omega-3 Fatty Acids

Omega-3 fatty acids comprise a large and important portion of brain cell membranes, where they participate in a wide variety of cellular functions. Indeed, **30** to **50%** of the fatty acids in brain cell membranes are long-chain polyunsaturated fatty acids that include the vital *omega-3* group. Brain cell membranes are especially rich in **DHA,** an essential fatty acid derived only from the diet.[59,60]

Omega-3s have many functions that help protect brain cells. Omega-3 fats are known to enhance the brain's relaxing functions.[61] This protects brain cells from overexcitation, which is a major cause of brain cell damage that occurs with aging.[62] Omega-3s also help preserve brain cell function by increasing the production of anti-inflammatory signaling molecules in the brain.[59,63] Similarly, omega-3 fats in brain tissue protect cells from damage induced by stress and elevated stress steroids.[63]

The importance of this protection is especially seen when there's not enough of this vital nutrient. Indeed, abnormal distributions of fatty acids in brain cells are associated with a variety of mental health disorders, particularly major depression and bipolar disorder.[64]

It is not surprising, then, that age-related changes in brain cell omega-3 fat composition raise the risk of brain abnormalities as people age.[65] By contrast, studies show that a higher omega-3 index (which is the sum of the omega-3 fats EPA plus DHA), is correlated with larger brain volume.[66]

Unfortunately, aging is associated with a significant decline in DHA levels in the brain, a drop that is sharply worsened in Alzheimer's disease and possibly other neurodegenerative disorders.[67, 68] This highlights the importance of protecting your brain by supplementing with omega-3 fats.

Pomegranate

Pomegranates contain very high levels of polyphenols, which are plant-derived molecules with anti-inflammatory and neuroprotective properties.[69] Animal studies reveal that supplementing with pomegranate juice slows the development of Alzheimer-like disease, a major cause of brain atrophy.[69–71] This protection may arise from the ability of the polyphenols in pomegranate to slow or stop brain cell death.[72]

Human studies demonstrate significant improvements in cognition and memory with consumption of 8 ounces of pomegranate juice daily, and lab studies with human brain cells in culture show that pomegranate polyphenols protect cells against changes that occur in other neurodegenerative diseases.[73,74]

Resveratrol

Resveratrol is a major component of red grapes and certain other dark fruits; it has seen widespread use in preventing aging and age-related cardiovascular and neurologic conditions. Studies in a mouse model of chronic fatigue syndrome (which can produce brain shrinkage) show that four weeks of resveratrol therapy increased the animals' daily physical activity by more than **20%,** possibly as a result of reduced brain cell death.[75] In addition, the volume of the memory-intensive hippocampus was larger following supplementation.

Researchers are also exploring resveratrol as a potent neuroprotectant against the brain-shrinking effects of obesity and a high-fat diet. In studies of obese animals (obesity is a cause of brain shrinkage), resveratrol protected brain tissue from oxidative damage, a precursor to brain cell death.[76] And in mice fed a high-fat diet, resveratrol similarly protected against oxidative damage to the vital blood-brain barrier and decreased injury to the endothelial cells in the brain.[77]

These findings in animals may explain the results of a compelling human study in **2014,** which demonstrated that, in healthy overweight older adults, supplementing with **200 mg/day** of resveratrol improved the functional connections between the hippocampus and the frontal areas of the brain.[78] Such changes were accompanied by improved memory performance as well as better blood sugar control, again pointing to the complex interactions of metabolism and brain performance.

Summary

Brain shrinkage is a silent threat to our health and longevity. Loss of brain volume means loss of brain cells, which in turn means loss of memory and learning.

There are a myriad of threats to brain volume as we age. Virtually all of the chronic symptoms of aging have been associated with, and to some extent implicated in, brain shrinkage. In addition, lifestyle habits such as a high-fat diet, sedentary behavior, and smoking or excess drinking can further complicate matters.

Fortunately, like other symptoms of aging, brain shrinkage appears to be preventable through a combination of lifestyle changes and sensible supplementation. Start by identifying which aging symptoms most directly affect you, and then focus your supplement regimen on controlling or reversing those factors. With proper care, your brain can maintain its youthful volume and function for years to come.

References

1. Enzinger C, Fazekas F, Matthews PM, et al. Risk factors for progression of brain atrophy in aging: six-year follow-up of normal subjects. *Neurology.* 2005 May 24;64(10):1704–11.

2. Hedman AM. Human brain changes across the life span: a review of 56 longitudinal magnetic resonance imaging studies. *Human Brain Mapping.* 2012;33:1987–220.

3. Olesen PJ, Guo X, Gustafson D, et al. A population-based study on the influence of brain atrophy on 20-year survival after age 85. *Neurology.* 2011 Mar 8;76(10):879–86.

4. Guo X, Steen B, Matousek M, et al. A population-based study on brain atrophy and motor performance in elderly women. *J Gerontol A Biol Sci Med Sci.* 2001 Oct;56(10):M633–7.

5. Henneman WJ, Sluimer JD, Cordonnier C, et al. MRI biomarkers of vascular damage and atrophy predicting mortality in a memory clinic population. *Stroke.* 2009 Feb;40(2):492–8.

6. Johansson L, Skoog I, Gustafson DR, et al. Midlife psychological distress associated with late-life brain atrophy and white matter lesions: a 32-year population study of women. *Psychosom Med.* 2012 Feb-Mar;74(2):120–5.

7. Olesen PJ, Gustafson DR, Simoni M, et al. Temporal lobe atrophy and white matter lesions are related to major depression over 5 years in the elderly. *Neuropsychopharmacology.* 2010 Dec;35(13):2638–45.

8. Debette S, Seshadri S, Beiser A, et al. Midlife vascular risk factor exposure accelerates structural brain aging and cognitive decline. *Neurology.* 2011 Aug 2;77(5):461–8.

9. Stoub TR, Detoledo-Morrell L, Dickerson BC. Parahippocampal white matter volume predicts Alzheimer's disease risk in cognitively normal old adults. *Neurobiol Aging.* 2014 Aug;35(8):1855–61.

10. van der Veen PH, Muller M, Vincken KL, Mali WP, van der Graaf Y, Geerlings MI. Brain volumes and risk of cardiovascular events and mortality. The SMART-MR study. *Neurobiol Aging.* 2014 Jul;35(7):1624–31.

11. Draganski B, Lutti A, Kherif F. Impact of brain aging and neuro-degeneration on cognition: evidence from MRI. *Curr Opin Neurol.* 2013 Dec;26(6):640–5.

12. Akinyemi RO, Mukaetova-Ladinska EB, Attems J, Ihara M, Kalaria RN. Vascular risk factors and neurodegeneration in ageing related dementias: Alzheimer's disease and vascular dementia. *Curr Alzheimer Res.* 2013 Jul;10(6):642–53.

13. Grober U, Kisters K, Schmidt J. Neuroenhancement with vitamin B12-underestimated neurological significance. *Nutrients.* 2013 Dec;5(12):5031–45.

14. Alosco ML, Gunstad J, Jerskey BA, et al. The adverse effects of reduced cerebral perfusion on cognition and brain structure in older adults with cardiovascular disease. *Brain Behav.* 2013 Nov;3(6):626–36.

15. Anazodo UC, Shoemaker JK, Suskin N, St Lawrence KS. An investigation of changes in regional gray matter volume in cardiovascular disease patients, pre and post cardiovascular rehabilitation. *Neuroimage Clin.* 2013;3:388–95.

16. Cherbuin N, Leach LS, Christensen H, Anstey KJ. Neuroimaging and APOE genotype: a systematic qualitative review. *Dement Geriatr Cogn Disord.* 2007;24(5):348–62.

17. Ford AH, Garrido GJ, Beer C, et al. Homocysteine, grey matter and cognitive function in adults with cardiovascular disease. *PLoS One.* 2012;7(3):e33345.

18. Yang LK, Wong KC, Wu MY, Liao SL, Kuo CS, Huang RF. Correlations between folate, B12, homocysteine levels, and radiological markers of neuropathology in elderly post-stroke patients. *J Am Coll Nutr.* 2007 Jun;26(3):272–8.

19. Narayan SK, Firbank MJ, Saxby BK, et al. Elevated plasma homocysteine is associated with increased brain atrophy rates in older subjects with mild hypertension. *Dement Geriatr Cogn Disord.* 2011;31(5):341–8.

20. Rajagopalan P, Hua X, Toga AW, Jack CR, Jr., Weiner MW, Thompson PM. Homocysteine effects on brain volumes mapped in 732 elderly individuals. *Neuroreport.* 2011 Jun 11;22(8):391–5.

21. de Jager CA. Critical levels of brain atrophy associated with homocysteine and cognitive decline. *Neurobiol Aging.* 2014 Sep;35 Suppl 2:S35–9.

22. Sapkota S, Gee M, Sabino J, Emery D, Camicioli R. Association of homocysteine with ventricular dilatation and brain atrophy in Parkinson's disease. *Mov Disord.* 2014 Mar;29(3):368–74.

23. Herrmann W, Obeid R. Homocysteine: a biomarker in neurodegenerative diseases. *Clin Chem Lab Med.* 2011 Mar;49(3):435–41.

24. Gallucci M, Zanardo A, Bendini M, Di Paola F, Boldrini P, Grossi E. Serum folate, homocysteine, brain atrophy, and auto-CM system: The Treviso Dementia (TREDEM) study. *J Alzheimers Dis.* 2014;38(3):581–7.

25. Squire LR. Memory and the hippocampus: a synthesis from findings with rats, monkeys, and humans. *Psychol Rev.* 1992 Apr;99(2):195–231.

26. Vogiatzoglou A, Refsum H, Johnston C, et al. Vitamin B12 status and rate of brain volume loss in community-dwelling elderly. *Neurology.* 2008 Sep 9;71(11):826–32.

27. Nachum-Biala Y, Troen AM. B-vitamins for neuroprotection: narrowing the evidence gap. *Biofactors.* 2012 Mar-Apr;38(2):145–50.

28. Cade WT. Diabetes-related microvascular and macrovascular diseases in the physical therapy setting. *Phys Ther.* 2008 Nov;88(11):1322–35.

29. Toth C, Martinez J, Zochodne DW. RAGE, diabetes, and the nervous system. *Curr Mol Med.* 2007 Dec;7(8):766–76.

30. Biessels GJ, Reijmer YD. Brain changes underlying cognitive dysfunction in diabetes: what can we learn from MRI? *Diabetes.* 2014 Jul;63(7):2244–52.

31. Moran C, Munch G, Forbes JM, et al. Type 2 diabetes mellitus, skin autofluorescence and brain atrophy. *Diabetes.* 2014 Jul 22.

32. Roberts RO, Knopman DS, Przybelski SA, et al. Association of type 2 diabetes with brain atrophy and cognitive impairment. *Neurology*. 2014 Apr 1;82(13):1132–41.

33. Wisse LE, de Bresser J, Geerlings MI, et al. Global brain atrophy but not hippocampal atrophy is related to type 2 diabetes. *J Neurol Sci*. 2014 Sep 15;344(1–2):32–6.

34. Ashraf GM, Greig NH, Khan TA, et al. Protein misfolding and aggregation in Alzheimer's disease and type 2 diabetes mellitus. *CNS Neurol Disord Drug Targets*. 2014;13(7):1280–93.

35. Britton M, Rafols J, Alousi S, Dunbar JC. The effects of middle cerebral artery occlusion on central nervous system apoptotic events in normal and diabetic rats. *Int J Exp Diabesity Res*. 2003 Jan-Mar;4(1):13–20.

36. Smale G, Nichols NR, Brady DR, Finch CE, Horton WE Jr. Evidence for apoptotic cell death in Alzheimer's disease. *Exp Neurol*. 1995 Jun;133(2):225–30.

37. Adeghate E, Donath T, Adem A. Alzheimer disease and diabetes mellitus: do they have anything in common? *Curr Alzheimer Res*. 2013 Jul;10(6):609–17.

38. Moroz N, Tong M, Longato L, Xu H, de la Monte SM. Limited Alzheimer-type neurodegeneration in experimental obesity and type 2 diabetes mellitus. *J Alzheimers Dis*. 2008 Sep;15(1):29–44.

39. Kiliaan AJ, Arnoldussen IA, Gustafson DR. Adipokines: a link between obesity and dementia? *Lancet Neurol*. 2014 Sep;13(9):913–23.

40. Raji CA, Ho AJ, Parikshak NN, et al. Brain structure and obesity. *Hum Brain Mapp*. 2010 Mar;31(3):353–64.

41. Fotuhi M, Hachinski V, Whitehouse PJ. Changing perspectives regarding late-life dementia. *Nat Rev Neurol*. 2009 Dec;5(12):649–58.

42. Ho AJ, Stein JL, Hua X, et al. A commonly carried allele of the obesity-related FTO gene is associated with reduced brain volume in the healthy elderly. *Proc Natl Acad Sci U S A*. 2010 May 4;107(18):8404–9.

43. Lo JC, Loh KK, Zheng H, Sim SK, Chee MW. Sleep duration and age-related changes in brain structure and cognitive performance. *Sleep*. 2014 Jul;37(7):1171–8.

44. Sexton CE, Storsve AB, Walhovd KB, Johansen-Berg H, Fjell AM. Poor sleep quality is associated with increased cortical atrophy in community-dwelling adults. *Neurology*. 2014 Sep 3.

45. Kubota K, Matsuzawa T, Fujiwara T, et al. Age-related brain atrophy enhanced by smoking: a quantitative study with computed tomography. *Tohoku J Exp Med*. 1987 Dec;153(4):303–11.

46. Durazzo TC, Meyerhoff DJ, Nixon SJ. Chronic cigarette smoking: implications for neurocognition and brain neurobiology. *Int J Environ Res Public Health*. 2010 Oct;7(10):3760–91.

47. Durazzo TC, Insel PS, Weiner MW. Greater regional brain atrophy rate in healthy elderly subjects with a history of cigarette smoking. *Alzheimers Dement*. 2012 Nov;8(6):513–9.

48. Gu Y, Scarmeas N, Short EE, et al. Alcohol intake and brain structure in a multiethnic elderly cohort. *Clin Nutr*. 2014 Aug;33(4):662–7.

49. Kubota M, Nakazaki S, Hirai S, Saeki N, Yamaura A, Kusaka T. Alcohol consumption and frontal lobe shrinkage: study of 1432 nonalcoholic subjects. *J Neurol Neurosurg Psychiatry*. 2001 Jul;71(1):104–6.

50. Mukamal KJ, Longstreth WT, Jr., Mittleman MA, Crum RM, Siscovick DS. Alcohol consumption and subclinical findings on magnetic resonance imaging of the brain in older adults: the cardiovascular health study. *Stroke*. 2001 Sep;32(9):1939–46.

51. Varela-Moreiras G. Nutritional regulation of homocysteine: effects of drugs. *Biomed Pharmacother*. 2001 Oct;55(8):448–53.

52. Polyak Z, Stern F, Berner YN, et al. Hyperhomocysteinemia and vitamin score: correlations with silent brain ischemic lesions and brain atrophy. *Dement Geriatr Cogn Disord*. 2003;16(1):39–45.

53. Blasko I, Hinterberger M, Kemmler G, et al. Conversion from mild cognitive impairment to dementia: influence of folic acid and vitamin B12 use in the VITA cohort. *J Nutr Health Aging*. 2012 Aug;16(8):687–94.

54. Smith AD, Refsum H. Vitamin B-12 and cognition in the elderly. *Am J Clin Nutr*. 2009 Feb;89(2):707s–11s.

55. Healthy Quality Ontario. Vitamin B12 and cognitive function: an evidence-based analysis. *Ont Health Technol Assess Ser*. 2013;13(23):1–45.

56. Smith AD, Smith SM, de Jager CA, et al. Homocysteine-lowering by B vitamins slows the rate of accelerated brain atrophy in mild cognitive impairment: a randomized controlled trial. *PLoS One*. 2010;5(9):e12244.

57. Douaud G, Refsum H, de Jager CA, et al. Preventing Alzheimer's disease-related gray matter atrophy by B-vitamin treatment. *Proc Natl Acad Sci U S A*. 2013 Jun 4;110(23):9523–8.

58. de Jager CA, Oulhaj A, Jacoby R, Refsum H, Smith AD. Cognitive and clinical outcomes of homocysteine-lowering B-vitamin treatment in mild cognitive impairment: a randomized controlled trial. *Int J Geriatr Psychiatry*. 2012 Jun;27(6):592–600.

59. Singh RB, Gupta S, Dherange P, et al. Metabolic syndrome: a brain disease. *Can J Physiol Pharmacol*. 2012 Sep;90(9):1171–83.

60. Nguyen LN, Ma D, Shui G, et al. Mfsd2a is a transporter for the essential omega-3 fatty acid docosahexaenoic acid. *Nature*. 2014 May 22;509(7501):503–6.

61. Sagduyu K, Dokucu ME, Eddy BA, Craigen G, Baldassano CF, Yildiz A. Omega-3 fatty acids decreased irritability of patients with bipolar disorder in an add-on, open label study. *Nutr J*. 2005 Feb 9;4:6.

62. Scrable H, Burns-Cusato M, Medrano S. Anxiety and the aging brain: stressed out over p53? *Biochim Biophys Acta*. 2009 Dec;1790(12):1587–91.

63. Hennebelle M, Champeil-Potokar G, Lavialle M, Vancassel S, Denis I. Omega-3 polyunsaturated fatty acids and chronic stress-induced modulations of glutamatergic neurotransmission in the hippocampus. *Nutr Rev*. 2014 Feb;72(2):99–112.

64. Tatebayashi Y, Nihonmatsu-Kikuchi N, Hayashi Y, Yu X, Soma M, Ikeda K. Abnormal fatty acid composition in the frontopolar

cortex of patients with affective disorders. *Transl Psychiatry.* 2012;2:e204.

65. Virtanen JK, Siscovick DS, Lemaitre RN, et al. Circulating omega-3 polyunsaturated fatty acids and subclinical brain abnormalities on MRI in older adults: the Cardiovascular Health Study. *J Am Heart Assoc.* 2013 Oct;2(5):e000305.

66. Pottala JV, Yaffe K, Robinson JG, Espeland MA, Wallace R, Harris WS. Higher RBC EPA + DHA corresponds with larger total brain and hippocampal volumes: WHIMS-MRI study. *Neurology.* 2014 Feb 4;82(5):435–42.

67. Torres M, Price SL, Fiol-Deroque MA, et al. Membrane lipid modifications and therapeutic effects mediated by hydroxydocosahexaenoic acid on Alzheimer's disease. *Biochim Biophys Acta.* 2014 Jun;1838(6):1680–92.

68. Zhang C, Bazan NG. Lipid-mediated cell signaling protects against injury and neurodegeneration. *J Nutr.* 2010 Apr;140(4):858–63.

69. Hartman RE, Shah A, Fagan AM, et al. Pomegranate juice decreases amyloid load and improves behavior in a mouse model of Alzheimer's disease. *Neurobiol Dis.* 2006 Dec;24(3):506–15.

70. Kumar S, Maheshwari KK, Singh V. Protective effects of Punica granatum seeds extract against aging and scopolamine induced cognitive impairments in mice. *Afr J Tradit Complement Altern Med.* 2008;6(1):49–56.

71. Rojanathammanee L, Puig KL, Combs CK. Pomegranate polyphenols and extract inhibit nuclear factor of activated T-cell activity and microglial activation in vitro and in a transgenic mouse model of Alzheimer disease. *J Nutr.* 2013 May;143(5):597–605.

72. Choi SJ, Lee JH, Heo HJ, et al. Punica granatum protects against oxidative stress in PC12 cells and oxidative stress-induced Alzheimer's symptoms in mice. *J Med Food.* 2011 Jul-Aug;14(7–8):695–701.

73. Bookheimer SY, Renner BA, Ekstrom A, et al. Pomegranate juice augments memory and FMRI activity in middle-aged and older adults with mild memory complaints. *Evid Based Complement Alternat Med.* 2013;2013:946298.

74. Forouzanfar F, Afkhami Goli A, Asadpour E, Ghorbani A, Sadeghnia HR. Protective effect of Punica granatum L. against serum/glucose deprivation-induced PC12 cells injury. *Evid Based Complement Alternat Med.* 2013;2013:716730.

75. Moriya J, Chen R, Yamakawa J, Sasaki K, Ishigaki Y, Takahashi T. Resveratrol improves hippocampal atrophy in chronic fatigue mice by enhancing neurogenesis and inhibiting apoptosis of granular cells. *Biol Pharm Bull.* 2011;34(3):354–9.

76. Rege SD, Kumar S, Wilson DN, et al. Resveratrol protects the brain of obese mice from oxidative damage. *Oxid Med Cell Longev.* 2013;2013:419092.

77. Chang HC, Tai YT, Cherng YG, et al. Resveratrol attenuates high-fat diet-induced disruption of the blood-brain barrier and protects brain neurons from apoptotic insults. *J Agric Food Chem.* 2014 Apr 16;62(15):3466–75.

78. Witte AV, Kerti L, Margulies DS, Floel A. Effects of resveratrol on memory performance, hippocampal functional connectivity, and glucose metabolism in healthy older adults. *J Neurosci.* 2014 Jun 4;34(23):7862–70.

Critical Thinking

1. How are middle aged men and women addressing the issues associated with brain shrinkage in their everyday lives?

2. What could we change in our daily diet to impact our brains as we age?

3. Is brain shrinkage an inevitable aspect of aging?

Internet References

Brain Food: 6 Snacks That Are Good for the Mind
http://www.telegraph.co.uk/news/science/science-news/11364896/Brain-food-6-snacks-that-are-good-for-the-mind.html

Brain Shrinkage
http://www.mayoclinic.org/diseases-conditions/mild-cognitive-impairment/multimedia/brain-shrinkage/img-20006725

Eat Smart for a Healthier Brain
http://www.webmd.com/diet/eat-smart-healthier-brain

Frontotemporal Dementia
http://www.alz.org/dementia/fronto-temporal-dementia-ftd-symptoms.asp

Study: 4 Factors That May Shrink Your Brain
http://healthland.time.com/2011/08/03/study-4-factors-that-may-shrink-your-brain/

Protect Your Brain Against Aging
http://alzdiscovery.org/cognitive-vitality

Article   Prepared by: Claire N. Rubman, *Suffolk County Community College, Selden, NY*

The Shock of Elder Abuse in Assisted Living

If you're like many recently surveyed, what you don't know may surprise you.

Lois A. Bowers

Learning Outcomes

After reading this article, you will be able to:

- Describe the nature of abuse in assisted living environments including medication errors and inappropriate sexual behavior.

- Discuss the discrepancy between nurse aides and executive directors with regard to rates of abuse.

- Articulate preventative measures suggested by the author.

Executive directors of assisted living communities may not be aware of all of the cases of elder abuse—especially sexual incidents—occurring in their communities. That's the conclusion of Marguerite "Marti" DeLiema, a doctoral candidate at the University of Southern California's (USC's) Davis School of Gerontology.

DeLiema discussed elder abuse with the more than 100 people attending the Assisted Living Federation of America (ALFA) Executive Director Leadership Institute (EDLI), held in conjunction with ALFA's annual meeting in May.

As part of her session, she polled attendees about their observations or suspicions of staff members' physical mistreatment of residents, mismanagement of resident medication (stealing residents' medication for themselves, giving medication intended for one resident to another resident or withholding medication from a resident) and inappropriate sexual behavior with residents within the past year.

When it came to physical mistreatment of residents or mismanagement of medication, EDLI participants' reporting of

observed or suspected incidents was similar to that of assisted living nurse aides surveyed by Nicholas Castle, PhD, and Scott Beach, PhD, for a large study published in the *Journal of Applied Gerontology.* Concerning sexually inappropriate behavior between a staff member and a resident, however, the executive directors reported a much lower frequency of this type of abuse than did the nurse aides, DeLiema says.

All but one responding executive director said they had never observed or suspected a staff member of such behavior, she says; one reported observing or suspecting one case. By comparison, the Castle and Beach study of nurse aides, DeLiema says, had "a lot more shocking results." For instance, three percent of the nurse aides surveyed said they knew of staff members' "unwelcome fondling" of a resident, and seven percent said they were aware of staff members who had exposed a resident's body part as a form of abuse.

"What really surprised me was the reaction of the audience to the Castle and Beach study results" related to sexual abuse, DeLiema says of EDLI participants. "They were really shocked by how high those rates were. They were shaking their heads and putting their hands over their mouths. They were really surprised. So that speaks to the fact that they just are not aware that this is going on in their communities."

Why does this apparent discrepancy exist between executive directors and nurse aides? One possibility, she says, is that the aides are closer to the delivery of care and so may see more incidents of inappropriate sexual interaction.

"It's my guess that it's just that [the executive directors are] further removed," DeLiema says. "These nursing aides are literally with [residents] 24/7, and they are the ones who have to manage the more difficult behaviors and do all of the personal care work. You would hope that the executive director would hear about these things if they're being reported, but perhaps not."

Also, DeLiema adds, perhaps some incidents of abuse are handled within the nursing department and are not communicated to the executive director. Or perhaps the EDLI survey-takers hesitated to respond honestly to the question, even though they were submitting their answers electronically and anonymously during the EDLI session.

Elder abuse takes many forms—financial, sexual, physical and emotional/psychological abuse as well as neglect. What can be done to prevent and address such abuse in long-term care (LTC) settings, whether it be perpetrated by a staff member, a family member or another resident? Increased awareness—through educational programs such as the EDLI and events such as World Elder Abuse Awareness Month, observed every June, and World Elder Abuse Awareness Day, observed every year on June 15—is one solution. Others, according to DeLiema:

- Develop and maintain a good working relationship with the LTC ombudsman in your state. "Sometimes, the cases we see, the facility can only do so much. They really need to pull someone in from the outside, and sometimes, the best option is more of a mediator than the police or adult protective services," she says, noting that ombudsmen usually take a person-centered approach.
- Educate residents, family and staff members that reporting abuse is a good thing. "You really need buy-in from the older adults if you're going to try to 'protect' them," DeLiema says. "And the same with physicians, getting them to feel that reporting is the best option" rather than trying to address incidents directly themselves.
- Train direct care staff who work with combative residents so that they don't react in an abusive way to

behaviors that, because of a cognitive disease process, may be beyond a resident's control. "It's important that they have a good understanding of the disease process," DeLiema says. Training, she adds, can answer these questions: "What is cognitive impairment, how does it manifest, what kind of behaviors can they expect?"

- Establish a system to address suspected or confirmed incidents of staff mistreatment of residents to ensure that such incidents don't recur.

The USC Davis School of Gerontology touts that it is the oldest and largest such school in the world. DeLiema also points executive directors and others to the school's website (gero.usc.edu) and its Guide for Elder Abuse Response (GEAR) app (guideforelderabuse.org) as additional resources. The app, she notes, has some elements of particular interest to those working in California, but it also contains information of wide potential interest.

Critical Thinking

1. Do families recognize when abuse may be occurring in assisted living homes?
2. Under what circumstances does a family use an assisted living facility for their loved one?
3. Are families generally satisfied with the quality of care at assisted living facilities?

Internet References

Elder Abuse
   http://www.cdc.gov/violenceprevention/elderabuse/index.html
Elder Abuse
   https://www.nia.nih.gov/health/publication/elder-abuse
What is Elder Abuse?
   http://www.aoa.gov/AoA_programs/Elder_Rights/EA_Prevention/whatIsEA.aspx

Article   Prepared by: Claire N. Rubman, *Suffolk County Community College, Selden, NY*

Unique Magnesium Compound Reverses Brain Aging

Jamie Rivington

Learning Outcomes

After reading this article, you will be able to:

- Explain the essential role of magnesium in brain development.
- Discuss the concept of brain plasticity as we age.

Scientists have been surprised by the discovery that magnesium plays an essential role in supporting brain plasticity, which is the sign of a youthful, flexible brain primed for optimal learning, memory, and cognitive function.[1]

The good news is that raising brain magnesium levels has been proven to restore critical brain plasticity and improve cognitive function.[1] In a just-published landmark human study, researchers showed that they could reverse brain aging by as much as 9–14 years in magnesium supplemented people.[2]

Scientists at the Massachusetts Institute of Technology (MIT) found a novel way of overcoming the problem of getting magnesium loaded into the brain due to poor absorption.[1]

These researchers tested a unique compound called magnesium-L-threonate and found it boosted brain magnesium levels by an approximate 15 percent.[1]

When comparing various forms of magnesium, they found that magnesium-L-threonate had the highest bioavailability and brain magnesium-loading ability.

As a result, studies show that magnesium-L-threonate improves brain plasticity, leading to direct and significant improvements in memory, learning, and cognition.[3]

The Foundation of Learning and Memory

The human brain is capable of forming new connections between neurons. When we take in new information, an electrochemical signal is sent across the space between neurons (called the synaptic space). This ability of the brain to form new connections or neural pathways to communicate with each other is often referred to as brain plasticity.

Think of it as the ability to learn a new skill, like a dance move. Our brains generate new neural pathways or "wires" to master the particular skill. On the contrary, when these "wires" become faulty or deteriorate, memories start fading and individuals can forget simple things like names or phone numbers.

Brain plasticity is now understood to be the very foundation of learning and memory.[4] This means that changes in memory (including the formation of new memories and learning of new concepts) requires changes in those synaptic connections, hence the term, *plasticity.*

As you are reading this article, your brain is forming and reforming new neural connections.

With aging, we lose brain plasticity, which results in a loss of cognitive function.[5] That's why a young person, with an active, *flexible* brain, easily latches on to new ideas and simply thinks faster than an older person whose brain has lost plasticity and is more fixed in its patterns.

As recently as a decade ago, scientists thought that loss of vital brain plasticity was inevitable due to age.

But they were wrong.

Recent studies have shown that increasing brain magnesium levels can reverse deteriorating brain plasticity. The result is considerable restoration of cognitive function both in healthy adults and in those with neurodegenerative diseases.[1,6–8]

What You Need to Know
Magnesium Improves Brain Plasticity

- Brain plasticity, the ability to remodel connections between brain cells, is the physical foundation of memory and cognition.
- Loss of memory and cognitive function in old age and in neurodegenerative diseases is the result of lost brain plasticity.
- Studies show that raising brain magnesium levels restores lost plasticity and improves cognitive function in aging animals and in models of neurodegenerative diseases.
- But conventional magnesium supplements fail to significantly raise brain magnesium levels.
- A novel form of magnesium, magnesium-L-threonate, has been developed, which is capable of rapid absorption and superior delivery to brain tissue, raising brain magnesium levels by up to 15 percent.
- Animal studies reveal marked and significant improvements in memory, learning, and cognition with magnesium-L-threonate supplementation, and lab studies show corresponding improvements in synaptic structures that correlate with improved brain plasticity.
- New human data shows promising results in older adults with cognitive impairment after supplementing with magnesium-L-threonate.
- Regular supplementation with magnesium-L-threonate is essential for anyone concerned about age-related loss of cognitive function or neurodegenerative diseases.

The Magnesium Connection

Magnesium is absolutely critical for maintaining healthy brain plasticity. This is because magnesium regulates how brain cells form those critical connections that are the foundation of learning and memory.

In fact, magnesium ions control tiny electrical switches (technically, "ion channels") in brain cells.[9] The more signals that these electrical switches transmit, the stronger the connections between cells, and the stronger the formation of the resulting memory. Thus, magnesium concentrations are an essential part of brain plasticity—the ability to add, remove, or revise cell-to-cell connections to regulate learning and memory.

Numerous studies demonstrate the dangerous impact of insufficient magnesium on brain health.[9,10] Lab studies show us that depriving brain cells of sufficient magnesium impairs their ability to participate in optimal plasticity.[10,11] In animals and humans, we are now able to see that this loss of plasticity leads directly to a poorer performance on tests of memory.[12,13]

The reason memory is impacted is because low levels of magnesium create decreases in the *strengthening* of connections between brain cells that lead to memory formation.[10]

In addition to impacting memory, chronically low calcium and magnesium levels in the diet have also been shown to correlate with a high incidence of neurodegenerative diseases.[14]

Basic lab studies have shown that boosting magnesium concentrations at excitatory synapses can enhance brain plasticity.[15] In brain cells cultured from the hippocampus (the part of the brain where we store and retrieve memories), these changes led to more permanent enhancements of brain plasticity, demonstrating *long-lasting* improvement.[15] (It is important to note that the levels of magnesium needed to improve plasticity are well within the normal physiological range, not exceedingly high.)

Studies in diabetic rats provide further support for magnesium's ability to reverse losses in brain plasticity and restore cognitive function.[11]

Like diabetic humans, these rats have a high risk of developing Alzheimer's disease. Researchers found that elevating brain magnesium levels with injected magnesium protected learning and memory in diabetic rats with spontaneous Alzheimer's-like symptoms. Elevating brain magnesium levels also *reversed* impairments in synaptic function and *long-term potentiation* (the cellular equivalent of learning).[11]

These studies make it clear that elevating brain levels of magnesium helps to improve cognition by improving plasticity (the ability to make connections between brain cells) and long-term potentiation(the strengthening of those connections).

But, one of the biggest challenges that researchers have encountered is delivering sufficient amounts of magnesium into the brain. Fortunately, scientists at the Massachusetts Institute of Technology (MIT) have found a solution.

A Breakthrough Form of Magnesium

Scientists at MIT set out to find a better-absorbed form of magnesium that also could boost concentrations of the mineral in the brain.[1] After testing numerous compounds, they found what they were looking for in a unique compound called magnesium-L-threonate. This is a complex of magnesium along with *threonic acid*, a breakdown product of vitamin C.[1,16]

Figure 1 shows the dramatic results of treating rats with magnesium-L-theronate compared with untreated control animals and with those supplemented with two other forms of

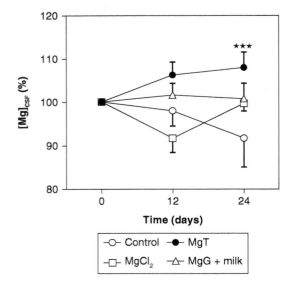

Figure 1. Raising brain magnesium levels with various compounds. Effects on spinal fluid (CSF) magnesium levels following supplementation of rats with various magnesium compounds. Magnesium-L-theronate (MgT) was the only one capable of significantly raising magnesium levels.[1]

magnesium.[1] Only magnesium-L-theronate proved capable of significantly raising magnesium levels in spinal fluid, which is a measure of brain magnesium.

Magnesium-L-theronate's effects were even more remarkable on short- and long-term memory performance in live rats (Figure 2). Compared with the other forms of magnesium, the animals that were supplemented with magnesium-L-theronate demonstrated significantly greater *memory retention* over 10 minutes and 12 hours (see Figure 2 charts A and B).[1]

In addition to short- and long-term memory improvements, rats supplemented with magnesium-L-theronate demonstrated *enhanced learning abilities* and *enhanced working memory,* which are essential for normal cognitive function.[1]

And in aged rats, supplemented animals were better at pattern completion (ability to retrieve memories based on incomplete information) compared with control animals.[1]

Microscopic examination of brain tissue explained the reason for these dramatic improvements. As expected, the rats supplemented with magnesium-L-theronate had higher densities of synaptic proteins associated with memory formation, especially in the hippocampus. These findings correlated with the animals' improved memory performance on testing.[1]

In addition, the magnesium increased the number of release sites at the presynaptic nerve endings, but reduced their overall probability of releasing neurotransmitters. This reconfiguration enabled synapses to more finely tune their transmissions,

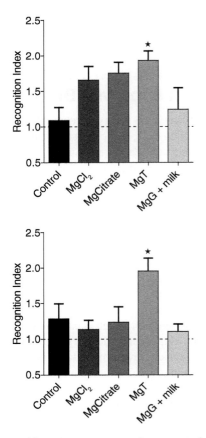

Figure 2. Short- and long-term memory enhancements by various magnesium preparations.[1] A. Short-term (10 minutes) memory performance in rats following supplementation with various magnesium preparations. Only magnesium-L-theronate showed significant improvements. B. Long-term (12 hour) memory performance in rats following supplementation with various magnesium preparations. Only magnesium-L-theronate showed significant improvements.

resulting in greater plasticity. The synapses were, in effect, "trained" to respond only to the "right" stimuli, producing improved memories in the live animals.[1]

Finally, the increase in brain magnesium levels enhanced *long-term potentiation,* which is the process that refers to the *strengthening* of connections between brain cells based on recent patterns of activity that is associated with enhanced learning and memory.[1,10]

Alzheimer's Disease

The ability of magnesium-L-theronate to enhance brain plasticity is of tremendous interest to researchers studying Alzheimer's disease. As tangles of toxic beta *amyloid protein* develop in Alzheimer's patients, they trigger brain cell death and the loss of brain *synapses*.[8,17-19] This hinders brain plasticity and ultimately impairs cognition.

magnesium-L-theronate has now been tested in a widely accepted mouse model of Alzheimer's disease. In this type of study, mice are bred to show brain structural problems and cognitive defects that closely resemble those in human Alzheimer's.[17]

When the researchers treated mice early in their disease progression with magnesium-L-theronate, it *prevented* the loss of synapses and the decline of memory that occurred in untreated animals. To the researchers' surprise, the supplemented animals showed these effects even when the magnesium-L-theronate was given at the end-stage of their cognitive decline.[17]

This surprising result might be related to magnesium's ability to help *prevent* and *clear* the accumulation of toxic *beta amyloid* plaques. In one particular study, magnesium-L-theronate supplementation suppressed the expression of the enzyme responsible for beta amyloid deposits by an impressive 80 percent.[20]

The researchers determined that, based on these results, magnesium could play a role in the prevention of Alzheimer's.[20]

New Findings for Posttraumatic Stress Disorder

While Alzheimer's is the most urgent demonstration of restoration of brain plasticity by magnesium-L-theronate, it is far from the only potential application for this supplement.

Researchers also found that magnesium-L-theronate has beneficial effects for those suffering from posttraumatic stress disorder (PTSD).[6]

Sometimes when our brains form connections, they aren't good ones. For example, certain objects or events linked with a previous danger triggers fear memories. In healthy people, these fear memories fade in time as the object triggering them is experienced in a safe environment. (Perhaps this is the likely scientific explanation for the phrase "time heals all wounds.")

For example, if you experienced a house fire, hearing fire engines could reproduce the feelings of fear experienced from the fire itself. In time, that feeling will fade when the triggering event is experienced in a safe environment.

Unfortunately, in people who suffer from posttraumatic stress disorder, that fear response does not fade with time. This is likely due to the fact that posttraumatic stress disorder induces a sharp reduction in brain plasticity.[21-24]

Exciting research has demonstrated that magnesium-L-theronate can help speed up this recovery process in people suffering from posttraumatic stress disorder.

Scientists studied magnesium-L-theronate in rats with conditioned fear responses (the animal equivalent of posttraumatic

stress disorder). Amazingly, the magnesium-L-theronate treatment helped the fear memory fade with time, *without impacting the original memory*.[6,25]

Research shows that magnesium-L-theronate enhances brain plasticity in *specific* regions of the brain most affected by traumatic events.[6] Because of these dramatic results, scientists are suggesting that magnesium could be a novel supplement for those suffering from posttraumatic stress disorder, anxiety, or depression.[6,25]

What Is Magnesium?

Magnesium, the fourth most abundant mineral in the body, is known to be a co-factor for more than 300 reactions catalyzed by enzymes, including those essential for energy release from food and conversion to cellular work through formation of adenosine triphosphate, or ATP, in mitochondria. Magnesium is also required for the synthesis of DNA and RNA.[27]

Magnesium is especially important in all of our bodies' electrical and electrochemical activities, including muscle contractions, heart rhythm, nerve conduction, and brain cell activity.[27]

The most common disturbance of magnesium in our bodies is hypomagnesemia, or low blood magnesium levels, which is widely recognized as a cause of seizures, hypertension, stroke, migraine headaches, attention deficit hyperactivity disorder, and metabolic conditions such as insulin resistance and type II diabetes.[27]

In addition to all of these known functions, magnesium has been found to be the controlling and essential factor in regulating synaptic plasticity in the brain, which is the physical process that underlies what we perceive as learning and memory.[1]

Recent Human Study

A remarkable human study on magnesium-L-theronate was released late in 2015 with compelling results that corroborate and extend all of the previous laboratory findings.[2]

Men and women aged 50 to 70, who reported cognitive problems (e.g., memory and concentration) were enrolled in the study. They were randomly assigned to receive either placebo or a supplement containing magnesium-L-theronate. Subjects took 1.5 grams per day of the supplement if they weighed less than 154 pounds, and 2 grams per day if they weighed more.

Subjects were evaluated before starting the supplement and again at weeks six and 12 (end of the study). At each evaluation, subjects participated in a series of tests of cognitive function, while blood and urine tests were performed to calculate total body magnesium status.[2]

By 12 weeks, lab results showed that magnesium-L-theronate was effective at loading magnesium into the body, as well as into cells (red blood cells were used because it is impossible to safely sample brain cells in humans).[2]

This form of magnesium was shown to be effective at loading magnesium into the brain and at enhancing brain function. This was made clear by results of cognitive testing. Already by week six, supplemented subjects demonstrated significantly increased speed in tests of executive function (e.g., reasoning, problem-solving, and planning). By week 12, that increased speed reached an approximate 20 percent improvement over baseline, while placebo recipients experienced no significant change.[2]

There was also a significant 13.1 percent improvement in supplemented subjects' working memory (the memory we use, for example, to remember where we put things) and a significant 37.6 percent improvement in episodic memory (for example, the ability to put new faces and names together). And composite scores of overall cognitive ability rose significantly from baseline and compared with placebo at both weeks 6 and 12.[2]

Tellingly, magnesium loading into red blood cells was significantly correlated with enhancement in overall cognitive ability in supplemented patients. This was a strong validation of earlier animal studies in which raising brain magnesium levels boosted cognitive function.[1]

An unexpected benefit was also demonstrated when the researchers examined fluctuations in cognitive performance over time. Such a fluctuation is known to be an early sign of impending cognitive impairment.[2,26] Not only did supplemented patients experience less cognitive fluctuation, but the changes that they did experience were primarily positive (performing better than usual).

All of these data provide impressive support for the use of magnesium-L-theronate to improve cognitive function. But the real shocker comes with an analysis of this study's subjects in the context of normal brain aging.

The researchers compared results of their study with data from a second study of cognitively normal subjects. They determined that cognitive performance fell about 1.04 percent per year in the cognitive normal subjects. Researchers established that baseline performance in the first study was about 10 percent lower than that of age-matched controls. But after 12 weeks of supplementation, the average *increase* in performance was 10.3 percent, essentially restoring performance to that of age-matched people without cognitive decline.[2]

A still more remarkable finding became evident when researchers used the normal cognition study to assign a "brain age" to each of their own study subjects. Using this calculation, for example, a 50-year-old with a 10 percent worse performance on cognitive testing would have a brain age equivalent to that of a cognitively normal 60-year-old (approximately 1 percent function loss per year).[2]

Using that calculation, the researchers found that even though the average chronological age of subjects who completed their study was 57.8 years, their average brain age at baseline was 68.3 years. But by 12 weeks, the brain age of the supplemented subjects had fallen by an average of 9.4 years, while that of placebo recipients fell by less than a year.[2]

In other words, supplementation with magnesium-L-theronate resulted in an effective reversal of brain age to near normal. The brain age reversal in subjects who had significant increases in red blood cell magnesium was still higher, at 14.6 years, moving those individuals into a brain age in fact younger than their actual age in years!

Summary

The loss of brain plasticity is at the heart of age-related loss of cognitive function. As our brains lose flexibility, we lose the ability to learn new concepts, to make sharp judgments, and to develop new skills.

Loss of brain plasticity is implicated in both the "natural" loss of brain function with aging and with accelerated cognitive decline as seen in Alzheimer's and other neurodegenerative diseases.

Restoring brain plasticity has become a major focus of neuroscientists aiming to slow or eliminate the loss of brain function over time.

Studies show that boosting brain magnesium levels dramatically renews the ability of brain cells and, in animals, to form new memories and discriminate between existing ones. But conventional magnesium supplements are inadequately delivered to brain tissue, challenging our ability to effectively raise brain magnesium levels.

The development of magnesium-L-theronate appears to have shattered that barrier. Studies show that this compound enters brain tissue more effectively than other magnesium preparations, and is significantly more effective at restoring memory functions and brain plasticity in numerous animal models, including those of Alzheimer's disease.

Recent new human data on magnesium-L-theronate shows promising results in older adults with cognitive impairment. Those interested in preventing cognitive decline and in restoring active, flexible brains should consider daily supplementation with magnesium-L-theronate. No other magnesium preparation comes close to its performance.

References

1. Slutsky I, Abumaria N, Wu LJ, et al. Enhancement of learning and memory by elevating brain magnesium. *Neuron.* 2010;65(2):165–77.
2. Liu G, Weinger JG, Lu ZL, et al. Efficacy and safety of MMFS-01, a synapse density enhancer, for treating cognitive impairment in older adults: a randomized, double-blind, placebo-controlled trial. *J Alzheimers Dis.* 2015;49(4):971–90.
3. Mickley GA, Hoxha N, Luchsinger JL, et al. Chronic dietary magnesium-L-threonate speeds extinction and reduces

spontaneous recovery of a conditioned taste aversion. *Pharmacol Biochem Behav.* 2013;106:16–26.

4. Mahncke HW, Bronstone A, Merzenich MM. Brain plasticity and functional losses in the aged: scientific bases for a novel intervention. *Prog Brain Res.* 2006;157:81–109.

5. Wang D, Jacobs SA, Tsien JZ. Targeting the NMDA receptor subunit NR2B for treating or preventing age-related memory decline. *Expert Opin Ther Targets.* 2014;18(10):1121–30.

6. Abumaria N, Yin B, Zhang L, et al. Effects of elevation of brain magnesium on fear conditioning, fear extinction, and synaptic plasticity in the infralimbic prefrontal cortex and lateral amygdala. *J Neurosci.* 2011;31(42):14871–81.

7. Basheer MP, Pradeep Kumar KM, Sreekumaran E, et al. A study of serum magnesium, calcium and phosphorus level, and cognition in the elderly population of South India. *Alexandria J Med.*

8. Li W, Yu J, Liu Y, et al. Elevation of brain magnesium prevents and reverses cognitive deficits and synaptic loss in Alzheimer's disease mouse model. *J Neurosci.* 2013;33(19):8423–41.

9. Palacios-Prado N, Chapuis S, Panjkovich A, et al. Molecular determinants of magnesium-dependent synaptic plasticity at electrical synapses formed by connexin36. *Nat Commun.* 2014;5:4667.

10. Danysz W, Parsons CG. The NMDA receptor antagonist memantine as a symptomatological and neuroprotective treatment for Alzheimer's disease: preclinical evidence. *Int J Geriatr Psychiatry.* 2003;18(Suppl 1):S23–32.

11. Xu ZP, Li L, Bao J, et al. Magnesium protects cognitive functions and synaptic plasticity in streptozotocin-induced sporadic Alzheimer's model. *PLoS One.* 2014;9(9):e108645.

12. Murphy T, Dias GP, Thuret S. Effects of diet on brain plasticity in animal and human studies: mind the gap. *Neural Plasticity.* 2014;2014:32.

13. Bilbo SD, Smith SH, Schwarz JM. A lifespan approach to neuroinflammatory and cognitive disorders: a critical role for glia. *J Neuroimmune Pharmacol.* 2012;7(1):24–41.

14. Taniguchi R, Nakagawasai O, Tan-no K, et al. Combined low calcium and lack magnesium is a risk factor for motor deficit in mice. *Biosci Biotechnol Biochem.* 2013;77(2):266–70.

15. Slutsky I, Sadeghpour S, Li B, et al. Enhancement of synaptic plasticity through chronically reduced Ca2+ flux during uncorrelated activity. *Neuron.* 2004;44(5):835–49.

16. Available at: http://www.fda.gov/downloads/Food/IngredientsPackagingLabeling/GRAS/NoticeInventory/UCM400322 (http://www.fda.gov/downloads/Food/IngredientsPackagingLabeling/GRAS/NoticeInventory/UCM400322). Accessed February 26, 2016.

17. Li W, Yu J, Liu Y, et al. Elevation of brain magnesium prevents synaptic loss and reverses cognitive deficits in Alzheimer's disease mouse model. *Mol Brain.* 2014;7:65.

18. Yu J, Sun M, Chen Z, et al. Magnesium modulates amyloid-beta protein precursor trafficking and processing. *J Alzheimers Dis.* 2010;20(4):1091–106.

19. Bisel BE, Henkins KM, Parfitt KD. Alzheimer amyloid beta-peptide A-beta25-35 blocks adenylate cyclase-mediated forms of hippocampal long-term potentiation. *Ann N Y Acad Sci.* 2007;1097:58–63.

20. Yu X, Guan PP, Guo JW, et al. By suppressing the expression of anterior pharynx-defective-1alpha and -1beta and inhibiting the aggregation of beta-amyloid protein, magnesium ions inhibit the cognitive decline of amyloid precursor protein/presenilin 1 transgenic mice. *Faseb j.* 2015;29(12):5044–58.

21. Chao LL, Tosun D, Woodward SH, et al. Preliminary evidence of increased hippocampal myelin content in veterans with posttraumatic stress disorder. *Front Behav Neurosci.* 2015;9:333.

22. Cominski TP, Jiao X, Catuzzi JE, et al. The role of the hippocampus in avoidance learning and anxiety vulnerability. *Front Behav Neurosci.* 2014;8:273.

23. Powers MB, Medina JL, Burns S, et al. Exercise augmentation of exposure therapy for PTSD: rationale and pilot efficacy data. *Cogn Behav Ther.* 2015;44(4):314–27.

24. Wingo AP, Almli LM, Stevens JJ, et al. DICER1 and microRNA regulation in post-traumatic stress disorder with comorbid depression. *Nat Commun.* 2015;6:10106.

25. Available at: http://www.abstractsonline.com/Plan/ViewAbstract.aspx?sKey=9415df25-4759-4d28-a789-5945ea5355d1&cKey=a899d2d6-6d4e-4201-8d26-6a3c82145103&mKey=%7b081F7976-E4CD-4F3D-A0AF-E8387992A658%7d# (http://www.abstractsonline.com/Plan/ViewAbstract.aspx?sKey=9415df25-4759-4d28-a789-5945ea5355d1&cKey=a899d2d6-6d4e-4201-8d26-6a3c82145103&mKey=%7b081F7976-E4CD-4F3D-A0AF-E8387992A658%7d#). Accessed February 29, 2016.

26. Palop JJ, Chin J, Mucke L. A network dysfunction perspective on neurodegenerative diseases. *Nature.* 2006;443(7113):768–73.

27. Grober U, Schmidt J, Kisters K. Magnesium in Prevention and Therapy. *Nutrients.* 2015;7(9):8199–226.

Critical Thinking

1. How do our dietary needs change as we age?

2. What are the normal signs of aging in the brain?

Internet References

8 Nutrients to Protect the Aging Brain
   http://www.newswise.com/articles/8-nutrients-to-protect-the-aging-brain

Ageing and the Brain
   https://www.ncbi.nlm.nih.gov/pmc/articles/PMC2596698/

Magnesium Levels Vital to Brain Health as Population Ages
   https://www.sciencedaily.com/releases/2013/11/131104142343.htm

Novel Magnesium Compound Reverses Neurodegeneration
   http://www.lifeextension.com/magazine/2012/2/novel-magnesium-compound-reverses-neurodegeneration/page-01

Article   Prepared by: Claire N. Rubman, *Suffolk County Community College, Selden, NY*

Could Cooking a Different Dinner Save You from Alzheimer's?

Pioneering New Research Suggests It's Possible

SARAH KLEIN AND CATHERINE PRICE

Learning Outcomes

After reading this article, you will be able to:

- Discuss the possibility that the food that we eat could contribute to Alzheimer's disease.
- Articulate the relationship between insulin levels and Alzheimer's disease.
- Compare the Mediterranean diet and a high carbohydrate diet in relation to Alzheimer's disease.

Seven years ago, **Myriam** Marquez was driving home when she came to a four-way stop. She wasn't far from her own driveway; she had stopped at this same intersection countless times. Yet she didn't know where she was.

"I called my daughter, panicked," Marquez says. A few excruciating minutes passed before she finally remembered where she was, and by that point she was sure she had Alzheimer's.

Her fears were soon validated: A battery of tests, including one for a gene that essentially guarantees Alzheimer's, confirmed her suspicions. She wasn't shocked; at least five of her father's siblings died with Alzheimer's symptoms. Two of her siblings have it, and her 47-year-old daughter is already beginning to show signs.

"I feel very blessed I'm still in the early stage," says Marquez, now 69 and living in Seattle. After her diagnosis, she charged into what she calls "warrior mode," campaigning to raise awareness of Alzheimer's while also working to stave off her own decline. Step one: Overhaul her "junky" diet. Instead of pasta, pizza, and fast food, she now eats Mediterranean style, loading up on veggies; focusing on chicken, fish, and tofu for protein; and limiting refined sugars and grains.

Dietary changes may seem inconsequential in the face of a diagnosis as monstrous as Alzheimer's, but there's reason to believe they're crucial. At a lab at Wake Forest School of Medicine, Suzanne Craft, a professor of gerontology and geriatric medicine, is studying how what we eat affects our brains and, in the process, revolutionizing the way we think about preventing and treating dementia.

Alzheimer's is the most common form of dementia, and the National Institutes of Health's National Institute on Aging estimates that it's the sixth-leading cause of death in the United States. It often runs in families, but fewer than 5 percent of Alzheimer's cases are directly caused by a genetic variation such as the one Marquez carries. There's usually no way to tell who will get it—in part because no one really knows what causes it.

Today, most Alzheimer's research is based on the hypothesis that symptoms are triggered by abnormal deposits of proteins in the brain called amyloid plaques and tau tangles. With no confirmed cause and no effective long-term treatments for the disease, researchers have turned to other factors that might be at play. It's likely, says Laurie Ryan, chief of the Dementia of Aging Branch of the National Institute on Aging's division of neuroscience, that Alzheimer's does its damage via multiple pathways.

One of those pathways seems to involve type 2 diabetes. People who have it are at least twice as likely to develop Alzheimer's as those who don't—an association so strong that in 2005, a neuropathologist named Suzanne de la Monte suggested that Alzheimer's could be referred to as "type 3 diabetes." That term, while controversial, has gained traction among some scientists as a way to focus attention on why the diseases often coexist.

Whatever you call it, the connection is worth exploring: Nearly 30 million Americans have diabetes, and 40 percent of people born today are expected to develop the disease in their lifetimes. If we want to protect America's mental health, we'd better figure out what the link is. Fast.

Ann Simpson is a Vivacious woman with a cheerful smile and an easy laugh. Ask her about Alzheimer's, though, and she quickly grows serious. "It's a nasty, nasty disease," she says quietly.

Simpson, 69, has already lost her mother and one sister to the disease; another sister has developed it as well. The sister living with Alzheimer's no longer remembers Ann's name or what money is. She ripped up a photo of a dear grandchild. "It's devastating," Simpson says, "and I'm scared to death that I may get it."

Given her family history—her deceased sister had both Alzheimer's and type 2 diabetes—Simpson was a perfect fit for a study, led by Craft, focusing on the role of insulin. Craft believes that much of the connection between Alzheimer's disease and type 2 diabetes has to do with this hormone.

Secreted in response to food, insulin removes sugar (glucose) from your blood and moves it into your cells, where it's used for energy. But sometimes the body doesn't use insulin as efficiently as it should. This is called insulin resistance, which means your body needs to release more insulin than normal to respond to the same amount of glucose. That might work for a while, but it's like using a leaky bucket to put out a fire: Because your body can pump out excess insulin for only so long, you'll eventually end up with chronically elevated blood sugar levels. That's type 2 diabetes.

The disease is well known for the havoc it wreaks on the body, but Craft and a growing number of researchers are more interested in what type 2 diabetes does to the brain. They're also exploring the role of insulin and blood sugar levels on memory in people who don't have diabetes—at least not yet. And the No. 1 factor that affects your blood sugar levels, and thus determines how much insulin you need, is your intake of carbohydrates.

The idea that there's a connection between diet and health may sound like old news, but Craft has gone beyond traditional observational studies.

"I'm an experimentalist by nature," she says, "and I wanted to do a very tightly controlled diet study to see whether we could affect people's cognition and the Alzheimer's markers in their spinal fluid by giving them a 'Western' diet high in sugar and saturated fat for 30 days."

That's exactly what she did. She took 49 older adults, 29 of whom had early signs of Alzheimer's disease and 20 of whom

did not, and randomly assigned them to one of two diets. The first, high in saturated fat and easily digested carbohydrates, was meant to mimic the stereotypical American diet. The second was more Mediterranean, with less saturated fat and a focus on complex carbs (like whole grains and legumes) that take a longer time to be absorbed and therefore don't cause the same spike in insulin as simple carbs do.

By the end of the month, the people who had been assigned to the Western-style diet performed worse on memory tests than they had at the beginning of the trial, and Alzheimer's-related beta-amyloid proteins showed up in their spinal fluid. Those who'd been assigned to the Mediterranean-style diet, on the other hand, did better on the tests, and their spinal fluid contained fewer Alzheimer's-related proteins. The effects reversed once participants returned to their normal eating patterns at the end of the study.

In a different trial, Craft found that people's cognitive abilities temporarily decreased—and that beta-amyloid in their spinal fluid temporarily increased—following a single high-carb meal. "It's surprising to see changes in these markers after just one meal," says Ryan.

The question is, how does this happen?

When craft started her research on Alzheimer's some 20 years ago, "the idea that there was an important connection between insulin and the brain—let alone insulin and Alzheimer's—was viewed as so novel as to be fringe," she says. Instead, researchers were focused on glucose. At the time, neurologists knew that the brains of people with Alzheimer's disease didn't use glucose properly. So Craft designed a small trial that tested whether giving people a boost of glucose via a sugary beverage could temporarily improve their performance on a cognitive test.

She was happy to find that it did. But it wasn't for the reason she had expected.

When the release of insulin was blocked, the memory benefit vanished. "The transient benefit to memory was tied not to the glucose but to elevations in insulin that happen naturally when people are given glucose," Craft says.

Scientists still don't understand why. But they do know that insulin is essential to the hippocampus, a seahorse-shaped structure in which our memories are created. Without adequate insulin, the hippocampus can't access the energy it needs to do its job—and memories can't be recorded efficiently. Insulin also acts as a neurotransmitter, a chemical that enables brain cells to communicate with each other. It modulates the levels of other brain chemicals that interact with memory. It also reduces inflammation, directs blood flow, and helps repair and create brain cells.

It might seem, therefore, that having extra insulin circulating in your body would be good for your mind. But that's not the case. When insulin levels in the body are abnormally high, the brain protects itself by restricting how much insulin it can absorb. In the short term, this shields the brain from the fluctuations in insulin levels that occur after meals. But when insulin levels are consistently elevated, as they are when you're insulin resistant, this process backfires and an insufficient amount of insulin reaches the brain. Ironically, the more insulin there is circulating in the bloodstream, the more likely it is that your brain isn't getting enough of it.

Craft isn't ready to say that less insulin in the brain actually causes Alzheimer's disease, in part because *Alzheimer's* is a highly specific term. Usually diagnosed after death, it means a person had the classic plaques and tangles as well as memory symptoms. And not everyone with age-related memory changes has Alzheimer's. "What we're studying is really the role of insulin in Alzheimer's *symptoms*," Craft says.

Craft and her team are now wrapping up a larger version of their original diet trial. She's also running a study she believes will prove that an ultra-low-carb diet is superior to the low-fat diet recommended by the American Heart Association when it comes to preserving brain health.

So far, Craft's findings offer a possible rationale for why a diet high in processed carbs (which promote insulin resistance) and type 2 diabetes (characterized by insulin resistance) increases the risk of Alzheimer's disease. They provide a plausible explanation for why several recent observational studies have found an association between a relatively low-carb, Mediterranean-inspired eating pattern called the MIND diet and a lower risk of Alzheimer's. Most important, they suggest that each of us can take steps to reduce our risk of developing Alzheimer's, starting with our next meal.

Like any responsible scientist, Craft has caveats. Her studies are ongoing, and she doesn't yet know how powerful the effects of dietary patterns on Alzheimer's risk may be. There is no question, however, that diet can affect our minds, she says—and that the typical American diet doesn't appear to be healthy.

Other researchers are also cautiously optimistic. While these are preliminary findings, says Martha Clare Morris, a professor of nutritional epidemiology at Rush University Medical Center who studies the role of diet in preventing chronic diseases like Alzheimer's, it's now an "aggressively studied" area

of research, as scientists and hopeful families alike clamor for a cure.

"People need to recognize that everything they put in their mouths has an impact on their brains," Craft explains. "Eating poorly and depriving your brain is absolutely going to affect how it functions over time."

She knows that some people will be skeptical. "Patients say to me, 'I ate well and exercised my whole life, and I'm 80 and I have Alzheimer's,'" Craft says. "What I say to them is that if you hadn't done that, you might have gotten Alzheimer's at 60."

Her advice: Eat a Mediterranean-style diet featuring lots of produce and fatty fish. Avoid refined grains and processed foods. Exercise. ("Diet and exercise work synergistically," Craft says.) Basically, do everything in your power to avoid becoming insulin resistant.

"How diet works in the brain is complicated, but what to do is not," Craft says. "To a large extent, the health of our brains is under our control."

Critical Thinking

1. How could we better educate our aging population on the benefits of a healthy diet to prevent or delay diseases such as Alzheimer's or dementia?

2. Does our aging population eat a healthy diet for our brain?

3. What are the signs of early Alzheimer's disease?

Internet References

10 Early Signs and Symptoms of Alzheimer's
http://www.alz.org/10-signs-symptoms-alzheimers-dementia.asp

About Alzheimer's Disease: Symptoms
https://www.nia.nih.gov/alzheimers/topics/symptoms

Alzheimer's: Can a Mediterranean diet lower my risk?
http://www.mayoclinic.org/diseases-conditions/alzheimers-disease/expert-answers/alzheimers-disease/faq-20058062

Eating for Alzheimer's Prevention
http://www.epicurious.com/archive/healthy/news/alzheimers-prevention

Insulin Resistance Increases Risk for Alzheimer's Disease, Study Finds
https://www.sciencedaily.com/releases/2015/07/150727130816.htm

Article   Prepared by: Claire N. Rubman, *Suffolk County Community College, Selden, NY*

No Country for Old People

U.S. market ideology is undermining human rights for elders.

DAVID BACON

Learning Outcomes

After reading this article, you will be able to:

- Think about the elderly, discuss the percentage of their annual salary that they spend on "living costs."

- Explain the guidelines for the "Supplemental Poverty Measure" (SPM).

- Define the term "economically vulnerable."

Is there a human right to age in dignity? Some countries think so. Unfortunately, ours isn't one of them. The Organization of American States (OAS) recently adopted the first international convention on the human rights of older people (though the United States did not endorse it). The Organization of African Unity is debating its own convention, and is expected to adopt it next year.

It is ironic that the world's poorer countries, presumably those with the fewest resources to deal with aging, are in the vanguard of establishing this set of rights. Meanwhile, the richest countries with the most resources, including the United States and members of the European Union, are arguing against applying a human rights framework to aging. In part, their contrarian stance reflects the dominance of market ideology. In a corporate economy, people lose their social importance and position when they are not working and producing value. In the United States, the resulting set of priorities has a devastating impact on older people.

While some countries are creating a new definition of human rights to include aging, and passing conventions that incorporate it, millions of seniors in the United States live in very vulnerable and precarious conditions, which are violations of their human rights as viewed in this context.

In another 15 years, 18 percent of the people in the United States will be over 65 years old. Though their numbers may be increasing; however, their security is not. In fact, the future of the nation's elders is growing ever more precarious.

According to a recent study, "Senior Poverty in America," by Rebecca Vallas, director of policy in the Poverty to Prosperity Program at the Center for American Progress, 10 percent of seniors (4.6 million people) fall below this country's official poverty line. In 1966, it was 29 percent. That sounds like progress. Vallas attributes the decline mostly to Medicare, Medicaid, and other programs established during this period. But this appearance of progress, she says, doesn't account for the desperate situation of millions of seniors today. The programs have helped people, but their success at lowering poverty among some seniors masks the desperate situation of millions of others. The official poverty line is too low, has grown increasingly out of whack over the years from the real cost of living, and uses a faulty method (being originally defined as three times the basic food budget) that does not correspond to current spending patterns for low-income people.

The official poverty line defines poverty for a single person as an income less than $ 11,770, and for a couple, $15,930 (for Alaska and Hawaii it's slightly higher). Rent alone absorbs a huge portion of this. Even seniors at 125 percent of the poverty line spend more than ¾ of their income on rent, Vallas found—$11,034 for singles, and $14,934 for a couple. It's hard to imagine finding an apartment in many urban areas with rent that low.

According to Vallas, seniors across the board spend 14 percent of their income on medical costs. Adding that to rent, poor seniors are left with about 10 percent of their income for food, bus fares, and everything else. It's no wonder that so many people in line at county food banks are old.

Even an income of twice the official poverty line is hardly enough to make ends meet, and the number of seniors under this line is much greater—32 percent of those over 65 and 40 percent of those over 75.

A better criterion for poverty is the Supplemental Poverty Measure (SPM). The U.S. Census Bureau created this yardstick in response to criticism that the official poverty line grossly underestimates poverty (see Jeannette Wicks-Lim, "Undercounting the Poor," *Dollars & Sense,* May/June 2013). The SPM is based on real-life expenditures for basic necessities like food, housing, clothing, and utilities. It varies from place to place and isn't meant to qualify or disqualify people for government programs. Vallas found that about 15 percent of seniors fall below this line, and 45 percent are "economically vulnerable"—below twice the SPM.

Poverty is no more evenly distributed among seniors than it is among people in general in the United States. Nearly 12 percent of older women (3.1 million) live below the official poverty line (vs. 7 percent of men), and 17 percent live below the SPM (vs. 12 percent of men), according to a 2015 Kaiser Family Foundation report. "The typical woman suffers an earnings loss of $431,000 over the course of a 40-year career due to the gender wage gap," Vallas says. "The gap is even larger for women of color." Black and Hispanic seniors are poorer in general—19 percent and 18 percent respectively are under the official poverty line, and 22 percent and 28 percent are under the SPM.

The income of seniors is overwhelmingly dependent on Social Security. The number of seniors who receive pensions from employers is declining rapidly, as corporations divest themselves of the "defined benefit" plans that, for an earlier generation, pegged payments to preretirement earnings for an earlier generation. Today, the average Social Security benefit is just over $16,000 per year—not far above even the official poverty line. "For nearly two-thirds of seniors, it is their main source of income, and for one-third it is their only income," Vallas notes. Without it, half of all seniors would fall below the SPM.

The official poverty statistics do not even account for people who have been left out of the Social Security system entirely. Many workers do not make contributions, including workers in the informal economy, like day laborers.

Human Rights for Elders

Two million seniors get Supplemental Security Income (SSI) benefits, which are based on low income rather than contributions made while they were working. But the maximum is $8,796 per year, well below the official poverty line. According to the Center for Budget and Policy Priorities, "for nearly three-fifths of recipients, SSI is their only source of income."

Getting left out of the safety net has devastating consequences. As of 2010, roughly 45,000 adults over age 65 were homeless, according to Vallas, who projects that this figure will increase by 33 percent by 2020 and more than double by 2050. The homeless population is getting older as well. The median age of single homeless adults was 35 in 1990, and 50 in 2010.

Immigration status is an even greater barrier to benefits. According to the Migration Policy Institute, about five million immigrants 65 and over make up 12 percent of the total U.S. immigrant population. For those who haven't become citizens, the safety net has huge holes.

Most lawful permanent residents can't receive SSI or food stamps (SNAP) for their first five years in the United States, although they can collect Social Security if they've managed to accumulate any qualifying earnings. People with no legal immigration status (an estimated 11 million people) can't even apply for a Social Security card. In order to work they have to give an employer a Social Security number they've invented or that belongs to someone else. Payments are deducted from their paychecks, but these workers never become eligible for the benefits the contributions are supposed to provide.

The Social Security Administration estimated in 2010 that 3.1 million undocumented people were paying about $13 billion per year in contributions into the benefit fund. Undocumented recipients, mostly people who received Social Security numbers before the system was tightened, received only $1 billion per year in payments. Stephen Goss, the chief actuary of the Social Security Administration, told VICE News in 2014 that surplus of payments versus benefits had totaled more than $100 billion over the previous decade.

Excluded undocumented immigrants, however, get old like everyone else. Without Social Security, they have to find some other way to survive—primarily by continuing to work or relying on family.

According to Lia Daichman, president of the Argentina chapter of the International Longevity Alliance, and the ILA's representative at the United Nations, "governments should guarantee that all people have a non-contributory pension, to be able to live without the support of younger people." Her own country, Argentina, began paying nearly every old person a pension in 2003, with medical and social benefits, even those who made no contributions. "This is good for women," she emphasizes, "because we often work in the home and weren't able to contribute, or because we worked in the informal economy." Even Nepal, one of the world's poorest countries, has instituted a noncontributory pension of 700 rupees a month.

Daichman doesn't view elders as needy people asking for charity. "People have a right to income and a dignified life," she asserts. "They worked all their lives for it." This perspective underlies her work trying to convince the international community to codify this right. The convention adopted by the OAS is a step toward the goal, she believes, in part because it will cover such a large area. In Latin America and the Caribbean, nearly 71 million people were older than 60 in 2015; by 2030 that figure will increase by over 70 percent, to 121 million people, according to a 2015 United Nations study of the aging of the world population.

Adopting new definitions and conventions on human rights (especially economic ones), even if they are not immediately implemented, helps to set a goal—a vision of how we want the world to work. Passing human rights treaties is also an important step in establishing rights in international law.

The OAS convention enumerates 27 specific rights, with many subcategories, from the right to independence, political participation, and freedom from violence to the right to a healthy environment. Some of the key rights it asserts are economic. Older people, it says, "have the right to social security to protect them so that they can live in dignity," and governments should provide income "to ensure a dignified life for older persons." Seniors also have the right to "dignified and decent work" with benefits, labor, and union rights, and pay equal to all other workers. Older people have the right to healthcare, housing, education and to "participate in the cultural and artistic life of the community, and to enjoy the benefits of scientific and technological progress."

The U.S. government does not recognize many of these rights, however—to housing, income, education, and healthcare, for instance. In this country these are all commodities, bought and sold on the market. Yet Social Security itself is a product of an earlier era in U.S. political life, in which President Franklin Roosevelt postulated that all people had the right to "freedom from want." Today a "cost/benefit analysis" is the more likely framework—weighing the need to ensure a dignified life for seniors against the cost of providing it.

Social welfare programs in the United States are the product of popular struggle against the inherent dynamic of a market economy to demand as high a rate of profit as possible. Old people, children, the disabled, and others who don't immediately produce profit are a social cost, and vulnerable in a system like this. Popular struggle is necessary to demand their needs be met. When popular movements weaken, the safety net then starts getting pulled apart. U.S. opposition to a human rights treaty for the aged is based not on a lack of morality, uncaring politics, or bad intentions, but on the way the system functions.

In declining to endorse the OAS convention on aging, the U.S. government inserted a note declaring: "The United States has consistently objected to the negotiation of new legally binding instruments on the rights of older persons . . . We do not believe a convention is necessary to ensure that the human rights of older persons are protected . . . The resources of the OAS and of its member states should be used to identify practical steps that governments in the Americas might adopt to combat discrimination against older persons." In other words, instead of having to abide by a binding agreement, each country should be free to do as it chooses.

As radical as they might sound to U.S. ears, these economic rights don't even test the limits of the ways a globalized economy now affects the aged. Enormous movements of people, for instance, fleeing war and poverty, have led to the separation of families. UN conventions, and almost all countries, recognize the right to migrate because of war and persecution. Should this be expanded to recognize a right of old people to reunite with their families, if they're separated by war or previous migration? Should the United States recognize the right of a migrant in California's Central Valley, for instance, after a lifetime working in the fields, to travel home to Mexico, and then return to their family putting down roots in Fresno?

"Of course it should," says Susan Somers, president of the International Network for the Prevention of Elder Abuse. "All we need is a little political will. But get it into a convention? That's a hard road, because of every nation's immigration laws. We're not trying to force countries to change their culture or ways of life. But when they come into conflict with harm, culture and tradition are no excuse."

A proposed U.N. convention has been stalled over these disagreements, and Daichman and Somers say opposition is coming from the United States, Australia, Israel, and the European Union. "They are really trying to push us back," Somers fumes. "They think it's going to cost them something, and that older people aren't deserving. Yet the budget item for treaties is so small compared to peace keeping and the Security Council—almost nothing."

A growing and vocal constituency is not simply waiting for wealthy nations to come around, however. Among Asian countries, Malaysia, Indonesia, Thailand, Bangladesh, and even Myanmar have made statements about the human rights of older people. "Human rights are at the core of everything," Daichman says. "The rights of people getting old should be considered human rights because they're human beings."

Sources: Draft Resolution—Inter-American Convention on Protecting the Human Rights of Older Persons; Organization of American States, "The Americas Becomes First Region in the World to Have an Instrument for the Promotion and Protection of the Rights of Older Persons," press release, June 15, 2015 (oas.org); Rebecca Vallas, "Senior Poverty in America: The Looming Crisis No One's Talking About," Center for American Progress (americanprogress.org); Interview with Rebecca Vallas, November 2015; Juliette Cubanski, Giselle Casillas, and Anthony Damico, "Poverty Among Seniors: An Updated Analysis of National and State Level Poverty Rates Under the Official and Supplemental Poverty Measures," Kaisar Family Foundation, June 10, 2015 (kff.org); Social Security Administration, "Effects of Unauthorized

Immigration on the Actuarial Status of the Social Security Trust Funds" (ssa.gov); Roy Germano, "Unauthorized Immigrants Paid $100 Billion Into Social Security Over Last Decade," VICE News, August 4, 2014 (news.vice.com); National Immigration Law Center, "Overview of Immigrant Eligibility for Federal Programs" (nilc.org); National Immigration Law Center, "A Quick Guide to Immigrant Eligibility for ACA and Key Federal Means-tested Programs," (nilc.org); Interview with Susan Somers, November 2015; Interview with Lia Daichman, November 2015; Center on Budget and Policy Priorities, "Policy Basics: Introduction to Supplemental Security Income"(cbpp.org); United Nations Department of Social and Economic Affairs, "World Population Ageing 2015" (un.org/en/development/desa).

Critical Thinking

1. How would you actualize Roosevelt's concept of "freedom from want" for our senior citizens?
2. How does the United States' treatment of our seniors compare with outer countries around the world?

Internet References

Aging and Socioeconomic Status
http://www.apa.org/pi/ses/resources/publications/age.aspx

Economic Hardship among Older People in New Zealand: The Effects of Low Living Standards on Social Support, Loneliness, and Mental Health
http://www.psychology.org.nz/wp-content/uploads/NZJP-Vol392-2010-6-Stephens.pdf

The New Retirement: "My Big Fear Is Being Old and Poor"
https://www.irishtimes.com/life-and-style/people/the-new-retirement-my-big-fear-is-being-old-and-poor-1.3168564

Taking Care: Ethical Care Giving in Our Aging Society
http://www.thenewatlantis.com/docLib/20091130_taking_care.pdf

Thinking about Retirement? Time to Think about Your Psychological Portfolio
http://www.apa.org/research/action/retire.aspx

David Bacon is a journalist and photographer covering labor, immigration, and the impact of the global economy on workers. For this article, he received a Journalists in Aging Fellowship, a program of New America Media and the Gerontological Society of America, sponsored by The Scan Foundation.
